John Ellis

Skepticism and Divine Revelation

John Ellis

Skepticism and Divine Revelation

ISBN/EAN: 9783337418908

Printed in Europe, USA, Canada, Australia, Japan

Cover: Foto ©Thomas Meinert / pixelio.de

More available books at **www.hansebooks.com**

SKEPTICISM

AND

DIVINE REVELATION.

BY

JOHN ELLIS, M.D.,

Author of the "Avoidable Causes of Disease," "Address to the Clergy,"
"The Wine Question in the Light of the New Dispensation," Etc.

THE TRUE HOPE OF MANKIND AT THIS DAY IS NOT IN LOOKING
BACK—TO JUDAISM, ROMAN CATHOLICISM, OR ANY OF THE
FORMS OF THE PAST—BUT FORWARD AND UPWARD TO THE
NEW JERUSALEM, WHICH IS NOW, IN THIS NEW AGE, DESCEND-
ING FROM GOD OUT OF HEAVEN.

———————

NEW YORK:

PUBLISHED BY THE AUTHOR.

1882.

PREFACE.

IT has been our aim in writing and compiling this work to show, in the light of revelation, to human reason—

1st. That there is a known personal God, who has revealed Himself to us as a Divine Man in His Word; and also in man and in the works of creation which surround us, when the latter are viewed in the light of revelation.

2d. That the material universe and man have been created from the spiritual world, and that all material objects and forms are but manifestations of affections and thoughts primarily from God, even if secondarily from man, either as a true or perverted image of God. As all of man's words and works spring from, or are caused by, his affections and thoughts, which are spiritual, the former necessarily correspond to the latter, as an effect does to its cause. So all of God's words and works must spring from, or be caused by, His affections and thoughts, and the latter must necessarily correspond to the former, as effects do to their causes; therefore, as God's works are infilled with life, and in this respect differ totally from the works of man, so if He has given us a Word, containing spiritual knowledge, it must differ from the words of man by being full of spirit and life, like His works.

3d. That the Sacred Scriptures are written according to this science of correspondences between natural and spiritual things; consequently God's Word and His works can never conflict, whatever the appearance.

4th. That the Lord at this day has revealed to us the correspondences in accordance with which the Sacred Scriptures were written, and by which they must be interpreted, if man is to be able to see and know the interpretation to be true, as he knows any of the interpretations of the natural sciences to be true. By the aid of this newly revealed science, we find that the Sacred Scriptures have a connected spiritual sense which is never contradictory.

5th. That this revelation of the spiritual sense of the Divine Word, and True Doctrines, is the fulfillment of the prophecies in regard to the Lord's Second Coming.

Our chief object has been to call the attention of the reader to the revelations made by the Lord for the benefit of this new, this crowning and endless age which is dawning upon us.

CONTENTS.

SECTION PAGE

I. A Personal God..................................... 1

II. Special Revelation from a Personal God 3

III. Have we any Special Revelations from a Personal
God?............................ 5

IV. The First Chapters of Genesis...................... 21

V. Genesis, Chapter First, and Creation 26

VI. Brief Exposition of the Internal Sense of the First
Chapter of Genesis......................... .. 29

VII. The Creation of Man and Woman (as described in the
First Chapter of Genesis, and as described in the
Second). 37

VIII. Eve.. 45

IX. The Garden of Eden—Its Trees and River.......... 47

X. The Fall of Man—The Serpent and Curse Introduced
into the World............................... 53

XI. Cain and Abel 61

XII. The Flood—General Remarks..................... 65

XIII. Noah 69

XIV. Shem, Ham, and Japheth 71

XV. The Flood of Waters 74

XVI. The Ark 81

XVII. The Tower of Babel.............................. 88

XVIII. Sun Worship and Idolatry—Their Origin........... 94

XIX. Spiritualism...................................... 105

XX. Mediate Revelation by the Word, or Immediate by
Spirits—Which is Preferable? 116

SECTION   PAGE

XXI. An Appeal to Spiritualists in behalf of the Writings
        of Emanuel Swedenborg........................ 123

XXII. Doctrines of the New Jerusalem.................... 129

XXIII. The Incarnation—Was there any Violation of the
        Laws of Nature?—Why the Lord came to this
        Earth?—" What became of the Universe, during
        His Incarnation?" 133

XXIV. The Divine Trinity, and the Trinity in Man........ 153

XXV. Sacrificial Worship—Its True Significance 170

XXVI. The Cross.. 180

XXVII. A True and Heavenly Life............. 184

XXVIII. The End of the World, and the Second Coming of the
        Lord.. 191

XXIX. The Resurrection—When It Occurs 202

XXX. The State of Infants in the Other Life 218

XXXI. On the State of the Heathen and Gentiles in Another
        Life... 221

XXXII. The New Jerusalem—The Church of the Future—
        The Crown of all Churches 229

XXXIII. The Divine Promise to those who receive the New
        Jerusalem at the Second Coming of the Lord 247

XXXIV. Emanuel Swedenborg, the Seer............ ... 257

SKEPTICISM

AND

DIVINE REVELATION.

I.

A Personal God.

THAT there is a personal God, or Creator, it would seem must be manifest to every enlightened and thoughtful individual who has ever had the idea of such a being properly and truly presented to him, and who observes and reflects upon the works of creation. In all created things, in the animal, vegetable and mineral kingdoms, he sees evidences of design, of careful thought, and the most wonderful adaptation of individual parts, and their uses to whole structures. There is nothing in the works of man which will compare in this respect with the works of creation, which we behold around us on every hand, from the smallest atom, vegetable and insect, to the vast suns and their surrounding planets. If we were to find a beautiful piece of man-made machinery which we had never seen before, what would be our first thought? Would it be that it had either come by chance, or was the work of the general mind of men, or would it not be that it was the work of some individual or personal man or men. Do we ever find anything of human production, manifesting thought and design, which has not been made by some individual or personal man or men? How unreasonable then to think for a moment that the beautiful forms and structures, filled with life, around us, manifesting in an infinite degree thought and design, are not the works of a personal being or Creator. Geology shows that they did not always exist.

If there is a personal Creator, it is evident that he must have had some object, design, or end in view, in creating the universe, worthy of such a being. Unaided by revelation from our Creator, we might have wandered in darkness and never have been able to see or comprehend the reason why the universe was created, for a goodly number of our scientific men of this day, who ignore Divine Revelation, have manifested to us how utterly impossible it is for men, engrossed in scientific investigations and pursuits, unaided by revelation, to comprehend or even perceive spiritual truths, or the spiritual side of creation and of man's nature.

But the sacred Scriptures intimate to us, and the revelations made by the Lord for the benefit of this perverted and skeptical age, through Emanuel Swedenborg, teach us that the object of the material creation and universe was that man might be created in the image and likeness of his Creator, capable of loving, reverencing, and serving Him and his fellow or neighbor; and that from man an angelic heaven of intelligent, rational, and happy beings might be created, who should forever reverence, reciprocate His love, and serve, by doing good to each other, and worship Him, not for His own sake or glory, but for their own good, that they might realize that they individually are but recipients of life, all brethren—God the giver of all life, all truth, and of all goodness. Can we imagine a more worthy object for the creation of the universe than this?

If, then, we are prepared to admit that this wonderful universe has been created by an intelligent Personal Being for the sake of making man in his own image, capable of becoming by the proper use of the freedom of will with which he is endowed, intelligent, wise and happy, can we for a moment suppose that such a Creator, after endowing man with rationality, conscience, and freedom of will, capable of the most terrible perversions and suffering, could by any possibility, if he is a wise and loving Father, as all His works manifest, leave man without any more special manifestation of His will, than he can gather from the dim light of nature—without any direct positive instruction as to his destiny, or on whom he is dependent for his existence, or how he should conduct himself so as to reach the highest state of intelligence, goodness and happiness? Would an earthly parent thus leave the child he loves, to grope in darkness? And if he would not, how can we attribute such an unnatural course to our Heavenly Father? It would seem, then, if there is a personal God, as enlightened reason plainly assures us, and he is our Creator, an intelligent and loving Father, that He should have given to his children some knowledge of Himself and some manifestation of His will, some rules of life to guide them here and to heaven hereafter. Would it seem unreasonable that a Father, who in his great love has created this vast and wonderful universe for man, that he might be the recipient of His love, should *personally manifest Himself* to His creatures whom he has created and endowed with rationality, freedom and conscience? The yearning heart of every earthly parent and of every child of an earthly parent answers No. That He should not only manifest himself in a personal form to the children whom he has created, that they may have an object for reverence and worship, and not bow down to an impersonal or unknown God, but also give them, as He may see they need, line upon line and precept upon precept of useful instruction, seems evident. Has He done it? and first as to special revelations.

II.

Special Revelations from a Personal God.

BY special revelations from the Lord are meant revelations either to or through individual men or women. The first thought which occurs is, "why should our Creator, if He is impartial, good, and merciful, reveal truth

to one man, or apparently favor him more than others, in
this respect ? " There are many reasons for His selecting
individual men for such a mission, either one of which
would seem satisfactory. Revelations are not made simply
for the benefit of the individual, but that the truths may
be taught to others, and handed down to posterity either
by tradition or in a written form; and, to say the least,
it is often doubtful whether the revelator is specially
favored at all or not. A man to be benefited by truth
must receive it in freedom, and not only receive it into his
understanding, but he must also live according to it, and
thus weave it into the very fibres of his spiritual organization, or it will do him no good. If he fails to shape his
life, or walk according to the truth, he will profane it; or,
in other words, by the light which he has received he will
be enabled to sink himself deeper into evil and consequent
suffering. If direct revelations were made to all men,
irrespective of their state, it is certain that many might be
compelled, as it were, to believe who have no desire to live
a good and true life, and therefore would be very seriously
injured by such revelations; but when the truth is taught
to them by their fellow-men, or handed down by tradition,
or in a written form, it comes with less authority, and does
not interfere with their freedom or compel them to believe,
and they can receive or reject it, according to the state of
their affections;—having eyes they can see not, having ears
they may hear not—not receiving the truth they do not
profane it, and consequently it does them comparatively
little harm. The " flaming sword " of self-love is placed at
the east of the garden, in the mind of the evil man, to protect the truth from profanation; fortunately, it is rarely
sheathed except by repentance, faith in the Lord, and a
sincere effort to lead a good life. Consequently, as a general rule, an evil man cannot see genuine spiritual truths,
which is very fortunate for him. Here then would seem
to be a very satisfactory reason why the Lord does not
directly reveal truth to all men. Then, all men are not in

a proper state, but our Creator seeing the hearts and capacity of all can select the best, or the one least likely to be injured by the truth to be revealed. If it is simply to write the words dictated by Him, it would seem possible that the man chosen need not necessarily be a good man, but one protected by the flaming sword of self-love from seeing the truth revealed in its true light, and thus from being injured by it; and the love of glory or fame might lead such a man to proclaim the truth with zeal, and others be benefited thereby, and himself not injured.

III.

Have we any Special Revelations from a Personal God?

THIS is a practical question, and one which no sensible man will hastily decide in the negative. The certainty of there being a personal Creator, and the equal certainty, if there is such a being, of whom man when regenerated is the image and likeness, that He would reveal to mankind such truths as are essential to be lived by us, that we may be happy here and hereafter, have been considered already. It becomes then, every man who is skeptically inclined, with due reverence and humility, to look for such a revelation, or such revelations; and, as far as possible, not to look with a combative or negative spirit, for such a spirit is of necessity almost, if not quite, a bar to the truth being seen. You attempt to show a man a house—yes, a beautiful house for human habitation—he, unfortunately, is naturally, as most men are spiritually, a little near-sighted; and instead of waiting until he has seen the entire house and can form a general idea of it, as you approach the gate or the outer door he begins to cavil and deny that that door is a house, or any part of a house, as it does not swing in the direction or manner the door to his house has always swung; or his house has no outer door. You call his attention to a beautiful window,

Gothic perhaps in form; but this is not like the window
in his house, it is obstructed with glass, which to you has
a use, but without waiting to understand this use, he
decides at once it is no part of a house, or at least of a
suitable house for him to live in; and so you go on
throughout your entire house, showing him all parts of it,
its halls, its rooms, its furniture, etc., and he denying and
combating at every step. Can you convince such a man?
Never! In our Father's house are many beautiful mansions, but from a negative and combative state a man can
never see or reside in one of them. We must come like
little children, in a teachable spirit, not to believe blindly
everything which is told us, or which we read, but to use
the reason with which God has endowed us, to judge after
a fair survey between truth and error. If we come in
such a spirit, and shape our lives according to the truth,
the Lord will lead us into one of His many beautiful mansions.

As it will be our aim not to write this treatise from a
negative spirit, but from an affirmative state, we will here
make a general statement, and afterwards consider it more
fully in detail. Not that we expect in the short space we
have allotted to ourselves to set before the reader evidence
enough to satisfy all, but we do hope to call the attention
of many an earnest enquirer to a serious examination of
the writings which have, after a patient and careful examination, so fully and happily satisfied us, and increasing
thousands of intelligent men and women.

Although born and educated in a Christian country, and
accustomed to read the Bible from childhood, and to sit
under the ministrations of religious teachers, not a few,
owing to the apparent conflict which seems to exist between the Word of God in its letter and His works, which
has been so clearly developed by the scientific researches
of this day, have been led to doubt, and some unfortunately openly to deny, that the sacred Scriptures are either
revelations from God, or entitled to any more respect than

the acknowledged writings of men. It is not to be supposed for a moment, by any liberal-minded man, that all
such doubters are either dishonest or that they do not
desire the truth ; the young, especially in the flush of scientific investigations, are liable to be led into such doubts,
and it is but too evident that religious teachers, by the
light afforded by the letter of the Bible alone, have not
been able to either shield them or deliver them from such
doubts.   But the Lord does not leave Himself without a
witness ; consequently in the Gospels and Book of Revelation, He promises a second coming in the clouds of
Heaven—not the clouds of earth, please bear in mind.
When on earth, our Saviour declared that He had many
things to tell men, but mankind then were not in a state
to receive them.   As a kind parent does to his child, so
our Heavenly Father adapts His instruction, or revelations, to the capacity and needs of His children.   At an
age when the earth seemed to men, and was believed to be
the centre of the universe, and the sun, moon and stars
were supposed to make a journey around it daily, the
Lord was supposed to be angry, revengeful, even hating
some of the creatures He had made.   Such was the language of God's works and of His Word to the untutored
men of those dark ages—the one in strict harmony with
the other.   But the enlightened science of this day shows
that the supposed motion of the sun, moon and stars was
only an apparent truth—not a real truth, the real truth
being that day and night are caused by the motion of the
earth—when it turns from the sun it is night. So a
spiritual revelation in keeping with the natural science of
to-day, must show that the supposed anger, revengefulness
and hatred attributed to God, are but apparent truths,
adapted to the state of mankind when given ; and men
were permitted to dwell in such apparent truths for the
sake of being restrained by their fears, and because they
were not capable of comprehending or being benefited by
real truths.   The real truth being, that God is never

angry, never hates and is never revengeful, but He is love and unchangeable, the same yesterday, to-day and forever. His tender mercies are around all His creatures; but when man turns from the Lord to himself, and seeks selfish ends, instead of regarding the rights of others, and perverts his God-given passions and appetites to purely sensual and selfish gratification irrespective of their legitimate use, making their gratification the chief object of his life, thus turning from the Lord to self, mental darkness overshadows him; and when he begins to suffer the legitimate consequences, or, if you please, punishments which necessarily follow from the violation of the spiritual and physical laws of his being, which the Lord has ordained for his good, it seems to him that God is angry with him and hates him; and who will not say that it is well that he has been permitted to remain in this apparent truth.

But the men of this day are rapidly outgrowing the state in which they can be restrained by the apparent truths of God's Word, for they are fast losing their belief in and reverence for a personal God and all revelations from such a being. Even the fears of a literal hell are being shaken off, and men no longer tremble before the anathemas of the most venerable churches, or the denunciation of their clergymen.

Look around, reader, upon the confusion in the religious world, the manifestations of sectarianism, the love of rule in spiritual things, the growing skepticism, the Lo here and Lo there, and tell us if it is not time for us to be looking for the sign of the Son of man in the clouds of heaven, and for the new order of things which he has promised us in His Word, when He declared, "Behold I make all things new." Look at the wonderful strides being made in the mechanical arts and in the sciences, and remember the order of creation and regeneration is, first that which is natural and afterwards that which is spiritual. This is the true order with the individual man, and it is true with the race.

Emanuel Swedenborg, the son of a Bishop of the Church of Sweden, who lived over a century ago, was thoroughly educated and trained in the sciences of his day, and devoted his life until he was over 54 years of age to scientific and mechanical pursuits, when, he assures us in his writings, he was called by the Lord from his scientific labors to the important mission of revealing to the world for the benefit of all Christians and others, the truths of a New Dispensation, or of the Second Coming of the Lord. He assures us that his spiritual sight was opened, as it was with the prophets, St. Paul and John the revelator; that he was permitted to see the inhabitants of the spiritual world, including those of heaven and hell, and to describe them and their condition, and to show the relation which the acts and deeds of this life have upon the future life; and he wrote a work entitled, "Heaven, the World of Spirits and Hell; from things seen and heard;" full of the most useful and practical instruction. Interspersed throughout his other works are relations of what he claims to have seen and heard in the spiritual world. He shows conclusively that the spiritual world is the world of causes, the real, the living world, and the natural world the world of effects: from this it follows that there is a strict correspondence between every object in this world and its cause in the spiritual world.

As is truly said by the Rev. George Field, in his work entitled "The Two Great Books of Nature and Revelation," which work will richly repay both the theological and scientific student for a careful perusal, and from which we shall not unfrequently quote in the following pages:

"The natural universe is therefore but an outer form of the Divine mind; and all its multitudinous contents are but so many symbols of the varied truths and affections existing in the world of mind. Thus the creation is, as it were, the alphabet of the Creator; and it is by its types that the Creator speaketh! Or, as the apostle wrote, 'The invisible things of Him [God] from the creation of the world, are clearly seen, being understood by the things that are made' (Rom. i. 20). A doctrine as old as the world, and taught by *Hermes Trismegistus* (the Egyptian *Thoth*, some 2000 years before it was thus reiterated by Paul. His words in English are, '*All things that are in heaven, are in the earth in an earthly form ; and all things that are in the earth, are in heaven in a heavenly form.*' Which sentiment is thus transferred to poetry by Milton:

> ' What if earth
> Be but the shadow of heaven : and things therein
> Each to other like, more than on earth is thought.'

"How immense—how wonderful is the idea that the *works* of the Creator should be the *signs* for the *words of His revelation !* and that the one is to the other as the soul is to the body, and the mystic chain which binds them is *correspondence,* or the relation which exists by creation between spiritual and natural things.

"'To the most ancient people,' says Mr. Kirby, 'the creation was a Book of Symbols, a sacred language of which they possessed the key, and which it was their delight to study and decipher.' (*Introduction to Entomology.*) *Correspondence* is the necessary relation subsisting between things spiritual and things natural, or between thoughts and their outward images : thus, not as might be inferred, that one *natural thing* corresponds to another natural thing, as this would be merely arbitrary or speculative, for though one may illustrate the other, it does not correspond to it, or have any necessary relation to it. Actions correspond to feelings: words correspond to thoughts: sounds or intonations correspond to the quality of the affection, because they actually produce them. So every object in nature corresponds first to its prototype in the Divine mind, and secondarily to its antitype in the human mind, by as fixed and immutable a law as that effects are produced by causes.'"

In a work by the late Prof. Agassiz on Lake Superior, he says: "There will be no scientific evidence of God's working in nature, until naturalists have shown that the whole creation is the expression of a thought, and not the product of physical agents;" and he adds, "Let the naturalists look at the world under such impressions, and evidence will pour in upon us, that all creatures are expressions of the thoughts of Him whom we know, love, and adore unseen."

That Man is not only the final end of Creation, but that God, the Creator, must have been the Infinite Divine Pattern—the self-existent Divinely Human Fountain, is also thus forcibly presented by Agassiz: "Man (he says), is the end to which all the animal creation has tended from the first appearance of the first Palæozoic fishes." But, says Hugh Miller, "No longer, however, the natural, but the DIVINE MAN—occupying what is at once its terminal point, and its highest apex."—*Testimony of the Rocks*, pp. 229–235.

In the late Mr. Bancroft's speech before the New York Historical Society he says: "The comparative anatomist has shown that all created vertebræ, without exception, are analogous, so that the induction becomes irresistible that *an archetype existed previous to the creation, of the first of the kind.* Shall we then hesitate to believe that the system of law likewise pervades the moral world? We cannot shut our eyes to the established fact that *an ideal, or archetype, prescribed the form of animal life;* and shall we not believe that the type of all intellectual life, *likewise exists in the Divine Mind?*"

According to this science of correspondences—which Swedenborg has shown is the science of all sciences—the sacred Scriptures were written, consequently they can only be correctly interpreted in accordance with this universal science. A correct interpretation therefore cannot be arbitrary, but it must be in accordance with rules and laws, and can never conflict with natural science, nor can

one portion of the Word of God, when correctly interpreted, ever conflict with another portion. He has shown,
consequently, that the Word of God, like His works, is
filled with life, and differs as much from the writings of
men as His works do from the works of men. The sacred
Scriptures then have not only a literal sense, but also a
connected spiritual sense running throughout, and within,
as the soul is within the body.

The Lord intimates in many passages that the sacred
Scriptures, or His words, contain a spiritual sense, as in
the following: "It is the spirit that quickeneth; the flesh
profiteth nothing; the words that I speak unto you, they
are spirit and they are life." "The letter killeth, but the
spirit giveth life."

"The Lord," says the Rev. John Hyde, "spoke in
parables to the Jews; and further it is declared that,
'Without a parable spake He not to them' (Matt. xiii. 34).
All that the Lord uttered was a parable; and was a parable because it possessed an inner meaning recognizable by
the instructed, but veiled from the unbelieving. That He
adopted this method, even with His disciples, is evident
from many passages. 'If thine eye offend thee, pluck it
out. If thy hand offend thee, cut it off.' 'Except ye eat
the flesh of the Son of man, and drink His blood, ye have
no life in you.' 'He that hath no sword, let him sell his
coat and buy one.' There was a *Divine* signification in
His words, because He was Divine who uttered them.
The words were but the outer covering of the Divine
meaning, just as His flesh was but the outer covering of
the Divine man. It was this inner 'spirit and life' that
profited them, and that will profit us to know. In this
inner or higher sense, all the Scriptures testified of Him.
'The spirit of prophecy was the testimony of Jesus.'

"Paul, in like manner, interprets the Sacred Word. To
him, the 'Jews after the flesh' were but types of 'the Jews
after the Spirit;' 'circumcision after the flesh' the
symbol of 'circumcision of the heart.' He asserts that

the *rock* from which the Israelites drank was the figure of the 'spiritual rock, which is Christ;' the tabernacle and its ceremonies, the holy of holies and its yearly entrance, were but 'symbols of the true;' that Jerusalem below was the type of 'Jerusalem that is above, the mother of us all;' that the earthly Zion was but the figure of 'the Mount Zion, the city of the living God, the heavenly Jerusalem,' to which.all the disciples of Christ had come; that Abraham and his two sons were '*an allegory;*' that Melchisedec was a type of Christ, as also were the high priests.

"The whole of the Hebrews is but an exposition of typical or symbolic interpretation, and it abounds in confirmations of the statement of David, that the history of the Israelites was 'a PARABLE.' Into the sublime halls of such spiritual interpretation he conducts us, and justifies our belief in an everywhere-present spiritual sense, by many a glimpse of its presence, where else it had lain concealed. He teaches us as he taught his disciple Timothy, that 'all Scripture is God-breathed (given by inspiration of God), and is profitable for doctrine, for reproof, for correction, for instruction in righteousness; that the man of God may be thoroughly furnished unto all good works' (2 Tim. iii. 16, 17); given by God to every man, that every man may thus become perfect; of universal importance because of universal application. Every word of it, consequently, treating of spiritual things, eternal in its interests, and to be spiritually understood."

The early Christian Fathers, "Clement of Alexandria, and Origen, understood that the sacred Scriptures have a spiritual sense; and Origen, when the shrewd enemy of Christianity, Celsus, ridiculed the stories of the rib, the serpent, etc., as childish fables, reproaches him for want of candor in purposely keeping out of sight, what was so evident upon the face of the narrative, that the whole is a *pure allegory.* Indeed so universal was this sentiment, that De la Bigue in his *Bibliotheca Patrum,* after quoting a number of testimonies to this effect, says: 'For these

reasons the interpreters whom we have mentioned, under·
standing all that is said of Paradise in a spiritual manner,
affirmed that divers heresies had arisen, because certain
persons had understood what is said of God and Paradise
after a carnal manner.' So that it is certain that, in the
primitive days, the *heretics* were those who interpreted
this part of Scripture according to the *letter*."—*Noble's
Plenary Inspiration.*

Aside from the relation of what he saw and heard in
the spiritual world, Swedenborg assures us that he received
from the Lord, while reading His Word, the true interpretation of the sacred Scriptures, in accordance with the
science of correspondences, and also the true Christian
doctrines—which had become during the dark ages seriously perverted by the evil inclinations, the conflicting
opinions and doctrines of men, which had too frequently
made the Word of God of none effect. He claims that
without Divine aid he could never have discovered the
science of correspondences, the true and rational interpretation of the Word in accordance therewith, and the true
Christian doctrines, and he most solemnly assures us that
he received nothing of all he has revealed to us upon these
subjects from any spirit or angel even, but from the Lord
alone while reading His Word.

Swedenborg also shows us that the Lord has never left
any nation or people without some knowledge of Himself
and of His will—enough, if they will but hearken and
obey, to lead to some of the innumerable mansions in His
heavenly kingdom.

Swedenborg says : "That religion has existed from the
most ancient times, and that the inhabitants of the globe
everywhere know of God with something about the life
after death, has not been from themselves and from their
own acuteness, but from the ancient Word mentioned
above, and afterwards from the Israelitish Word. * * *
It is well known that they had a knowledge of Paradise,
of the flood, of the sacred fire, and of the four ages—from

the first or golden age to the last or iron age—by which
the four states of the church are signified in the Word, as
in Daniel ii. 35. It is also known that the Mahometan
religion which succeeded and destroyed the previous religions of many nations, was taken from the Word of both
Testaments." "They who do not believe the Word from
the Word, can neither believe anything divine from nature;
for the Lord teaches, they have Moses and the prophets,
let them hear them; if they do not hear Moses and the
prophets, neither will they be persuaded if any of the dead
were to rise (Luke xvi. 29–31). It is the same if any one,
rejecting the Word, will believe from nature alone what
certain of the ancients, who were Pagans, have written,
such as Aristotle, Cicero, and others, concerning the existence of God and the immortality of the soul; this they
did not first know from their own natural light, but from
the religion of the ancients, among whom there had been
a divine revelation, which was successively propagated to
the heathens."

To the people of the most ancient or the Adamic age
He gave open vision and direct revelations, and they
understood the correspondence between spiritual and
natural things; and a knowledge of correspondences and
essential spiritual truths, after men began to sink voluntarily into evil, and open vision ceased, were handed down
by tradition among all nations; and from this source have
originated Mythology, Idolatry, Masonry and sacrifices as
the latter have existed among Gentile nations. Objects and
images once used to remind men of spiritual truths, the
spiritual signification of the objects and images being
gradually lost, men came at length to worship the natural
object or image, or to use the same in sacrifices. In a
more or less perverted form the Ten Commandments have
been handed down by tradition among many nations
previous to their ever seeing the written word, and some
knowledge of spiritual subjects among all nations. When
our missionaries come to perceive the fact and act accord-

ingly, that heathen nations are not all heathen after all, and come to recognize the truth and good there is already among them, they will be more successful in converting them to Christianity.

Through Moses and the Prophets, the Evangelists and St. John, were given special revelations in a written form, adapted to the times and wants of the men for whose benefit they were given, all written according to the correspondence between spiritual and natural things; every object, image, and word used representing spiritual ideas, perceptions, affections, and thoughts. Swedenborg claims to have given, or more strictly speaking, that the Lord gave through him, the key for unlocking all these various books written by different men in different ages, and to demonstrate to man's rational perceptions that God was in very deed their author, and from the vast store-house of God's Word he brings forth things new and old for the benefit of the men of this age. Has he accomplished all this? If he has, the Lord has indeed been mindful of and merciful to the men of this age. Swedenborg asked no man to receive the truth on his say so, in fact he expressly teaches that no one can really receive the truth into his life any further than he perceives it to be true, and if not brought into life it is of no use, and soon vanishes from his mental vision, even if he hears it. With him there is no salvation by truth or faith alone, for all genuine religion has relation to life, and the life of religion is to do good. But the Rev. J. C. Ager says truly and justly:

"The real proof of the existence of anything is to see the thing itself. As soon as we begin to see the spiritual sense which is reflected in the letter, and to see the boundless vista of truth which it opens, and especially when we begin to feel the searching and discriminating power of this higher truth, penetrating to the most hidden motives and springs of action, we need no argument to convince us that there is such a sense in the Bible, and that the Bible is Divine and Infinite by virtue of that sense.

"Whether there be such a sense, therefore, is mainly a question of fact. You cannot tell whether it is there or not until you look for it.

"The system of interpretation by which this higher sense is unfolded is set forth in the writings of Emanuel Swedenborg. It is not an arbitrary system, but is based upon the relation which everywhere exists between the spiritual and the natural; in other words, it is based upon an ontological law, or a law of being. What this law is, and how it is manifested in all nature and in all languages, cannot be explained in a brief space. The fundamental idea of it is this: that as the body not only clothes but *reveals* the soul, so does the material or natural universally both clothe and *reveal* the spiritual. The body reveals the soul because it in every way *corresponds* to it—is the type of it. This is true not only of its form, but of its constitution and the laws by which it is governed. As soon as the relation between the spiritual and the physical is clearly discerned, the study of the body becomes the most fruitful source of information respecting the soul.

"And this correspondence between the spiritual and the natural is universal. The natural is the outcome of the spiritual, and therefore reveals it, when the language in which it speaks is understood. That is, the natural corresponds to the spiritual, and to the extent that this correspondence is perceived does the spiritual become manifest in and through the natural.

"The various bearings and applications of this law or relation are thoroughly discussed and clearly explained by Swedenborg. He shows that this is the law of Divine revelation alike in the works of God and in the Word of God.

"Every natural object is the form and embodiment of some spiritual idea or principle; and, therefore, it is the most perfect expression or type or picture of that idea. This higher significance of nature man has always seen dimly and partially; and the recognition of this corres-

pondence forms the basis of all poetry.   But the Lord sees
this higher side of nature in all its infinite fulness; hence
in Divine language this correspondence finds full and perfect expression.   And it is in accordance with this law that
the Divine Truth finds its ultimation, in human language,
in the Divine Word.

"When we apply this principle of interpretation to the
Bible we find how completely it removes all the difficulties
which have been the occasion of so much doubt and skepticism.

"Take the first chapter of Genesis, for instance, which
the theologians have tried in vain to reconcile with the
conclusions of modern science.   When interpreted by this
law, it is seen to be, not an erroneous or imperfect account
of the creation of the natural world, but a typical description of man's spiritual creation, that is, of his spiritual
development from the state of spiritual or mental chaos to
the paradise or heavenly state.   And the instruction it
contains applies equally to the regeneration or development of the race, and to the regeneration of the individual.

"So the description of Eden is seen to be, not the description of some place on the earth's surface, all traces of
which have been lost, but a picture of the heavenly state
of mind to which we may all aspire.   Hence it is full of
instruction for all who would reach that state.

"So, again, the account of the 'fall' is a picture of what
occurs to every man who rejects Divine guidance, and
accepts in place thereof sensuous knowledge, which is the
'serpent.'   This sensuous or materialistic spirit is just as
active to-day as it was when mankind was in the Eden
state, and the world is full of the victims of its seductions.
And when our eyes are opened to the spiritual lessons of
the third chapter of Genesis, we find it full of warning and
instruction in respect to the present state of the world.

"Most Christian scholars agree that true history, in the
Scriptures, begins with Abraham, and that the preceding

chapters are compiled from ancient documents. This Swedenborg declared more than one hundred years ago, showing this first part of Genesis to be pure parable, without literal historical sense, but depicting in typical language the early *spiritual* history of the race, its development from the chaos or animal state, and the mental experiences which led to its spiritual decline. The numbers mentioned in these chapters are also symbolical; hence we have no chronology of this period.

"It will be seen, not only that this recognition of a spiritual sense in the Divine Word opens to our view limitless treasures of spiritual instruction therein, but also that it lifts the Bible out of the arena of scientific controversy. Science and Revelation have each its province, and the two need not conflict. It is the province of Science to investigate truth relating to our physical nature, and the material world which is its home. It is the province of Revelation to teach truth respecting our spiritual nature, and the spiritual world which is its home. Or, as is often said, it is the province of Science to deal with effects, and of Revelation to deal with causes; for the physical world is the world of effects, and the spiritual world, that of causes.

"But it is also true that while the two are distinct, neither can be rightly comprehended without the other. A true conception of Christianity—that is, of religion—is now possible, because true science is now beginning to be discovered and accepted. The foundation is being laid upon which the superstructure can rest. A false or imperfect science and a false or imperfect religion have always gone hand in hand. Man rises from sensuous thought to spiritual thought, and if his sensuous thought be wrong, his spiritual thought must needs be erroneous or imperfect.

"On the other hand, if a man stops in the sensuous plane of thought, he sees but one side of the truth, and that the lower; and to accept that as complete, is to falsify all his conceptions."

Thanks be to the Lord for the revelations made through Swedenborg; from this time forth the sacred Scriptures will be reverenced as they have never been before since the age of Noah, for in the light of this newly-revealed science of correspondences they are taken out of the regions of theory and speculation, and placed in that of absolute knowledge; their Divine origin by those who have a reasonable knowledge of correspondences will no more be questioned than the existence of the French, German or Italian language by those who have patiently acquired a knowledge of the key or grammar and dictionary of such language. The Word then becomes holy, for it is seen to be from God, who is shown therein in very deed to be our Father—who, from His great parental love for His children, has revealed to us in it the spiritual history of our race and the laws of spiritual life, in accordance with which we must live if we would have heaven within us, and consequently reach a state of happiness and heaven hereafter.

"We are satisfied," says a recent writer, "that could many of the heartiest opponents of such a view of the Word of God perceive that there is such a rule and such a key,—that, unlocked by this consistent key, the darkest places of Scripture are opened to the light, with results not only not trivial, but of high importance to the spiritual progress of man,—they would gladly receive what would so entirely vindicate the divinity of the Scriptures and at the same time thoroughly sweep away the basis of all infidel objections. It would neither impugn the correctness nor depreciate the value of the literal sense. Every fact and every principle which they now learn they could still revere, as we do. But, added to this, they would find the Word filled with a grander significance, and derive from it fuller instruction."

IV.

The First Chapters of Genesis.

THESE chapters, as is well known, have given rise to a serious controversy between scientific men and theologians. Believing that both parties have been in error, and contending against each other when there is no occasion or real ground for such controversy, we propose to consider them briefly in the light of the revelations made through Swedenborg. But before doing this, we desire to say that these chapters belong to the revealed Word of God, had Him for their author, and consequently contain divine truths adapted to the wants and understandings of the men for whom they were written, long before the days of Moses, and copied by him. It matters little by what man's hand they were first penned, the simple question is, Have they a connected spiritual sense? if so they have the Divine imprint, and their authorship is placed beyond question. These chapters contain the early spiritual history of the golden age and of our race, and they were copied by Moses more especially for the benefit of this and coming ages, when, in the good providence of the Lord, a knowledge of correspondences has been restored to men. We make this statement at the commencement as to the sacred character of the contents of these chapters, for we should be exceedingly sorry to lessen, by any thing we may write, any man's reverence for a single moment for the Word of God, of which we know these chapters to be a part.

It would seem that, unaided by further revelation, an intelligent man, if he could divest himself of the prejudices and preconceived ideas derived from education (a very difficult thing to do), on carefully reading these chapters in Genesis, might ask both the scientist and the theologian a few practical questions, which would be worthy of their serious consideration.

To the scientist he might say: "You assume that there
is no other earth but the material earth and no other creation but the material creation, and because you have found
by your investigations into the works of creation, espe
cially in your geological researches, that the earth was not
created in six days, and the order of creation was not such
as the order described in Genesis, you have come to the
conclusion that this portion of the Bible, as applied to the
creation of the material universe, is not true, and consequently your faith in the entire volume as containing
divine revelations, is impaired if not destroyed; but have
you never heard of a mental earth, an earth which can
hear, fear, be joyful, mourn, be corrupt, and be judged?
If you have not, you will not have to read the sacred
Scriptures long before you will find that, whether they
ever treat of the material earth or not, they certainly do of
a mental or spiritual earth; for you will read, even in
Genesis: "The earth also was corrupt before God." Surely
the material earth was not corrupt; and elsewhere you
will read, "Hear, O earth, the words of my mouth;" "Let
earth hear;" "Hear, O earth, I will bring evil on this
people;" "The earth feared;" "The earth mourneth and
fadeth away;" "Let the earth rejoice;" "Sing, O heavens,
and be joyful, O earth;" "The earth is full of the goodness of the Lord;" "The earth shall be full of the knowledge of the Lord;" "Look unto me, and be ye saved, all
the ends of the earth;" "The earth is utterly broken
down, the earth is dissolved;" "The earth and all the inhabitants thereof are dissolved;" "He uttered His voice,
the earth melted;" "Arise, O God, judge the earth."
Surely you can but perceive that it was not the material
earth which was meant in the above and a multitude of
other passages you will find. You scout the idea that the
days of creation in Genesis were vast indefinite periods of
time and not literal days, as the language certainly implies if we take the narrative literally, and I do not see
how any sensible man, untrammeled by preconceived ideas,

can differ from you in this respect; but having satisfied yourself that this narrative is not a correct literal history of the creation of the material universe, and especially of our earth, do you see nothing in it worthy of your careful consideration? Its very existence, coming down as it does from time immemorial, must be as much of a mystery to you as any you can find in the material universe, if you ignore its divine origin. Professing to be a Divine revelation, it certainly is written in an orderly and systematic manner, and is a beautiful history, and I think you will admit that it did not come, or was not written, by chance or by an impersonal being. The writer certainly was an intelligent being undoubtedly in the form of man, and it is evident he, or the being who wrote through him, had a design, which was to convey useful and practical infor-mation for men. There certainly is too great a manifes-tation of intelligence for us to suppose that the author of these chapters either did not know what he was writing about, or did not understand his subject. What object could he have had, if it is to be understood literally?

To the theologian he would say: "Why do you assume that the first chapters of Genesis treat of the creation of the material earth and the first physical men on it? Is there not enough in the very language itself to show unmistak-ably that it was never intended by the writer as a history of the material creation—in fact, could not in the very nature of things have been so intended? Look at it pa-tiently for a moment. A material earth without form and void, or empty. Could matter possibly be without form and void?" "And darkness was upon the face of the deep—abyss." If the earth was without form and void, where could there have been a deep or abyss? Literally, as the narrative reads, there was light, day and night, on earth before the creation of the sun, moon and stars, and vegetation appeared on earth before the sun was created. The sun, moon and stars were not created until the fourth day, and then apparently simply to give light and heat to

the earth.   No wonder that the astronomer, viewing the
heavens with his telescope, the geologist carefully examin-
ing the record in the strata of the earth, reading their
wonderful revelations of a vast past history for the earth,
and the photographer analyzing the light of the sun,
showing almost beyond question that the sun is the physical parent of the earth—no wonder, I say, that they, in
the light of recent discoveries, cannot accept the record in
Genesis as a correct history of the creation of the material
universe, and especially when, according to theologists, the
creation was crowded into six days, and occurred only
about 6000 years ago.   If you abandon the literal days
you give up the whole as a literal narrative; for if the days
so carefully described were not literal days, what right
have you to assume that any part of the record was literally
true, as to the material creation?   But taking the record
as a history of the material creation, your difficulties have
but fairly commenced with the first chapter; but I shall
only hastily call your attention to a few of them, such as
the garden eastward in Eden.   The tree of life also in the
midst of the garden, and the tree of knowledge of good
and evil, were these literal trees? do not their very names
show that they were not, but that they were mental or
spiritual trees?   Nothing would seem to be more absurd,
surely, than in the very face of their significative names to
assume that they were literal trees, unless it may be to suppose that woman was made from a literal rib taken from
man.   Now, is it true that the serpent is more subtle than
any beast of the field, and that he can talk, or that he eats
dust?   What reason have you to suppose he ever talked or
could reason?   After Adam and Eve had eaten of the forbidden fruit their eyes were opened; what does this mean?
had they not their eyes open before this? and did they not
know that they were naked before this event?   Then we
read, "The Lord God made coats of skins and clothed them."
Now, I ask you in all sincerity, if it is possible to regard
the passages to which I have referred, and a large number

more, as a part of a literal history of the natural creation, or to suppose for a moment, on a careful and unbiased reading, that they were ever intended as such by their author?"

In the revelations made by the Lord through Emanuel Swedenborg, we are clearly shown that the Word of the Lord was not given to teach man natural sciences, or a history of the material creation, for such knowledge, by patient research, is already within man's reach, and he will be benefited by his investigation; but Divine Revelation has a higher and nobler use to perform; in other words, by it the Lord our Creator reveals to man a knowledge of Himself and of spiritual truths, which man, unaided, by searching could never find out, for they are entirely above the reach of the natural man. Man cannot build a tower, by his self-derived intelligence, which will reach to heaven, and thus scale its walls and obtain heavenly wisdom and goodness. If he would reach heaven or heavenly knowledge, he must ascend by the ladder let down from heaven, or by living a life according to the truths revealed by the Lord through or from heaven in the sacred Scriptures, to guide him. All genuine knowledge of the Lord and of spiritual truths possessed by man has been revealed to man by the Lord, and handed down either in a written form or by tradition; but in the latter case, often more or less perverted.

The first chapters of Genesis, according to Swedenborg, are a pure Allegory, written according to the correspondence between natural and spiritual things. They contain a spiritual history of the most ancient church, denominated Adam, and of the ancient church denominated Noah, which was established after the fall of mankind, and after our race became overwhelmed by a flood of falses and evils. It is not of the physical creation that they treat, but of the spiritual creation or regeneration of men, and even of the regeneration of the men of our day, for the Word of the Lord is applicable to all men of all times.

2

The most beautiful and important lessons of spiritual truth are contained in these chapters for our use; compared with which, natural sciences and the physical history of our earth sink into insignificance.

In what follows, we propose to give the reader simply a glimpse of the contents, or spiritual sense of these chapters. To do justice to them, or to fully illustrate the meaning and show its correctness by quotations from other portions of the sacred Scriptures—for all parts of the Word must be interpreted or explained in harmony with every other part, the Word being practically its own interpreter —would require a volume. Such a volume has already been written by a man specially prepared and illuminated by the Lord for the purpose. In the first volume of Swedenborg's *Arcana Cœlestia*, containing 568 pages, the reader will find an explanation of the first eleven chapters of Genesis which will satisfy his highest reason. We are authorized to say that this volume will be sent, postage paid, to any one who may desire it, on the receipt of seventy-eight cents by the American Swedenborg Printing and Publishing Society, 20 Cooper Union, New York City. The regular price, until recently, has been one dollar and fifty cents, or nearly double the present price.

V.

Genesis, Chapter First, and Creation.

IN his preface or introduction to this chapter Swedenborg says:

"1. That the Word of the Old Testament includes arcana of heaven, and that all its contents, to every particular, regard the Lord, his heaven, the church, faith, and the things relating to faith. no man can conceive who only views it from the letter. For the letter, or literal sense, suggest only such things as respect the externals of the Jewish church; when, nevertheless, it everywhere contains internal things, which do not in the least appear in those

externals, except in a very few cases, where the Lord
revealed and unfolded them to the apostles—as that sacrifices are significative of the Lord—and that the land of
Canaan and Jerusalem are significative of heaven, on
which account they are called the heavenly Canaan and
Jerusalem—and that Paradise has a like signification.

"2. But that all and every part of its contents, even to
the most minute, not excepting the smallest jot and tittle,
signify and involve spiritual and celestial things, is a truth
to this day deeply hidden from the Christian world; in
consequence of which little attention is paid to the Old
Testament. This truth, however, might appear plainly
from this single circumstance: that the Word being of the
Lord, and from the Lord, could not possibly be given
without containing interiorly such things as relate to
heaven, to the church, and to faith. For if this be denied,
how can it be called the Word of the Lord, or be said to
have any life in it? For whence is its life, but from those
things which possess life? that is, except from hence, that
all things in it, both generally and particularly, have relation to the Lord, who is the very Life Itself. Wherefore
whatsoever does not interiorly regard Him, does not live;
nay, whatsoever expression in the Word does not involve
Him, or in its measure relate to Him, is not divine.

"3. Without such a living principle, the Word, as to
the letter, is dead. For it is with the Word as it is with
man, who, as all Christians are taught to believe, consists
of two parts, an external and an internal. The external
man, separate from the internal, is the body, which, in such
a state of separation, is dead; but the internal is that
which lives and causes the external to live. The internal
man is the soul; and thus the Word as to the letter alone,
is like a body without a soul.

"4. It is impossible, whilst the mind abides in the literal
sense only, to see that it is full of such spiritual contents.
Thus, in these first chapters of Genesis, nothing is dis-
coverable from the literal sense, but that they treat of the

creation of the world, and of the garden of Eden which is
called Paradise, and also of Adam as the first created man;
and scarcely a single person supposes them to relate to
anything besides. But that they contain arcana which
were never heretofore revealed, will sufficiently appear from
the following pages; where it will be seen that the first
chapter of Genesis, in its internal sense, treats of the NEW
CREATION of man, or of his Regeneration in general, and
specifically of the most ancient church; and this in such a
manner, that there is not a single syllable which does not
represent, signify, and involve something spiritual.

"5. That this is really the case, in respect to the Word, it
is impossible for any mortal to know, however, except from
the Lord. Wherefore it is expedient here to premise, that,
of the Lord's divine mercy, it has been granted, now for
several years, to be constantly and uninterruptedly in
company with spirits and angels, hearing them converse
with each other, and conversing with them. Hence it has
been permitted me to hear and see things in another life
which are astonishing, and which have never before come
to the knowledge of any man, nor entered into his imagination. I have there been instructed concerning different
kinds of spirits, and the state of souls after death—concerning hell, or the lamentable state of the unfaithful—
concerning heaven, or the most happy state of the faithful—particularly concerning the doctrine of faith which is
acknowledged throughout all heaven: on which subjects,
by the divine mercy of the Lord, more will be said in the
following pages."

The greatest part, at this day, only attain the first state; some only to the second; others only to the third, fourth, and fifth; few to the sixth; and scarcely any to the seventh."

VII.

The Creation of Man and Woman.

(AS DESCRIBED IN THE FIRST CHAPTER OF GENESIS, AND AS DESCRIBED IN THE SECOND.)

"And the Lord God formed man of the dust of the ground, and breathed into his nostrils the breath of life; and man became a living soul."—GEN. ii. 7.

"IN considering the Divine wisdom contained in the first two chapters of Genesis," says the Rev. Dr. Bayley, "there are two particulars which are somewhat striking in themselves, and have served to confirm theories entirely incompatible with the authority of this portion of the Divine Word as a revelation from Infinite Wisdom. The first is, that notwithstanding in the preceding chapter it is said, that 'God made man, male and female, on the sixth day, yet in the present chapter (ver. 5) it is said, after the seventh day, 'there was not a man to till the ground.' No ingenuity can make it probable that all the proceedings related to have taken place, from the creation of Adam to the formation of Eve from his rib during his sleep, could be the work of one day only. He is said to have named all the animals in the time, and to have discovered that it was not good for man to be alone. Can it be supposed that all which is implied in these operations could be the work of twelve, or even twenty-four hours? Impossible. We must seek for a higher reason; and happily this is afforded. In the first chapter of Genesis, the regeneration of man is the theme, up to that state in which truth becomes his only law and guide. He is then a true man, and a free man, in the image of his God. His religion is not constrained now, as it is in all the states meant by the days preceding the sixth. Hence, at the conclusion of that day, all things are pronounced by the Divine Being to be very good. Man is in that state a truly spiritual man; he conquers in every trial to which he is subjected. But there is a state better still: it is that in which LOVE is the supreme law—in which man is more than conqueror: he is no longer the subject of temptation. There is no labor in this state; all is rest, not the rest of inactivity, but a rest from struggle—a state of interior peace—a sabbath of the soul. This is truly a celestial state. The former chapter traced man's mental creation,—his spiritual progress, up to the stage of his becoming fully spiritual; but this chapter is taking the description forward until he becomes celestial. Up to the period described in this verse there was no man to till THIS ground, —to cultivate the celestial state.

" We shall, perhaps, be able to see the interesting subjects of thought to which the spiritual sense here invites us more clearly, if we notice three remarkable features of distinction between the first chapter and the second, both of them apparently treating of the origin of things, and of man. In the first chapter *water* occupies the leading place; in the second chapter *ground* is the most important. God broods over the face of the water on the first day; he divides between the waters on the second; he distinguishes between land and water on the third; He made fishes and fowls from the water on the fifth day. This will readily be understood and its bearing be seen by the spiritually-minded student, who knows that water, in its varied forms, is the symbol of truth—that living, purifying power which is called the water of life (Rev. xxi. 1; John iv. 10, 14). Water in the sea is representative of truth in the memory; general, external, undiscriminated, capable of being tossed about by every wind of doctrine. Water, as gentle rain, is representative of truth as it descends from the intelligent mind of a loving teacher, or from the Lord the Divine Teacher; hence Moses said, ' My doctrine shall

drop as the rain, my speech shall distil as the dew, as the
rain upon the tender herb, as the showers upon the grass'
(Deut. xxxii. 2). Water, as a river, is representative of
truth when it has become elevated to the inmost affections
of the soul, and thence flows down again into the whole
mind and life, purifying, directing, fructifying, and blessing the whole man. This is the river of God, which is
full of waters (Ps. lxv. 9 ; xlvi. 4). In the second chapter,
the only water mentioned is the river which flowed *out of*
Eden, and which was divided into four heads: a river
which has never been found on earth. It is a symbol of
truth flowing from the heart, when man is in a celestial
state.

"In the second chapter, ground has the leading position.
Mist comes upon the whole face of the *ground;* man is
made of the dust of the *ground;* out of the *ground* grow
all trees pleasant to the sight and good for food, the tree
of lives and the tree of the knowledge of good and evil;
out of the *ground* fowls are formed (ver. 19), though in
the first chapter they are said to be formed from the water
(ver. 20). Ground is the symbol of goodness; for this is
the ground into which the seeds of truth should be received. The good ground is an honest and good heart,
said the Lord Jesus (Luke viii. 15). Those states are
properly spiritual, in which the spirit of truth is the principle from which man acts as the guiding rule of his life.
Those states are properly celestial, in which love or goodness is the leading characteristic. When a man is in
spiritual states, he is rigidly right, aims at constant correctness in the path of duty, is perhaps brilliant, and delights in pursuing the truth, but is comparatively cold.
When a man is in the celestial state, he is gentle, loving,
kind, merciful, easily entreated, long-suffering, ever regards goodness as the chief object of his care, and is in all
his religious duties, warm. The spiritual man regards the
water of heaven, or truth mainly; the celestial man, the
ground of heaven, or goodness mainly Hence the first

feature of distinction which the discriminating mind will notice between the two chapters.

"The next distinctive feature between them is in the different name employed to express the Deity. In the first chapter everything is done by God, Elohim; in the second, by the Lord God, Jehovah Elohim. This circumstance has led some to conjecture that the two are merely separate traditions of the creation collated by Moses, and giving only the speculations of the writers respecting the origin of men and of all things. But this idea, in order to explain the difficulty of finding the Creator designated by different names, leads us to the unspeakably greater difficulty of a denial of revelation. For, if we deny this portion of the Divine Word to be anything more than unauthorized traditions of unknown writers, we by implication deny the whole Bible to be a Divine revelation, for the whole proceeds upon the basis of this early part being divinely true. And what a result is this! To think that our heavenly Father has left His immortal children without a guide! that He who provides bounteously its food for the humblest insect has left man's spiritual demands unsatisfied! Oh, no! we cannot admit so terrible a result. Man, already an angel in embryo, asks for angels' food, and He who has provided for all his other wants must have provided for this. 'Man lives not by bread alone, but by every word that proceedeth out of the mouth of God.' 'Blessed are they who hunger and thirst after righteousness, for they shall be filled.' That which seems an imperfection in the divine revelation only appears so, because the spiritual character of that revelation is not seen. 'The law of the Lord is perfect, converting the soul' (Ps. xix.); and when its application to the soul is seen, its divine beauty and excellence at once are made manifest.

"But when we ascertain the spiritual sense of the names God and Lord, we shall find that their diversity is an example of the divine excellence and perfection of the Holy Word, as well as an illustration of the truth of our prin-

ciple of unfolding it.   The appellation God (Elohim, or
powers) is expressive of the divine truths, which manifest
the powers of God, and which, under the name of the
divine laws, really effect all which God does in the entire
universe.   The appellation Jehovah (he who is) designates
the inmost existence of Deity, the Divine Love.   God is
love.   The two grand essentials of Deity, Infinite Love, the
source of all the goodness of the Lord, and Infinite Wisdom, the source of all the truth from the Lord, are constantly referred to in the Old Testament, and discriminated
from each other by these two names Jehovah, or Lord, and
God.   'I will call upon God, and the Lord shall save me,'
means that we appeal to the Divine Truth, but Divine
Love really saves us.   'Yet I will rejoice in Jehovah, I
will joy in the God of my salvation,' directs our attention
to both divine principles as sources of interior joy.   By
noticing the use of these two appellations, and bearing the
signification in mind, a beauty and force will be found in
the Holy Word which was before unsuspected, but which
is eminently interesting and important.

"While man is in the spiritual states of his regeneration, truth is the spring of his conduct—his guiding star,
his impelling power.   He follows it, he bows to it; it rules
him, fights for him, recreates and renews him.   Hence
God does all for him in these states.   Although Divine
Love is really within the Divine Truth at all times, man
is not consciously aware of this.

"When, however, man has entered into a celestial state,
and, in all he does, *goodness* has the lead, a great change
is gradually effected in his mode of thinking.   He does
not value truth less, but he esteems Christian love and
goodness more.   He is no longer prone to dispute about
truth, but is only careful to practise it.   The law is written upon his heart; it is no longer the object of reasoning.
He sees it by light from within; he says, Yea, yea, to what
he inwardly perceives to be right, or Nay, nay, to the reverse   He is now at peace, and has but to cultivate and

preserve the virtues Divine Love and Wisdom have unfolded within him. He is in Eden, and has only to dress
and to keep it. In all the divine dealings with him now
he sees the Divine Love as manifest as the Divine Wisdom.
He discerns not only the right of Providence in all things,
but its mercy. It is no longer God only, but Jehovah
God, who leads him. It is the Deity as his Father that
he rejoices to hear. He feels his LOVE around him, and
within him, and he is happy. He lives in his Father's
house; his Father's commands are no hard laws to him,
but delightful directions. He loves the law, and has great
peace (Ps. cxix. 165). This, therefore, is the sufficient
reason for the name of the Lord being Jehovah God in
the second chapter, and simply God in the first.

"The third distinctive peculiarity is, that man is described in the first chapter as being created male and
female, on the sixth day. In the second, after the seventh
day is described, he is created as Adam, alone, and not
until many proceedings are narrated which cannot be supposed as having taken place in twelve or twenty-four
hours, is it found not to be good for man to dwell alone,
and during Adam's sleep Eve is formed. We do not mean
it to be inferred that we think man's physical creation is
related in either the first or the second chapter. An inquiry into that is the proper subject of natural science,
not of divine revelation. God's Word has to do with
souls, churches, and man's spiritual career, not with
earthly questions, which scientific lore is quite adequate to
solve. There are sufficient indications of the existence of
other inhabitants of the world in the time of Adam and
Eve, to show that their history is not the account of the
single solitary family of human beings then inhabiting
the globe. Cain went into the land of Nod, and there he
took a wife (chap. iv. 17). Whence came his wife, if there
were no other people yet existing than his own father and
mother? When he slew his brother Abel, and was convicted by Jehovah, he complained that when he was cast

out from his presence, every one that met him would kill him, and Jehovah set a mark upon him for his protection. Of whom could he be afraid, if there were no one on earth but his father and mother? He built a city, it is said, and called it after the name of his son Enoch (ver. 17). Whence did they get the building materials? Surely a city implies more than one family.

" In thinking, therefore, of Adam, we must dismiss from our minds the idea of the natural creation of man as the subject of our divine narrative at all. Doubtless God created the physical universe, and man upon it; but that is not the subject now, nor of that revelation whose grand purpose everywhere is not natural history, nor external events, except as the medium of conveying heavenly and divine instruction (Isa. lv. 8).

"Adam is the generic name for all human beings; in Hebrew it is equivalent to MAN. Hence it is said in the fifth chapter of the book before us (ver. 2), 'God created them male and female, and called THEIR name Adam in the day,' etc. This single appellation, Man, was expressive, among the wise ones of old, of human beings in a regenerated state; and as these, when presented together in the divine sight, compose one body (1 Cor. xii. 12), the Church, however numerous the members may be, are called by this one name, MAN or Adam.

"This is expressed very strikingly in the Hebrew of Ezek. xxxiv. 31: 'And ye my flock, the flock of my pasture, are Adam, and I am your God, saith the Lord Jehovah.'

"Let us resume, then, the inquiry for the spiritual reason why man is spoken of in the first chapter as having been created male and female, and in the second as Adam alone.

"In the spiritual states of man, which we have seen to be described in the first chapter, and in which truth in the intellect is the sovereign ruler, the two grand faculties of the mind are distinctly presented as male and female. The intellect is male, for intellect predominates in the properly developed manly character; the will, the seat of the affections, is female, for the heart is the predominating characteristic of the true womanly character. Both these grand faculties are, however, found in each mind, so that, in a certain sense, each mind is male and female, and when both the heart and the understanding are combined in the reception of true religion, in that mind there is a marriage, an interior union of the truth which is understood, with the goodness which is loved: their land is married (Isa. lxii. 4), they know the truth, and they are happy because they do it.

"Now, while man is in spiritual states, and has first to learn the truth by slow investigation and reasoning, and afterwards to bring his heart by further effort, to adopt the truth, and do it, he perceives these two faculties of his soul very distinctly, as though they were separate. He feels that he is male and female. But when he has entered into the celestial state, so that love from the heart rules every lower faculty and power, this divided consciousness disappears. He feels as one embodiment of love, from first to last. Heavenly love in him adores, love believes, love bears, love speaks, love acts. He becomes a form of holy love. That principle glistens in his eye, pervades his language, and if the spirit could be visibly presented to the sight, it would be a beautiful form of celestial affections embodied. Because this state, the celestial one, is the subject of the second chapter, Adam is presented up to the time when something *not good* is discovered, as dwelling in Eden, alone.

"We have a parallel presented in Deut. xxxiii. 28: 'Israel then shall dwell in safety, ALONE: the fountain of Jacob shall be upon a land of corn and wine; also his heavens shall drop down dew.' Here, Israel is treated as one person, and dwelling alone, when there was nothing foreign, or adverse there. The loneliness is not that of solitariness, but of unity. So is it in the celestial state of man, or of the Church. The ruling love, being heavenly, glows like a celestial fire in the highest region of the soul; wisdom, like a flame from that fire, illuminates the whole mind with a calm and holy light. All things below have been moulded to delightful and ready obedience, and happy order rules in every principle of the character and life. Then, man dwells in Eden, in safety, alone."

Such, then, are some of the lessons which are presented for our consideration in the divine account of man in Eden, spiritually understood, or when this portion of the Divine Word is unfolded according to the law of correspondences between spiritual and natural things, revealed by the Lord through Emanuel Swedenborg.

VIII.

Eve.

THE men of the most ancient Church were led by the Lord, and had a perception of that which was good and true, and they acknowledged the Lord as the giver and themselves as but recipients. They were said to dwell alone, because they were under the Lord's guidance as celestial men, and were not infested by evils or evil spirits. But their posterity began gradually to decline from this exalted state, and were not content to be led by the Lord, but desired also to be guided by themselves and the world.

By the woman which was formed and given to the man is signified selfhood, or what is properly one's own, or rather what appears to be one's own. The state of man, when he supposes his life to be self-derived, is compared to deep sleep, and by the ancients it was called deep sleep, and in the Word it is said of such that they have poured out upon them the spirit of deep sleep, and that they sleep the sleep. By a rib, which is a bone of the chest, is meant man's selfhood, or proprium, referred to above, in which there is but little vitality, as bones possess little

vitality or life. By to build is spiritually signified to raise
up what was fallen; by the rib, the comparatively dead
selfhood or love of self and the world; by a woman is
signified a selfhood vivified or made alive by the Lord;
by he brought her to the man is signified that a selfhood
or proprium was granted him. Their being naked and
not ashamed, signifies that they were innocent; for the
Lord had insinuated innocence into their selfhood or proprium, to prevent its being offensive to him. "The
posterity of this Church," says Swedenborg, "did not wish,
like their parents, to be a celestial man, but to be under
their own self-guidance, and thus inclining to selfhood;
it was granted to them, but still one vivified or made alive
by the Lord, and therefore called a woman, and afterwards
a wife." Instead of perceiving and feeling as their ancestors constantly did, that all life, all truth and goodness,
were from the Lord, and that they were living from Him,
they were still permitted to perceive that they lived from
the Lord, although when not reflecting on the subject
they knew no other but that they lived from themselves.
"It is not," says Swedenborg, "however, easy to perceive
how these things are, unless the state of the celestial man
is understood. In the celestial man the internal man is
distinct from the external; indeed, so distinct that he perceives what belongs to the internal, and what to the external, and how the external is governed by the internal
from the Lord. But the state of the posterity of this
celestial man, in consequence of inclining to proprium or
the affections which belong to the external man, was so
changed, that they no longer perceived the internal man
to be distinct from the external, but imagined the internal
to be one with the external; for such a perception takes
place when man inclines to proprium, or to the love of
self and the world."

The posterity of the Most Ancient Church, or of Adam
when he dwelt alone, was not evil but still good; and because they desired to live in the external man, or in pro-

prium, this was permitted by the Lord, but charity and innocence were insinuated; and men still made the external things subordinate to spiritual, and used the things of this world without placing their chief delight therein; the fall was not yet, but was to come.

It is impossible to give in a few words, touching here and there only, a very good or even clear idea of the wonderful practical treasures of spiritual knowledge contained in these divine chapters when spiritually unfolded according to the science of correspondences. If the reader would understand this part of the sacred Scriptures, he must read the first volume of Swedenborg's "Arcana Cœlestia," and he will there find every verse, sentence and word carefully unfolded, and will be able to see that the Word of the Lord is indeed infinite, and contains treasures for him vastly surpassing in value all earthly treasures.

IX.

The Garden of Eden—Its Trees and River.

"And the Lord God planted a garden eastward in Eden; and there he put the man whom he had formed. And out of the ground made the Lord God to grow every tree that is pleasant to the sight and good for food; the tree of life also in the midst of the garden, and the tree of knowledge of good and evil. And a river went out of Eden to water the garden; and from thence it was parted, and became into four heads."—GEN. ii. 8-10.

"THAT this garden," says the Rev. Dr. Bayley, "its trees, and fountain with four streams, were never intended to be otherwise than allegorically understood, the very names, as already intimated, themselves undoubtedly imply. What is a Tree of Life? The Book of Proverbs answers, Wisdom is a Tree of Life. And may we not ask the firmest adherent to the letter of the Scriptures only, Did you ever find life growing on any earthly tree? Has life more than one source, and do we not regard this to be Him who is the Life? Do we not find this same tree

declared in the Book of Revelation to be in the midst of
heaven? 'To him that overcometh,' it is said, 'I will
give to eat of the Tree of Life that is in the midst of the
paradise of God' (Rev. ii. 7). But can any rational mind
suppose that an earthly tree has been transplanted to a
spiritual and heavenly world? The idea is obviously unworthy of being rationally entertained. Again, we find the
Tree of Life in the midst of the New Jerusalem, and on
both sides of the river. 'In the midst of the street of it,
and on either side of the river, was there the Tree of Life,
which bare twelve manner of fruits, and yielded her fruit
every month; and the leaves of the tree were for the
healing of the nations' (Rev. xxii. 2). Is this at all com-
patible with the idea of a literal tree? Assuredly not.
But when on the other hand we reflect that from the one
source of life, the Lord, there descend two grand influences—Love and Wisdom—in the most intimate union;
and these form the inmost powers of light and blessing to
the regenerated soul—the soul in the state of paradise,
then we recognize the tree of two lives in the ancient
garden of Eden. We say the tree of two lives, for the
word rendered life, *hachayim*, is in the dual, not in the
singular, nor in the general plural, in the account of this
tree in our text. The holy influence of the Lord, in its
twofold character of love and light within, is the tree of
lives. This is in the midst of the garden of the soul.
This is the source of the joys of the angels. This is the
centre, and pervades all the principles of the New Church
called the New Jerusalem. The virtues it inspires in all
the varying states of man's regeneration—as his faith
waxes and wanes, and thus his spiritual months go on—are
the twelve manner of fruits it bears. On its holy branches
grow acts of patience for seasons of affliction, of gratitude
for those of prosperity, of trust and fortitude in the storms
of life, of benevolence, charity, and justice in our daily
walk, and of hope, ever speaking of better things, like an
inward gem glittering in all the golden fruit of this divine

tree. Its leaves are the truths, which are for the healing
of the nations.

"The tree of knowledge of good and evil is equally in-
dicative of a spiritual existence, not of a natural plant.
For on what tree does knowledge grow, save on the human
mind? The idle fancy that this tree was an apple-tree
cannot be called a thought, it is a fancy having no rational
ground. Can knowledge be cut from an apple, or squeezed
from a fig? We find knowledge grows only as we exercise
the desire to know.

"The knowledge of external things may well be called
the knowledge of good and evil, for it is the knowledge of
the results of order and disorder, of fitness and unfitness,
of truths and appearances. It is an acquaintance with the
outsides of things. This knowledge is useful for earthly
purposes, but is not the real truth. It is a tree that has
its uses in the garden, but its fruit is not to be eaten.
Our own sensations give us a knowledge of ourselves, but
that knowledge is full of fallacy, and needs the constant
correction of a higher wisdom. We feel as if our life were
our own. We are conscious of no origin of life out of
ourselves. We feel that we exist, but we do not feel the
stream of life from which our existence is momentarily
maintained. Judging from our own sensations, we are
self-existent. This, however, is an appearance, which we
must beware of confirming. Let the tree grow for its own
purposes, but do not eat the fruit. Our own knowledge
is good to know and to use, but not to eat, or to confirm,
and make part of ourselves. The perceptions of heavenly
wisdom are the other trees of the garden; and of these we
may freely eat—they are in accordance with eternal truth.
But, of the tree of our own self-perceived knowledge we
may not eat, for in the day, or state, in which we eat of it,
we enter upon the path of error, of self-will, of carnal-
mindedness, of spiritual death; 'For to be carnally
minded is death; to be spiritually minded is life and
peace.'

3

"Both trees can be rightly admitted into our garden, but each must have its proper place, and each its proper value assigned: the Tree of Lives must be in the midst of the garden; the tree of the knowledge of good and evil, at the circumference. That a garden, and especially the garden of Eden, is regarded in the sacred Scripture as symbolic of a regenerated, cultivated state of the soul, is manifest in the declarations of the prophets. The prophet Isaiah said: 'The Lord shall guide thee continually, and satisfy thy *soul* in drought, and make fat thy bones: and *thou shalt be like a watered garden*, and like a spring of water, whose waters fail not' (lviii. 11). Jeremiah adopts the same language of correspondence: 'Therefore they shall come and sing in the heights of Zion, and shall flow together to the goodness of the Lord, for wheat and for wine, and for oil, and for the young of the flock and of the herd: and their soul shall be as a watered garden; and they shall not sorrow any more at all' (xxxi. 12).

"This circumstance gives us the reason why the site of Eden has never been found. Persons who have had no higher idea of the Divine Word than the literal one, have sought everywhere to discover a land watered by four rivers flowing from one fountain: one of the rivers being the Euphrates. No satisfactory discovery has ever been made.

"But all have admitted that the exact site could not be found. And yet, according to the prophet, the king of Tyre had found it, and been in it many hundreds of years after the flood, if it also were a natural event. 'Son of man, take up a lamentation upon the king of Tyrus, and say unto him, Thus saith the Lord God; Thou sealest up the sum, full of wisdom, and perfect in beauty. Thou hast been in Eden, the garden of God; every precious stone was thy covering, the sardius, topaz, etc., * * * * thou hast walked up and down in the midst of the stones of fire' (Ezek. xxviii. 12–14).

"If the garden of Eden means a cultivated, enlightened,

and happy state of mind, this language is not difficult to
be understood. The precious stones represent precious
truths; the stones of fire, truths glowing with love, for
love is spiritual heat.

"Another mention of the trees of Eden is made by the
same prophet in chapter thirty-one, where the language of
the whole chapter is unquestionably allegorical. 'Behold,'
it is said, 'the Assyrian was a cedar in Lebanon, with fair
branches, and with a shadowing shroud, and of a high
stature; and his top was among the thick boughs' (ver. 3).
Of the Assyrian thus represented by a majestic cedar, the
prophet proceeds to say: 'The cedars in the garden of God
could not hide him: the fir trees were not like his boughs,
and the chestnut trees were not like his branches; nor any
tree in the garden of God was like unto him in his beauty.
I have made him fair by the multitude of his branches:
so that all the trees of Eden that were in the garden of
God envied him' (ver. 8, 9). Again: 'I made the nations
to shake at the sound of his fall, when I cast him down to
hell with them that descend into the pit: and all the trees
of Eden, the choice and best of Lebanon, all that drink
water, shall be comforted in the nether parts of the earth'
(ver. 16). Here, it is manifest, no natural trees can be
meant. These could not envy the Assyrian, or strive to
hide him. These could not be comforted when they went
down to the pit, with them that are slain. From every
consideration, therefore, it is clear, that in the Divine
Word, Eden and its trees are the types of a mental and a
spiritual paradise, not of a natural garden.

"The river which watered the garden, with its four
heads of subordinate streams, though nowhere found in
nature, is easily found in spirit. It is that Divine Truth,
which is called the 'river of the water of life' (Rev. xxii. 1),
which is meant by the River of God, which is full of
waters; and that holy stream which the prophet saw, and
which 'made everything live where it went' (Ezek. xlvii.
9). Divine Truth as it descends from the Lord comes as

one river, but as it is received by man it is parted into four great divisions, faith, knowledge, reason, and science; and these illustrate the different departments of the mind, which are like so many countries into which they flow.

"Happy is it with man when all these streams are received and harmonize together. His state is then an Eden indeed; a paradise of light, and love, and joy.

"We must return to the Eden state, or we can never attain the joys of Paradise. The Lord will sow the good seed of the Word in our souls, if we will permit Him. He will give us power to cultivate our minds, and make our souls like a watered garden. We must have His love and wisdom like a tree of lives in the centre of our garden, and of its fruits we may eat and live. This is the only way of securing Paradise. The kingdom of God must be formed within (Luke xvii. 21). It is indeed not meat and drink, but righteousness, peace, and joy in the Holy Ghost (Rom. xiv. 17). . How vain is the dream of those who fancy that to find happiness they must seek it in distant lands—some in Jerusalem, some in Mecca, some in Rome. Heaven and happiness are as near in our beloved land as on any spot of God's earth, and by them who seek faithfully, by help from our blessed Saviour, the Lord Jesus, to subdue the sources of misery in themselves, in their vices, their passions, and their follies, whether they dwell in a palace or in a cottage, in an island, or in distant lands, the divine promise will to them be realized: 'The Lord shall comfort Zion: he will comfort all her waste places; and he will make her wilderness like Eden, and her desert like the garden of the Lord; joy and gladness shall be found therein, thanksgiving, and the voice of melody" (Isa li. 3).

If the reader would understand this wonderful allegory of the Garden of Eden, as fully unfolded by the science of correspondences between spiritual and natural things, he must read the first volume of Swedenborg's "Arcana Cœlestia."

X.

The Fall of Man—The Serpent—And the Curse Introduced into the World.

(WRITTEN BY THE REV. DR. BAYLEY, OF LONDON.)

"And the Lord God said unto the woman, What is this that thou hast done? And the woman said, The serpent beguiled me, and I did eat."—GEN. iii. 13.

"THAT man is not now in the condition in which he must have been created seems evident if we reflect upon the perfections of his Divine Creator, or the manifest capabilities of the human constitution, and then notice the individual and social state of the race at present. When man came from the hands of his Maker, without the intervention of other human beings, he must have been complete and unperverted in his degree of life, and in his powers, though that degree and those powers were finite; since his Divine Creator must have been too good not to desire to make him complete for happiness, too wise not to know how to accomplish His purpose, and too powerful not to be able to carry it into effect. Man must, therefore, have been created, at first, in a state of order, and with every power to arrive at the possession of the highest, fullest bliss. But now, alas, how changed is the whole scene of mankind! Swarms of police and immense standing armies are required to prevent private and public ruffians from preying upon mankind. Wild passions are with difficulty restrained; now and then they burst all bounds, and like volcanoes which have been long pent up, but whose burning surges can no longer be held in, they pour forth their rivers of scorching death on all around. Universal imperfection is admitted, and testifies to an universal fall, seen from the outside of society. But when we regard man as he is within, he who watches his own heart and mind knows how much there is to subdue, reform, and to regenerate, before he can be happy. Others see, sometimes, what is done, but they see not what is resisted. 'The heart is deceitful above all things, and desperately wicked, who can know it?' (Jer. xvii. 9.) The human mind is like a magnificent building whose splendid arches and glorious proportions may be traced, but which lies in ruins. It is a volume of incalculable worth, on which the laws of eternal righteousness are to be traced in golden letters, but, alas! it is all torn and blotted, and can only, by a divine hand, be restored. The world within is like the world without. By the diligent hand of cultivation fair spots are formed of verdure and of beauty, lovely enough to show what is the intention of its Maker, and what are its capabilities, but at the same time it is actually deformed with jungle and desert, with marsh and quagmire, with thorn and briar. Wild beasts of every hideous and terrible form hide, and howl, and roar, and fight, and destroy there. Such is the human soul now. How came it thus? That is our present inquiry.

"The history of nations has no answer to our present question. Human philosophy is equally dumb. Divine revelation imports to give an answer, and the question upon which we are now engaged is, What does the answer mean?

"Those who take the early chapters of Genesis as a literal history inform us that a natural serpent seduced our first parents, and persuaded them to eat of a fruit which God had forbidden to be touched, and for this offence God cursed them and their posterity, the serpent, and the earth. But this is so strange an account, that if it had not first been childishly received in the dark ages, and continued to be taught us generally in childhood, it would not have been received at all. What a strange idea does it give of God, when it represents Him as placing a tree needlessly in paradise; for, according to this idea, its fruit was never to be tasted, it could only tantalize the inhabitants of the garden. What a character does it attribute to

infinite love, the best of Beings, when it describes Him as
so jealous of the fruit of this one tree, and so unfeeling to
His immortal children, as to curse them *and their unborn
posterity*, because this fruit was taken! What an improbable circumstance is narrated, when we are told that
our first parents in their perfect state could be seduced by
an animal, and be led away from God by a beast of the
field. This has been felt to be so improbable that many
have said the devil was in the serpent, but Moses says not
a word about any devil entering the serpent. His words
are simply, 'Now the serpent was more subtle than any
beast of the field which the Lord God had made' (Gen.
iii. 1). And if a devil was the real delinquent, how comes
it to pass that he escapes without a word, while the poor
serpent, his innocent tool, is punished? By this mode of
understanding the narrative the real culprit is never-men-
tioned, the beast is condemned to go on its belly and to
eat dust all the days of its life. And what is still more
wonderful, not only does the devil escape unnoticed, but
the serpent takes no notice of the sort of food he is condemned to live upon, and declines to eat dust any more
than other carnivorous animals.

"This serpent, too, according to a mere literal interpretation, should have its head bruised by the Messiah, and it
should bruise His heel (chap. iii. 15). But who ever
heard of its continuing to live four thousand years, until
the Saviour came, or then fulfilling this prediction?

"But it is said, God gave a law respecting the tree of
knowledge of good and evil: 'Thou shalt not eat of it, for
in the day that thou eatest thereof thou shalt surely die'
(Gen. ii. 17). And he was bound by His undeviating
truth to put this law into execution. But here the literal
interpretation meets with another difficulty, or rather with
several difficulties. For, taking the word death in the
natural sense, its advocates are compelled to admit Adam
did not die *on the day* he ate of the tree, and not until
nine hundred and thirty years after. If this death were a

curse, these advocates say, Christ took upon Himself the
curse inflicted upon man, and so saved the human race.
Of course then man ought not to die. Besides, in that
case, the law which it was said God was, by His undeviating truth, bound to enforce, was *not enforced after all;*
for the law was 'THOU shalt surely die.' It says not one
word of any one dying for him. The death of another
would not fulfil the law, THOU shalt surely die. Lastly,
all this argument respecting the inflexible law goes upon
the implied meaning of the law to be what it by no means
expresses. In the day thou eatest thereof, I will cause
thee to die, or I will put thee to death. There is, however, nothing of this kind in the announcement.

"Having seen the difficulties which crowd around a
merely natural interpretation of the serpent, and the circumstances which are connected with it in the sacred
Scriptures, and seen how full an illustration they
give of what the apostle calls 'the letter that killeth,'
let us now advance to the 'spirit which giveth life'
(2 Cor. iii. 6).

"That the serpent is used in the sacred Scriptures with
a spiritual meaning, is evident from this very Book of
Genesis, and almost from every other. We read, chap.
xlix. 17, 'Dan shall be a serpent by the way, an adder in
the path, that biteth the horse's heels, so that his rider
shall fall backward;' very obscure this language, unless
we apply to its interpretation the science of correspondence, in which each natural object bears a representation
which has an analogy to its nature and habits. The serpent lives and moves close to the earth. In warm countries it is to be found in great numbers, in great variety,
and often of great size. Some kinds are harmless, but
some are most deadly. They are generally insidious in
their movements, and they spring from under the grass or
leaves, or from their holes in the sand, ere the traveller is
aware that danger is near. Some species are said to exercise great power of fascination, and make it almost impos-

sible for the animal they have destined for their prey to
escape. From all these circumstances, we can easily
recognize their analogy with that affection of our nature
which disposes us to delight in the gratifications of sense.
The love of sensual things is useful, though its uses are of
a low kind. If it were not pleasant to us to observe the
beauties of our lovely world, to listen to the music of the
human voice and the harmonies which nature offers, to
enjoy the fragrancies with which the balmy air is loaded,
and to taste the savours of the food which Providence
bestows to sustain and strengthen us, our bodies could not
be maintained as a healthy base for the higher things of
life. The serpent, though a creeping animal, has his
proper place and use in the little world of the human
mind. Yet in the strong excitements of sense there is
a subtle tendency to excess, that needs the constant watch-
fulness of wisdom to preserve this principle in order.
'The serpent is more subtle than any beast of the field
which the Lord God has made.'

"Sensual love, when chosen and preferred above the
higher and holier principles that dignify the moral, the
rational, and spiritual departments of our nature, makes
the spirit of fiends and fiendish men, and hence is called
'that old serpent,' even the devil and Satan, which de-
ceiveth the whole world.' (Rev. xii. 9.) To oppose this
spirit, and destroy its direful power, the Lord came into
the world by assuming the seed of the woman, and thus
fulfilled the prophecy by bruising the head or chief power
of the serpent, when He conquered hell. The infernal influences bruised His heel or lowest part, His outward
human nature; while He became completely triumphant
by then glorifying His human nature, and subduing hell
and death.

"He gave His disciples, at first, and He still gives them,
power to tread upon serpents of sensuality in themselves,
as He says, 'I beheld Satan like lightning fall from heaven.
Behold I give unto you power to tread on serpents and

scorpions, and over all the power of the enemy: and nothing shall by any means hurt you.' (Luke x. 18, 19.)

"We have now the chief elements for understanding the divine account of man's fall. The tree of knowledge represents the knowledge we acquire by our senses; the serpent, the love of sensuous knowledge and experience, which may be good or bad, according as it is kept in its proper place, or raised to rule where it ought to serve. When the serpent is the servant of higher principles, it inspires its possessor with circumspection; when suffered to rule, it leads to sensuality.

"In the woman's reply a remarkable fact is to be noticed; she regards the tree of knowledge as in the midst of the garden, although as the Lord God arranged the garden, the tree of lives was in the midst (chap. ii. 9). She says, 'We may eat of the fruit of the trees of the garden, but of the fruit of the tree which is in the midst of the garden, God hath said, Ye shall not eat of it, neither shall ye touch it, lest ye die' (chap. iii. 3). In this declaration of the woman we have another change of state implied; she regarded the tree of knowledge, not the tree of lives, as the centre of all wisdom. When we have adopted our conclusions from the short-sighted appearances of sense, as being central truth, we are ripe for ruin, and such was the condition of the people represented by the divine record before us. There is an experience illustrative of this in the case of every one who falls. If divine wisdom were firmly held to, if the tempted fled for refuge from their own clouded fancies, to the Rock of ages, all would be well; but when they place the tree of their own knowledge in the centre of the mind, they find their fancied strength becomes the veriest weakness, and the issue is misery and death.

"The serpent next becomes bolder. The sensual principle strengthens itself, and suggests, 'Ye shall not surely die: for God doth know that in the day ye eat thereof, then your eyes shall be opened, and ye shall be as gods,

knowing good and evil.' When we determine to act upon
our own conceits, we deem ourselves singularly clever.
We conclude we shall take no harm; we shall know how
to elude all the dangers Divine Wisdom has predicted, and
all the world shall see how successful shall be our projects.
We shall no longer be hoodwinked; our eyes shall be
opened, and we shall be as gods, showing that we know
how to secure, in our own way, and by our own strength,
selfish indulgences and the goods of selfish and worldly
success, and avoid the evils of suffering, adversity and want.
We take then the fruit of the tree; it seems good, it seems
pleasant. It is a tree to be desired to make one wise. We
take it, but soon experience shows that this wisdom of the
serpent is the curse of the soul. Alas for such opening
of the eyes as then takes place! A sense of weakness is
soon unfolded; a sense of restlessness and loss; a sense of
blame, and necessity for covering. We desire to excuse,
and apologize. We cover ourselves with the fig-leaves of
idle pretences that we had no power to do otherwise, although we forsook the guidance and the strength which
were extended to save us. We have lost the bright day
of former light and love; it has become evening, and we
are cold and sad.

"It is the cool of the day. The hour of reflection has
come on. The merciful voice of the Almighty is perceived
moving in the garden of the soul, and asking the important question, 'Adam, where art thou?'

"Can any one conceive that the All-knowing needed to
inquire after man in an earthly garden? Surely not. But
He comes from His mercy into the conscience of every
one after sin. The question implies the divine impulse,
leading the sinner to ask himself, 'Man, where art thou?'
Remember where thou wast. Thou hast been innocent,
peaceful, and happy; how art thou now? Thou hadst
once the sweet lessons of heavenly wisdom shining brightly
within thee; these are all obscured and fled. 'Man, where
art thou?'

"The origin of evil was not the introduction of a new principle into human nature; it was only displacing the principles which were already there, and were all good, in their proper order. Natural evil is not anything original; it is but the perversion, or displacement, of what is otherwise good. Fire is a good thing as a servant, but bad as a master: water is excellent as rain, or in a river, but bad as a flood: every power of the human mind and body is good in its place and proportion, but each one becomes an evil, when unduly exalted. When the senses and the passions of the lowest degree of the soul were raised to undue importance, and the higher and holier principles of the soul were first neglected, and then despised and disbelieved, this constituted the fall, and it was a real and fearful fall—the higher principles of love to God and man were thrown down, and made to serve. The life's business of man now is to reverse this, and thus rise again by power from the great serpent-bruiser—the Lord Jesus Christ. Our serpents—our sensual principles, are now too fearfully impure, and too strong for us. He will give us power, however, to tread upon them. It is hard for us, at first, to resist our proneness to place the pleasures of time before the purities of eternity, the desires of the flesh above the principles of the spirit; but if we look to Him, the Divine and Perfect Man, virtue will go out from Him, and we shall be saved. 'Thou shalt call His name Jesus, for He shall save His people from their sins.' He will enable us to deny ourselves and all our faculties, and follow Him. By His power we shall not only subdue the sensual things of our nature, but they will be regenerated, filled with new heavenly life. We shall first tread upon the serpent, and then take it up, and join it to what is heavenly. 'These signs,' our blessed Lord says, 'shall follow them that believe; they shall take up serpents' (Mark xvi. 18).

"When we have thus struggled, and by the aid of the Captain of our salvation conquered, in the conflicts of the regeneration, the fall will be reversed in us; the love of

God and man, wisdom and faith, peace and happiness, will be restored to us. We shall realize those gracious words of the divine promise, and have paradise and the tree of life once more. 'To him that overcometh will I give to eat of the tree of life, which is in the midst of the paradise of God' (Rev. ii. 7).

"Feeling the loss of mankind, by separation from the source of all happiness, wisdom, and peace; feeling our own personal want of the divine Deliverer from sin and sorrow; let us lift our eyes and hearts to our only Saviour, and in the language of Milton say —

> 'Queller of Satan, on Thy glorious work
> Now enter; and begin to save mankind."'

How different the above ideas of the fall of man, drawn from the writings of Emanuel Swedenborg, from those generally entertained; whether more rational or not the reader can judge for himself.

XI.
Cain and Abel.

IN his introduction to the internal sense of the fourth chapter of Genesis, Swedenborg says: "Since this chapter treats of the degeneracy of the Most Ancient Church, or the falsification of its doctrine, and consequently of heresies and sects, under the names of Cain and his descendants, it is to be observed, that there is no possibility of understanding how doctrine was falsified, or what was the nature of the heresies and sects of that church, unless the nature of the true church be rightly understood. Enough has been said above concerning the Most Ancient Church, showing that it was a Celestial Man, and acknowledged no other faith than such as was connected with love towards the Lord, and the neighbor. By means of that love from the Lord, they obtained faith,

or a perception of all its truths, and were therefore unwilling to speak of faith, lest it should be separated from
Love. * * * Such was the nature of the Most Ancient
Church and of its doctrine; but the case is far different at
the present day, for now faith precedes charity, and by
means of faith, charity is given by the Lord, and then
charity takes the precedence. It hence follows, that doctrine became falsified in ancient times when men made
confession of faith, and thus separated it from love. Those
who falsified doctrine in this way, or separated faith from
love, or acknowledged faith alone, were denominated Cain;
and this thing was regarded by them as an enormous
(heresy).

"By the man and his wife the Most Ancient Church is
signified, as has heretofore been shown: its offspring, or
first-born, is faith, which is here called Cain; the saying,
I have gotten a man from the Lord, signifies that faith
with such as are called Cain, is known and acknowledged
in a distinct form." * * * They had been, as it were,
previously, ignorant of faith as a separate object of
thought, because they had a perception of what related to
it; but, when they began to make a distinct doctrine of
faith, they then collected together the truths which they
had heretofore perceived, and reduced them into doctrine,
calling it I have gotten a man, Jehovah, as if they had
found out something new; and thus, what was before in-
scribed on the heart became a mere matter of science. In
ancient times they gave every new thing a name, and explained what the name implied by particular sayings.
Thus the signification of the name Ishmael is explained
by the saying, 'Jehovah hath heard his affliction' (Gen.
xvi. 11); that of Reuben, by the expression, 'Jehovah
hath looked upon thy affliction' (Gen. xxix. 32); the
name Simeon, by the saying, 'Jehovah hath heard that I
was hated' (Gen. xxix. 33); and that of Judah, by 'Now
will I praise Jehovah' (ver. 35). The altar built by Moses
was called 'Jehovah my banner' (Exod. xvii. 15); and

in like manner the doctrine of faith is here denominated
'I have gotten a man, Jehovah,' or Cain."

"The second offspring of the church is charity, signified
by the terms Abel and brother. He is a shepherd of the
flock who exercises the good of charity, and a tiller of the
ground is one who is destitute of charity, although principled in faith separate from love, which is, indeed, no
faith." "Such persons as regarded corporeal and terrestrial objects chiefly, were said to till the ground, as is
evident from what is related in the second chapter of
Genesis, 19–23; where we read, that the man was cast out
of the Garden of Eden to till the ground."

But it will be remembered that Cain and Abel dwelt
together in comparative peace for a time, as brethren; or,
in other words, faith and charity were still united; thus
says Swedenborg, "At its origin faith was not so far separated from love as in the end of days, or in the progress
of time; which, indeed, is the case with every doctrine of
true faith." By Jehovah's having respect unto Abel and
his offering, is signified that works of charity, and all worship grounded in charity, were well-pleasing to the Lord.

"Abel signifies charity, as stated above. By charity is
meant love to the neighbor and compassion; for he who
loves his neighbor as himself, is also compassionate towards
him in his sufferings, as towards himself."

"The firstlings of the flock signify that which is of the
Lord alone, as appears from the statement that the firstlings or first-born, in the representative or Jewish Church,
were all holy, because they had relation to the Lord, who
is alone the first-born; and as all love is of the Lord, for
not the least portion of it is of man, therefore the Lord
alone is, in reality, the first-born. This fact was represented in the ancient churches by the first-born of man
and of beast being sacred to Jehovah."

"By Cain, as has been stated, is signified faith separate
from love, or such a doctrine as admits the possibility of
this separation."

"Cain's being very wroth, represents that charity had departed, as may appear from what is afterwards related of his killing his brother Abel, by whom charity is signified. Anger is a general affection resulting from whatever is contradictory to self-love and its lusts. This is manifestly perceptible in the world of evil spirits, for there exists a common feeling of anger against the Lord, in consequence of their not being principled in charity, but in hatred. Whatever does not favor self-love and love of the world, excites opposition, which is manifested by anger."

"Sin in general is called the devil, who, with his crew of infernals, is ever at hand when man is destitute of charity; and the only means of driving away the devil and his crew from the door of our minds, is love towards the Lord and our neighbor."

"Cain's rising up against his brother Abel, and slaying him, when they were in the field together, denotes that when both faith and charity took their origin from the doctrine of faith, then faith separate from love could not but disregard and thereby extinguish charity; as at the present day with those who maintain that faith alone saves, without any work of charity, for in this very supposition they extinguish charity, although they know, and confess with their lips, that faith is not saving faith unless it be grounded in love."

Cain's reply when asked, Where is Abel thy brother? "I know not, am I my brother's keeper?" signifies that he considered charity as nothing, and was unwilling to be subservient to it, consequently, that he altogether rejected everything of charity. Such at length became the doctrine of those who were called Cain.

"The most ancient people," says Swedenborg, "by Jehovah's speaking, understood perception, for they knew that the Lord gave them the faculty to perceive. This perception could continue no longer than whilst love was the ruling principle. When love towards the Lord, and neighborly love as a consequence, ceased, perception perished, for perception could only exist in the degree that love remained. This perceptive faculty was peculiar to the Most Ancient Church. When faith however became separated from love, as in the people after the flood, and charity was communicated through the medium of faith, . then conscience succeeded (in the place of perception), dictating to the mind, although after a different mode. Of this, by the divine mercy of the Lord, we shall speak at a future period."

The want of space will compel us to leave the reader who wishes to pursue this sublime spiritual history of our race to consult the first volume of Swedenborg's Arcana Cœlestia, and there he will find the spiritual signification of the historical record clearly given and abundantly illustrated from every part of the sacred Scriptures. This section has been composed almost entirely of short extracts from the above work. Taken from their connections and illustrations, they can give the reader but a faint idea of the depth and fullness of the knowledge contained in the spiritual sense of this portion of the Divine Word, as unfolded by the Lord through Swedenborg. The reader will be surprised to find this record full of the most useful and practical lessons of spiritual truth adapted especially to the wants of the men of this day, and that it has providentially been handed down to us for this very purpose— a pure allegory instead of a 'literal history of the first son born to earthly parents most foully murdering his innocent brother. With a short notice of the Flood and Tower of Babel, we shall have done with this part of our subject, or the first chapters of Genesis.

XII.

The Flood.

THERE exists among some nations who have not the Bible a tradition of a flood, and in Genesis we have a description of a universal flood so distinct and clear in all the particulars that it has been received and admitted as a record of a flood of material waters by the Christian world up to a recent date; and yet, on a more careful examination and comparison of the size of the ark with known facts in regard to the number of animals, birds, insects and reptiles which could not live in the water, the want of adequate ventilation, etc., to say nothing of the general opinion of scientists who have examined the subject, not a few theologians and theological writers have been compelled to admit that such a flood as is described in Genesis, with the preservation of animal life as there described, has never taken place. When men have a dogma or theory to sustain, it is very difficult for them to either heed or see the whole truth.

The late Dr. Pye Smith observed: "Ingenious calculations have been made of the capacity of the Ark, as compared with the room requisite for the *pairs* of some animals, and the *septules* of others; and it is remarkable that the well-intentioned calculators have formed their estimate upon a number of animals *below the truth*, to a degree that might appear incredible. They have usually satisfied themselves with a provision for three or four hundred species at most, as in general they show the most astonishing ignorance of every branch of natural history."

And yet even this writer, not being able to see anything in the description in Genesis more important than the literal record, was led by his reverence for the sacred Scriptures, to the invention of a theory of a local flood, which of course in no way answers the description in Genesis.

Could anything show more clearly the necessity, if the sacred Scriptures are to retain their hold on the minds of men as divine revelations, of a new and higher interpretation of their meaning? The Lord said to His disciples when on earth, "I have many things to say unto you, but ye cannot bear them now." Have not the wonderful scientific developments of this day prepared us for a higher unfolding of spiritual truth? Is it not clear that all things are being made new on the physical plane of life? and if so, is it reasonable to suppose the Lord has forgotten our spiritual wants? Reader, read carefully the writings of Emanuel Swedenborg, and a new world of life and light will be opened to you, and you will be ready to exclaim that the Second Coming of the Lord is indeed with power and great glory. It will be clearly shown to your rational comprehension that there are other floods than those of material waters, and more to be dreaded by men, of which we shall treat hereafter.

"But," says the Rev. Dr. Bayley, "it may now be asked, Why do you not receive the account of the flood as commonly taught? To this we reply, that, although we consider the divine account of the flood to be allegorical, we by no means make less of the Divine Word than others, but, in fact, more. We perceive immeasurably more in it than mere literalists admit, but we cannot accept the natural interpretation of the history, because we do not believe it was ever so intended to be understood. It is part of the series which describes spiritual creation under natural imagery, trees of life and knowledge, talking serpents, and a variety of other particulars which cannot be reconciled with reason or with science, if they are literally understood; and we have no doubt that true theology, true reason, and true science are in harmony. They come from the same divine fountain.

"In the letter, the Word was given to each people in the mode best accommodated to them, and in the early ages allegory was what they loved. They gave spiritual history in natural forms. Hence we have the account of the formation of the Church, like the creation of the world; we have trees of life and knowledge, and a speaking serpent. Hence the origin of parables, and mythology; and to this class of writing belongs the flood. But, again, it may be asked, Why not consider this history, in particular, literal? The geologists inform us that there are no vestiges of a

universal flood visible on the earth. The celebrated Professor Buckland, of Oxford, once thought otherwise, and
wrote his work 'Reliquiæ Diluviana,' but he recanted his
opinion, and himself condemned his former conclusions.
Professor Sedgwick, of Cambridge, also declared that there
were no appearances in nature from which to arrive at the
conclusion that there had been a flood affecting the whole
earth, during the period of human existence. On closing
his career as Professor, he said, ' Our errors were, however,
natural, and of the same kind which led many excellent
observers of a former century to refer all the secondary
formations of geology to the Noachian deluge. Having
been myself a believer, and, to the best of my power, a
propagator of what I now regard as a philosophical heresy,
and having more than once been quoted for opinions I do
not now maintain, I think it right, as one of my last acts,
before I quit this chair, thus publicly to read my RECAN-
TATION. We ought, indeed, to have paused before we first
adopted the diluvian theory, and referred all our old superficial gravel to the action of the Mosaic flood : for of
man, and the works of his hands, we have not found a
SINGLE TRACE among the remnants of a former world
entombed in these ancient deposits.'

"Some cling to the literal account of the flood, because
they find traditions among many ancient nations of such
a calamity having happened. But this would be the case
from a vast spiritual deluge. If a wild overspreading of
malignant follies and falsehoods took place, and an inun-
dation destructive of all that was sacred among men
existed, this, in the ancient manner of speaking, would be
called an universal flood, and in after ages, when the
spiritual meaning was forgotten, would be supposed to
have been a flood of earthly waters. This is clearly the
case with the Hindoo tradition. It was translated by Sir
William Jones from the Bhagavat, and is the subject of
the first Purana. It is sufficiently like the Bible account
of the deluge to show that it alludes to the same great

event. It is said to have taken place at the close of a
calpa, or dispensation, when there was a general destruction, owing to the sleep of Brahma, and his creatures in
different worlds were drowned in a great ocean. A holy
king, by name Satyavrata, is saved by the appearance of
the Deity in the form of a fish (scientific truth), with a
great horn (power), who slays a demon, and recovers the
sacred books. This remarkable tradition concludes with
these words: ' But the appearance of a horned fish to the
religious monarch was *maya*, or delusion, and he who shall
devoutly hear this important Allegorical Narrative will
be delivered from the bondage of sin.' Here, then, we
have a key to all these traditions. The most perfect of
them all states that it is an allegorical narrative. This is
in perfect harmony with our view of the flood in the
Bible; removes every difficulty, and gives a spiritual
divine lesson."

XIII.

Noah.

" THE history of Adam was not the history of an individual man, but of a Church represented as a man.
The elevation, temptation, and fall of humanity in general, are unfolded by the lot of Adam in Eden, his dealings with the serpent, and his expulsion from Paradise.
' Male and female created He them; and blessed them, and
called their name Adam' (Gen. v. 2). Under his name,
and in the short but wonderfully significant history of the
first man and his descendants, the first church, with its
offshoots, is delineated. These people, who are represented as living nearly a thousand years each, are shown
by Swedenborg to be types of the communities which existed in the golden age. That Most Ancient Church, like
all other great churches, had sects and varieties which
were its generations—its sons and daughters. Each name,
with the hundreds of years of existence, describes in the

brief Divine style some state and quality belonging to that church. And when it sank altogether with gigantic lusts, and immersed in floods of falsehood, it was succeeded by another church represented in the Divine Word by Noah.

"It will not be too difficult to think that, as the church is one body before the Lord, though consisting of millions of members, so its life may be described as the life of one man, however long the period assigned to it may be. The Jewish Church is generally described in the singular as Israel, although it subsisted for fifteen hundred years. It was the manner of the ancients thus to group all of one sentiment as if they were one being. It is derived from the Divine Wisdom, which views heaven as one angel (Ps. xxxiv. 7), the church as one body (1 Cor. xii. 37), a nation as one individual, as Assyria (Ezek. xxxi.), a heresy as one polluted form (Rev. xvii. 5), legions of infernal spirits as one devil (Mark v. 9).

"We find the same similarity with Genesis, as to the ages of the early fathers of mankind, in Egyptian, Chinese, and Hindoo mythologies. The first kings of Egypt, according to their traditions, reigned each more than twelve hundred years. In the Chinese books it is related that the primitive ancestors of mankind lived eighteen hundred years. The Hindoos, however, assure us that in the golden age the period of man's life was eighty thousand, and at its best period, one hundred thousand years. And one of their holy kings was two millions of years old when he began to reign, continued on the throne for a million of years, and then spent in retirement one hundred thousand years more (See Buckle, vol. I). No one in Christendom, certainly, would adopt these numbers literally, and yet, probably, they had a meaning well understood when they were written.

"The spiritual sense removes the difficulties, and itself presents admirable lessons concerning man's regeneration and interior life, fraught with instruction and edification.

"Noah, or Consolation, represents those who would form the nucleus of a New Church, the germ of a new age. Of these, it is said, he called his name Noah, saying, 'This same shall comfort us concerning our work and toil of our hands, because of the ground which the Lord hath cursed' (chap. v. 29). And by these words is meant that by means of this New Church the difficulties of cultivating the soul would be overcome, and spiritual rest would be attained, for another signification of the word Noah is Rest. Noah is said to have been just and perfect, or upright, in his generations, and to have walked with God, and these three qualifications are the essentials of every church. Justice is expressive of the essence of goodness, uprightness of the clear acknowledgment of truth, while walking with God is said in relation to the activity of a good life. These three are the essentials of all religion.

"The Church called Noah, then, as possessed of the three essentials of religion, the trinity of heavenly virtues, is described as just, upright, and walking with God."— *Rev. Dr. Bayley.*

XIV.

Shem, Ham, and Japheth.

"And Noah was five hundred years old: and Noah begat Shem, Ham, and Japheth."—GEN. v. 32.

"WE have seen," says Rev. Dr. Bayley, "that Noah was the representative of the Ancient Church. We will now proceed to investigate the Divine Allegory further, in relation to the three sons, Shem, Ham, and Japheth; for they and their wives also went into the ark, and were saved.

"These three represent the general features into which the church of Noah divided itself. Churches have sons and daughters just as individuals, and just as nations have. Each sect is as a child to the church out of which it sprung. Thus, out of the Church of Rome sprang the Church of England, the Lutheran and the Calvinistic Churches. From the Church of England arose the Puritans, the Methodists, the Baptists, the Independents, and all the numerous subdivisions which, as children, grandchildren, and great-grandchildren, have originated from her.

"Shem and Japheth appear to represent those portions of the Ancient Church who were actuated by that charity which hides the sins of others; this was manifested by their conduct in covering the nakedness of their father. Ham is clearly the representative of such as know indeed what is right, but use that knowledge rather to expose the failings of others than to hide or to heal them. Their wives represent the Affections for these forms of religion.

"The vineyard Noah planted and cultivated is the Church, where the heavenly vines of a true faith grow. His getting drunk represents the members of the Church giving themselves too much to speculations and selfish vanities, and becoming intoxicated with Pride.

"Spiritual drunkenness is more terrible than natural; it is being besotted with phantasies and errors, inflated with self-derived intelligence. When a person neglects practical religion, and forgets the humility of heart which fills us with distrust of ourselves, he is on the highway to some infatuation. He begins soon to be impatient of contradiction, goes from one paradox to another, until no conceit is for him too absurd. Errors of the most fearful kind creep in. He will have all the world to be occupied with some small idea of his, and he sees his one thought everywhere, and in everything, and thus by exaggerating what may be true in itself to an undue proportion, he shuts out other truths, and makes some form of monstrous fallacy exist where the fair proportion of a complete and well-formed faith ought to be. Thus comes spiritual drunkenness. When we are in this state we are never steady. We reel to and fro like a drunken man. We roll from phantasy to phantasy, for the sake of preserving our idol thought, until we lose sight of the great essential of religion; and instead of charity being our central principle, self-love and self-conceit are seen. Thus was it with Noah. He was drunken, and was uncovered within, or in the midst of his tent (ver. 21).

"Ordinarily the selfish are at great pains to cover themselves with appearances and pretexts. We have an instance of this in the case of Adam and Eve. When their eyes were open to their real fallen state, and they knew that they were naked (that is, were conscious of their having sunk into selfhood), they sewed fig-leaves together, and made themselves aprons (Gen. iii. 7). The fig-leaves represent the lowest forms of truth, such as they are in the letter of the Word. These may easily be arranged so as to cover any state, however evil. Every false religion is only an immense covering of the nakedness of the soul, and an elaborate device to put a fair face upon what is intrinsically bad. A man who clings to self still wishes to be saved, and he will hatch or favor any scheme that promises him salvation without the subjugation of self.

"Ham exposing his father's nakedness represents the spirit of those who have no charity. They see the nakedness of others, but instead of aiding them, or shielding them, they tell it to their brethren without. How sad it is that so much of the Ham spirit remains to the present day. It has been said, and not without some ground, that dwelling upon the failings of one another is the besetting sin of churches. Yet nothing can be more odious or more destructive of true charity. The spirit of heaven leads the angels to attribute good to every one, as far as possible, and if there be evil, to excuse it as much as can be. The spirit of evil accuses, attributes an evil motive even when good is done, and magnifies the least failing so as to make it a serious fault. Evil spirits are called the accuser of the brethren. 'The accuser of the brethren is cast down, which accused them before our God day and night' (Rev. xii. 10). This accusing spirit is typified by

4

Ham, and is often connected with a fair amount of learning and talent, but, alas! with the desire of raising itself at the expense of others. Indisposed to advance in purity and heavenly-mindedness, those who are represented by Ham cannot bear to see others esteemed better than themselves, however justly it is their due. If they gaze upon the sun, they mark only his spots. Desiring so much to detract from the virtues of others, it is a perfect jubilee to them to detect a fault. They mark it well; they see that its blackest features come out; they publish it far and wide. Alas! at the same time they know not how much they are proclaiming their own deficiency in that highest of Christian graces—angelic charity."

Shem and Japheth covering their father's nakedness represents such as in a spirit of charity and kindness desire to excuse and heal, rather than to accuse and proclaim the supposed or real faults of others.

"Let us ever strive and pray for that practical religion and sobermindedness that will preserve us in purity and order; lest, in the solemn words of Scripture, the 'shame of our nakedness appear.'"

XV.

The Flood of Waters.

IN treating of the true signification of the first chapter of Genesis, it was shown that by the Earth is signified, in the Divine language, the human mind; but that by the Earth is denoted the *earthy* or *natural mind*, as distinguished from the *spiritual* or *heavenly mind*, which latter is denoted by the *firmament* or *heaven*; and in each degree of the mind, there are the two faculties or Will and Understanding, denoted by the land and the water, and the heat and the light, or the male and the female:

"Water in its pure and unperverted state is a type or symbol of *Truth*, or of a specific kind of truth; for *iron*, a *sword*, a *rock*, *light*, etc., etc., are outward images of Truth, but always of fixed and specific kinds, and as different in their character as are their respective physical correspondents. Thus *iron* denotes Truth, *natural truth*, rather in the *abstract*, as silver denotes its relative *spiritual truth in the same way;* whilst a *Sword* denotes truth in a more specific sense, or as the sharp and powerful truth by which falsehood and evil are assailed, or by which characters and reputations are defended; so a *rock* in like manner denotes truth, but rather those postulates and principles which serve as a basis for an argument, or on which, as on a foundation, all other truths repose. *Light*, also, is truth, or that mental atmosphere in which specific truths become visible to the intellectual sight. It is the medium for rendering truths visible. And *water* is truth of still a different kind. The water from the earth, denotes that natural truth which is for the purifying and cleansing of the natural mind, from any incidental impurities or evils; it also relieves the cravings of the mental appetite, which thirsts for knowledge and information, and satisfies it with such truths as are adapted to its state. And water from the atmosphere above the earth being purer, less tainted with the dross of earth, denotes truth of a more elevated character, i. e., *rational* or *intellectual;* whilst the waters from heaven, in like manner, denote those which are of a yet higher, or more internal character."—*Rev. G. Field.*

The Water of Life signifies divine truths from the Lord through the Word.

But the waters of the Flood were not pure, harmless and useful to man; for they were destructive, therefore they do not correspond to truths but to falses, or to those perversions of truths, which, with their attendant evils, are injurious and destructive to man's spiritual life; and tend to destroy heavenly life, or love to the Lord and his neighbor in the soul.

"The account of the Flood," says the Rev. Dr. Bayley, "is such as to impress every reader of the Divine Word. It is the history of an appalling calamity. It was a fearful

consummation of great evils. But what was its nature?
What were its circumstances? Was it of water or of
wickedness? Those who have not reflected much on
spiritual things are startled even at the mention of a
spiritual flood, although the thing itself is not at all
unknown or unfamiliar. They have been so long accustomed to the common idea, and are habitually so persuaded
of the value of natural life, that although the destruction
of virtue and truth by torrents of iniquity is far more
appalling to the wise, to the heedless it seems of little
moment. Not so, however, is it regarded in the Word of
God. Throughout its divine pages a spiritual flood is
treated of as the soul's most awful calamity. And we may
here notice, that a spiritual assault of evil and error, is
undoubtedly meant by the term flood, in a very large
number of passages in the Scriptures. No other meaning
can be attached often to the expression. How manifest
this is in the Book of Psalms every one must have noticed.
Take, as a striking example, the sixty-ninth. 'Save me,
O God; for the waters are come in unto my soul. I
sink in deep mire, where there is no standing: I am come
into *deep waters,* where the *floods* overflow me' (ver. 1, 2).
Again, 'Deliver me out of the mire, and let me not sink:
let me be delivered from them that hate me, and out of
the deep waters. Let not the waterflood overflow me,
neither let the deep swallow me up, and let not the pit
shut her mouth upon me' (ver. 14, 15). Here there is a
cry which nothing but the agony of the bitterest temptation could produce. Not the death of the body, but the
fear of the more terrible death of the soul, could awaken
the agonizing expressions here uttered. 'Save me, O God,
for the waters are come in unto my soul.' In the eighteenth Psalm we have something of the same kind. 'The
sorrows of death compassed me, and the floods of ungodly
men made me afraid. The sorrows of hell compassed me
about; the snares of death prevented me' (ver. 4, 5).
And a little further: 'He sent from above, he took me,

he drew me out of strange waters' (ver. 16). These are evidently entreaties of the soul under bitter trials, which are described as floods of water. Such language, with such signification, is very frequent in the Scriptures; and the states it portrays belong to the experience of all, except those who yield themselves willingly to sin, and go constantly along with the stream. The Psalmist says again: 'For this shall every one that is godly pray unto thee, in a time when thou mayest be found: surely in the floods of great waters they shall not come nigh unto him' (Ps. xxxii. 6). In earthly floods, the righteous have no peculiar exemption. They are objects, like all others of divine care, for eternal ends; but while in ordinary life people recognize a great Providence in their escapes from danger, a wider and deeper view of Providence would reveal the truth that there is a Divine care and mercy over those drowned at sea, or dashed to pieces on a railway, equally with those who rejoice at being unhurt. 'The Lord is good to all, and His tender mercies are over all His works.'

"The end of a church is frequently in the Word described as accompanied by a flood, though certainly not by one of outward waters. Where the end of the Jewish Church is predicted by Isaiah, it is mentioned as being accompanied by the fearful circumstances of a flood, although no one supposes that such a catastrophe outwardly occurred.

"The prophet Daniel describes the end of the Jewish Church, which was completed by the crucifixion of the Lord, in like manner as attended by a flood. 'And after threescore and two weeks shall Messiah be cut off, but not for himself; and the people of the prince that shall come shall destroy the city and the sanctuary; and the end thereof shall be with a *flood*' (chap. ix. 26). A flood of impieties, falsehoods, and delusions, there was then, but we are not aware of any other. Such floods are adverted to by the Lord in the Gospel as assailing every one. The good come out of them, or ride over them; the wicked sink and perish. 'Whosoever heareth these sayings of mine, and doeth them, I will liken him unto a wise man, which built his house upon a rock : and the rain descended, and the *floods* came, and the winds blew, and beat upon that house, and it fell not; for it was founded upon a rock. And every one that heareth these sayings of mine, and doeth them not, shall be likened unto a foolish man, which built his house upon the sands: and the rain descended, and the floods came, and the winds blew, and beat upon that house; and it fell: and great was the fall of it' (Matt. vii. 24–27). The floods alluded to in both portions of this divine description of the temptations which must be endured in the discipline of life, are, as every one will admit, those influences which impel the soul to wrong; those assaults which like surging waves come again and again to try the principles of all, and under which such as trust in their own opinions only, and do not rest on the Rock of the Divine Word, will too surely fall. Similar floods of falsehood, it will be admitted, are meant when it is said, on the birth of the man-child, as mentioned in the Reve-lation, 'The serpent cast out of his mouth *water as a flood* after the woman, that he might cause her to be carried away of the flood. And the earth helped the woman; and the earth opened her mouth, and swallowed up the flood which the dragon cast out of his mouth' (chap. xii. 15, 16). *A flood from the mouth of the serpent* can surely only be understood to mean a torrent of erro-neous teachings, destined, if possible, to discredit the New Church meant by the woman, and the sublime doctrine she has produced for the world. It is, then, the undoubted usage of the sacred Scriptures to represent, under the figure of a flood, the streams of false and destructive errors which prevail at the end of a church, with the utmost virulence, and also at some period in the career of every man, are permitted to test the sincerity and fixedness of his religion.

"There are three sources of flood mentioned : the 'fountains of the great deep,' the 'windows of heaven,' and ' the rain.' In times of spiritual struggle there are opened awful deeps within man, which send up malignant, loathsome persuasions, scalding hot, which would hurry the soul to ruin. The deep-rooted selfishness of the fallen heart says, 'There is no God' (Ps. xiv. 7). The wicked bravado of insolent pride says within his heart also, ' There is no fear of God before his eyes' (Ps. xxxvi. 1). The horrid cravings of sensuality beg for their indulgence with importunate yells, and the poor soul knows hardly what to do. 'Deep calleth unto deep at the noise of thy waterspouts: all thy waves and thv billows have gone over me' (Ps. xlii. 7). The windows of heaven are the rational faculties of the soul. These are given to let in heavenly light. In an orderly state they are indeed the windows of heaven. The divine light of truth shines freely in. They are the eyes of the soul. But in sore temptation, at these same windows, false reasonings enter. Infidel spirits, perhaps infidel books and infidel friends, supply waterspouts of specious conclusions, all at the time seemingly powerful, weighty, with much truth in them, but all dishonoring to God, and degrading to man. Logic, appearing to the sad and darkened mind irresistible, seems to prove evil good, and good evil, religion to be only superstition, heaven a dream, hell a bugbear, virtue a farce, and all the glorious order of the universe a mere fortuitous jumble of atoms, brought together by blind chance, or equally blind necessity. Added to this, there is the rain, the unceasing pattering of false teaching from companions and associates, plying the spirit day by day with the scornful word, the vile jest, the wild jeer, the frequent invitation, the constant persuasion to wrong-doing, and often the bitter denunciation of the virtuous as hypocrites; the withering sarcasm, which, like storms of hail, comes down on the wearied, almost despairing soul with cruel force; all these make a storm—a flood of overwhelming force. Happy is

he who has a heavenly ark at hand, in which he can take
refuge and be saved.

"At the end of a church, the flood assumes fearful
power. Books of an irreligious character abound. The
church has first perverted the truth, and taught the traditions of men' for the commandments of God. Puerile
superstitions are common, from which the reason of mankind revolts. Morals are relaxed. Religious teachers are
too often unworthy of their name and office. They have
devised some scheme which they call religion, which dims
the holy light of that truth which says, 'Do justly, love
mercy, and walk humbly with thy God.'

"Others originate a philosophy which tries to make the
universe a self-acting machine—a science very learned and
very laborious, but learned and laborious about trifles;
dwelling for ever on forms of speech, but overlooking the
sense, the soul of speech ; solemnly and devotedly engaged
on worms and butterflies, on the affinities of atoms, and
the measurement of angles, but seldom entering upon
those aspirations of the angelic nature within, which raise
us from creeping through this outer life the denizens of a
day, to soar into the glorious regions of light and love,
which give us affinities with the holy and the true of all
ages, and enable us to become of the measure of a man,
that is, of an angel.

"Thus was it in the middle and latter half of the last
century. At the time when the Lord revealed to man,
through Swedenborg, the truths of the New Dispensation,
iniquity abounded. Love waxed cold. Faith was scarcely
to be met with anywhere. Works of amusement were dis-
gustingly vicious. From royal circles down to the poorest
hovels, vice under ten thousand forms reigned almost un-
challenged. Alison, the historian of that period, thus
describes it : 'Man's connection with his Maker was
broken by the French apostles of freedom: for they declared there was no God in whom to trust, in the great
struggle for liberty.' 'Human immortality,' says Chan-

ning, 'that truth which is the soul of all greatness, they
derided. In their philosophy man was a creature of
chance, a compound of matter, a worm soon to rot and
perish for ever. At last came the revolution, with its dis-
asters and its passions, its overthrow of thrones and altars,
its woes, its blood, and its suffering.' In the general
deluge, thus falling upon a sinful world, the mass of mankind still clung to their former vices. They were, as of
old, marrying and giving in marriage, when the waters
burst upon them, but an Ark of Salvation had been prepared by more than mortal hands. The hand on the wall
had unlocked the fountains of original thought. The
Lord at such seasons reveals New Truths from heaven,
and Old Truths in a new light. These serve as an Ark
of safety for the humbly good, who can then say, ' If it
had not been the Lord who was on our side, when men
rose up against us: then they had swallowed us up quick,
when their wrath was kindled against us: then the waters
had overwhelmed us, the stream had gone over our soul:
then the proud waters had gone over our soul. Blessed be
the Lord, who hath not given us as a prey to their teeth '
(Ps. cxxiv. 2-6). 'The floods have lifted up, O Lord, the
floods have lifted up their voice; the floods lift up their
waves. The Lord on high is mightier than the noise of
many waters, yea, than the mighty waves of the sea'"
(Ps. xciii. 3, 4).

XVI.

The Ark.

(WRITTEN BY THE REV. WM. B. HAYDEN.)

"AFTER having seen the kind of Flood which devas-
tated the earth in those early days, suffocating the
spiritual life of man, and actually sweeping off multitudes
of the human race through the intensity of their own vices
and lusts, it will be the more easy to understand the
meaning of the Ark which Noah was commanded to build.

The Ark has ever been a type of salvation. It is both a type of what man has to do for himself, in the way of building up a right frame of spirit and a holy character, in co-operation with the Lord; and also of that Divine care and protection watching over the believer, shielding him in temptation, and bearing him safely through the storms and trials of life, which the Lord ever vouchsafes to his faithful followers.

"The little ark of bulrushes was employed to protect and save the infant Moses from the suffocating waters of the Nile. The Ark which Moses afterwards was commanded to construct, according to the heavenly pattern shown him in holy vision in the Mount, received the two tables of the covenant, and after being placed in the most holy place in the Tabernacle, became thenceforward the type of Salvation to the Jews, the symbol of the Divine presence among them. And when the Apostle John, in Patmos, saw the Temple of the Tabernacle in heaven opened, he saw the holy Ark of the Covenant resting there in its place.

"The Tabernacle in the Wilderness and the Temple of Solomon signified similar things. We know with what particularity the building of these is described in the inspired narrative: all the dimensions of the former being specially commanded. We know that both those buildings represented the Lord our Saviour in His redeeming work, wherein the Humanity which he assumed having been glorified by Him, became ever after the Temple of the Living God and the supreme Ark of our eternal salvation.

"In His parable at the close of the Sermon on the Mount, the Saviour tells us how we may *build* upon the rock a house unto eternal salvation. It is by faithfully doing the sayings which we learn of Him, exemplifying them in the life. If we do not obey His precepts, we build on the sand, constructing a house that will not *stand against the flood*— forming a character, that is, which cannot resist temptation, but which will inevitably fall and be swept away whenever assailed from without.

"When therefore we consider the moral necessities of those very ancient times—human society being beaten upon by an overrunning flood of falsities and evils, we can readily understand the kind of *building* required to protect the good men of that time from being overwhelmed and swept away in the common destruction. It was something to take care of their moral habits, to shield their religious character, and secure their spiritual regeneration.

"Hence, in a collective sense, the Ark there meant was the church; and in an individual sense, each man or member of the church.

"In providing for the spiritual safety of the small remnant who were willing to remain obedient in that trying time, the Lord gave a Revelation of such truths as were needed for the times; enough for thorough instruction and guidance. The church, called Noah, 'was a preacher of righteousness,' and therefore taught its members to *build* on the right foundation. Like the ancient Egyptians, as well as all the earliest oriental peoples, it expressed its sacred truths by *hieroglyphics*. And the people among whom they taught perfectly understood them. The commandments concerning the building of the Ark, therefore, were to them a continuous parable, the *moral* of which they clearly saw and applied to heart. They learned them as commandments applying to their repentance, regeneration and spiritual life, and heeded and obeyed them accordingly. They saw how each detailed instruction applied to some trait of thought, feeling, or action, and so became a living divine rule for the regulation of their conduct. As they looked upon the picture, they saw it as a divine allegory, and beheld in it an impressive embodiment or programme of their *Whole Duty*, both to God and man. They knew that in obedience— in entering into the Ark or *Covenant*, there was safety. While to remain out of the line of duty in that corrupt

time was to be out of the ark, which was sure destruction
to their souls.   They needed the constant instruction and
influence of a divinely-founded church.

"As the curtains, cedar boards, veils, candlestick, and
gold and silver things of the Tabernacle, each represented
some holy truth or good connected with our Saviour and
His work of redeeming grace, so each thing that is said to
have entered into the construction of the Ark by Divine
command, as the gopher wood, the mansions, stories,
door, and window, represents some definite truth or good
connected with man's regeneration and spiritual life.   A
lucid exposition of their meaning may be found in the
first volume of the 'Arcana Cœlestia,' by Emanuel
Swedenborg, which cannot fail to throw light upon the
spiritual experiences of the reader ; and so, although
intended for those very ancient and childlike people, may
be of great practical value to-day and to us.

"Beasts are the scriptural types or emblems of man's
affections, while the birds, or 'fowls of the air,' are
typical of his thoughts, which are more soaring and irreg-
ular in their flight.

" We can see therefore what is meant by the clean beasts
and clean fowls which were to be gathered into the Ark
in sevens.   They are the purified affections and purified
thoughts of the upright or regenerated man.   And again,
we can see, too, that whereas unclean beasts and unclean
birds were likewise gathered in, though in single pairs.
that human nature then was as it is now.   The church
had its imperfections.   Church members had something
of the natural man still about them, their lower nature,
the 'law of sin' in the members.   Nevertheless, as the
'clean beasts' were to predominate in the Ark, so the
spiritual man, or spiritual part of man, was to bear rule in
the church ; and its unclean things, through divine grace,
kept in subjection and subordination.

"The 'door,' the 'window,' the sending forth of the
raven and the *dove*, as well as every circumstance related,

when understood aright, or according to the science of correspondences, conveys its beautiful and instructive lesson.

"Thus far, we have not alluded to the scientific and other difficulties which surround the literal interpretation of this account of the Ark, nor do we intend to enlarge upon them. They come more and more into view as the subject is carefully studied. They strike different minds as of different degrees of importance. But there can be no doubt that of late, in the full blaze of all that modern research has disclosed on the subject, thoughtful minds everywhere are sore pressed for an adequate solution.

"The incapacity of the Ark, from its size, to contain all the kinds of animals and birds, with food for a year; its want of light and ventilation; the wide dispersion of animals over the globe, their variety of climate, and the impossibility of collecting them from such immense distances in so short a time; are among what, to most minds, seem to be the insuperable difficulties in the way of a literal belief in the narrative.

"It ought therefore to be a satisfaction to every rational, devout, and believing mind, that the history is found to be constructed like a prophetic writing; divinely inspired, but giving the spiritual history of those times in a parable or allegory, in unison with the universal mode of writing in those very ancient or hieroglyphical ages."

———

¶ "Dear reader, in the foregoing pages concerning the Flood and Ark, we have wished to raise your views from carnal and curious speculations to spiritual and profitable ideas. You will be assailed by a flood, if you have not hitherto experienced its wild waves. False sentiments and deep trials await all persons at some periods of their lives. The Floods will come in upon your soul, and without a proper Ark, you must spiritually be drowned. Our Lord, at the end of His grand sermon on the mount, taught both of those who heard His words and did them, and of those who did them not, 'the rain descended, and the floods came, and the winds blew and beat upon that house' (Matt. vii. 24–27).

"Have you pondered upon this? Are you prepared with your ark? Are you clear in your own mind as to what you are to expect, and what you are to do? Remember, the same waves which overwhelmed the ungodly bore up the ark. The streams of iniquity will surge across your path and all around you, in the days of temptation; for this has been the experience of the servants of God in every age. See how pathetically the Psalmist describes the experience of the good but tried ones of his day: 'When the waves of death compassed me, the Floods of ungodly men made me afraid: the sorrows of hell compassed me about: the snares of death prevented me: in my distress I called upon the Lord, and cried to my God: and He did hear my voice out of His temple, and my cry did enter in His ears' (2 Sam. xxii. 5–7). 'He sent from above, He drew me out of many waters; He delivered me from my strong enemy, and from them that hated me; for they were too strong for me' (ver. 17, 18). Strange, wild, false states, like stormy waters, come to trouble us again and again. They assail our belief in God, in His providence, and in His care. They pour out strange phantasies and blasphemies against revealed religion, and against our Saviour. They increase for a time in virulence and power. They rage, and howl, and roll on, strange and dark, like the awful roll of waves mountains high. But be not afraid. Look to the Lord Jesus Christ, and trust in Him. Look up. Have faith, and persevere. He is the Divine man, God become a man, to be known to you and to save you. Thus it is written, 'A man shall be as a hiding-place from the wind, and a covert from the tempest; as rivers of water in a dry place, as a shadow of a great rock in a weary land' (Isa. xxxii. 2).

"Look in prayer and love to this living, loving, manifested God. He will teach you how to make an Ark. He will give you the pattern, the directions, and the materials. No storms can destroy those who trust in Him. They will seem at times to be in great danger. The awful roll and roar of the storm will threaten to overwhelm them,-but they are really quite safe. The ark of the Divine religion of the Lord Jesus, with its three stories, will never give way. You will be straitened for the time, but safe. 'The Lord sitteth upon the Flood; yea, the Lord sitteth King for ever. The Lord will give strength unto His people: the Lord will bless His people with peace' (Ps. xxix. 10, 11). 'For this shall every one that is godly pray unto Thee, in a time when Thou mayest be found: surely in the floods of great waters they shall not come nigh unto him. Thou art my hiding-place: Thou shalt preserve me from trouble: Thou shalt compass me about with songs of deliverance' (Ps. xxxii. 6, 7).

"How many thousands around us do we see engulphed in horrid streams of infidelity, falsehood, and corruption, in their thousand forms! Let us point all to the Ark of Safety. The three grand principles of love, faith, and obedience, accepted from the Lord Jesus, will rescue every one. Let us then love Him with all the heart, dear reader. He is our Creator, Redeemer, and Regenerator. He will never forsake you, but love, enlighten, and bless you. Have faith in Him. You are in His world. All its laws are under His command, and in His good time the storms will cease, the winds will howl no more, the Flood will no more threaten. Obey Him, and you will soon find life improving around you. You will come into enlightened freedom. The truth will make you free. The narrow bounds of the Ark, which once contained and saved you, but yet confined you, will let you come forth in safety, and the whole world will be a grander ark, in which you will be perfectly safe, while you are enjoying its blessings and adoring its Maker."—*Rev. Dr. Bayley.*

XVII.

The Tower of Babel.

"And they said one to another, Go to, let us make brick, and burn them thoroughly. And they had brick for stone, and slime had they for mortar. And they said, Go to, let us build us a city and a tower, whose top may reach unto heaven; and let us make us a name, lest we be scattered abroad upon the face of the whole earth."—GEN. xi. 3, 4.

"LIKE the garden of Eden, the Tower of Babel," says the Rev. Dr. Bayley, "has been a puzzle to geographers who look to the literal sense of the Bible alone. They have sought for its remains in different regions, but with most unsatisfactory results.

"If the sacred writings had only represented the people as designing to reach heaven by a tower, it would have been difficult for rational belief; but when it proceeds to state that the Deity came down and felt it necessary to stop their efforts by rendering them unintelligible to each other, surely it must induce every thoughtful person to say, this cannot be literal, this must have another signification.

"But, it must not be forgotten, that if the ages of these early personages were the ages of individuals (and not, as they really were, descriptive of communities, called by single names, as Israel was for more than a thousand years), then Noah, Shem, Ham, and Japheth, must have been among these people. They had come down from the mighty Ararat, more than three miles high. Could they have so childish a conceit as that they could reach heaven by a brick building, in a plain or a valley, when they had not found it in the regions of perpetual snow? Surely, if its forming part of that primeval history which we have seen, in relation to the other great subjects, can only be allegorically or spiritually understood, did not lead us to a spiritual sense, the inevitable difficulties of the letter in this instance alone, would lead us to look for some higher, some interior meaning. In this case, as in the others we have treated, we must say to the biblical student, 'Come up higher, friend.'

"We have mentioned that, like the site of Eden, the position of this tower has greatly perplexed the curious. It is like Eden with its Tree of Lives, in another respect. Paradise has a leading position at the beginning of the Bible, and we find it again in the last book (Rev. ii. 7; xxii. 2). It is thus represented as the blissful state from which men fell, and as that which, by regeneration, they · will again attain. In both, a spiritual blessing, not a natural place. So with Babel, it is here as the symbol of pride, building up superstition to scale heaven in its own way. It is the same in the book of Revelation. There, Babylon the great is the symbol of a selfish and superstitious church, a prostitution of religion, by mysterious doctrines and priestly craft, to the awful purpose of lording it over men's souls, as well as their bodies.* No one supposes that Babylon in the Book of Revelation means an earthly city; why then assign that meaning to Babel here?

"Let us turn now to the same history as opened by the divine science of correspondence, or analogy, revealed through Emanuel Swedenborg. The whole earth is said to be of one language, and of one speech. The earth, as in other cases, means the church, especially as to its external principles, worship, and practice. The earth at this time is said to have had one language, and the speech one, or as the latter part may be rendered, *the words united*, or *made one* (debarim echadim); because the church is represented in a state of charity and harmony. Where love rules, there unity prevails. Even if doctrines differ, kindness can find sentiments sufficiently in common to harmonize men's minds. When love animates and directs them, the tone of all and of each is directed to the production of use. Their language is one, and their words are one.

"But we are informed these people went from the east, and they found a plain (or valley) in the land of Shinar, and dwelt there.

"The east, in the divine language, is the symbol of a state of love to the Lord, because, in such a state of the heart, the Sun of righteousness, the Sun of the soul, arises, and gives its beams of light and warmth over the mind. Eden is said to be eastward (Gen. ii. 8).

"Valleys are the symbols of the lower affections of the soul, and mountains of the higher. Hence we read of the 'valley of bones' (Ezek. xxxvii. 1), which the prophet addressed, and which symbolized the natural mind full of the skeletons of religious teaching, long uncared for. The Psalmist blesses those who, passing through the valley of Baca (or weeping), make it a well; or, in other words, who are brought into troubles and sorrow externally, but make these the means of opening in themselves that well of salvation, whose bright waters sparkle with hope and consolation—that water of truth, which springs up forever, to quench the thirst of the faithful soul (John vii. 37, 38).

"When they are described as coming into a little broken valley, in the lion land, and dwelling there, it is to intimate that they had departed from their first love, and sunk into low and carnal states, in which they rejected all real high principles, all real goodness, which is the only real greatness, and boldly determined to make a religion for themselves, outwardly of the same appearance as before, but inwardly devoted to their own glorification, and to the gratification of spiritual pride. This is to leave the glorious mountains of the east, and to dwell in a little broken valley of our own, in the land of the lions, or Shinar. 'My soul is among lions,' David said, 'and I lie among them that are set on fire' (Ps. lvii. 4).

"'Let us build a city and tower, whose top may reach to heaven, and make us a name.' What a burst of arrogance and self-sufficiency is here! 'Let us build a city,' let us construct a system of doctrine, let us make a church. The true church of the Lord is a city which comes down from heaven, 'the city of the living God, the heavenly Jerusalem' (Heb. xii. 22). 'Let us build a city,' let us contrive a scheme, say they, which shall profess to honor God and save souls, but which shall really 'make us a name.' Let us seek influence with all our might. Let us teach men that we are the mediators between them and God. We will induce the Deity to be propitious. We will forgive them their sins. We will teach them a way to be saved, although they cling to evil and despise such of the divine commands as interfere with their sins.

"Let us now mark the materials which these Babel-builders used. 'And they had brick for stone, and slime had they for mortar.' Stone, as a natural production, affording a strong foundation, and the material for firm and solid walls, corresponds to truth; *brick*, as a human manufacture, and a substitute for stone, is the symbol of opinions fabricated by man's contrivance.

"TRUTHS will not serve the purpose of Babel-builders, so they make materials of their own; *brick* have they for *stone*.

"The false principles engendered by spiritual pride, which elevate man in the place of God, and substitute unintelligible ceremony in worship instead of enlightened adoration, are aptly represented by brick which the builders make themselves. Where, for instance, could the paraphernalia of superstitious religion—consecrated ground, holy water, sainted bones, etc., the worship of dead and living men, high-sounding names—His Holiness, Father in God, Right Reverend Father in God, and such-like pompous titles applied to mortals quite as frail and feeble as others, be obtained, unless they had made them themselves? The stones of divine truth would not do, and so they made brick. The whole of the persuasions which tend to the exaltation of priestly pride, are bricks of human contrivance substituted for the stones of a true spiritual building.

"They said also, 'Let us burn them thoroughly.' Fire
is the symbol of ardent affection. Heavenly fire is the
affection to do good (Ps. civ. 4). The fire of hell is the
affection or lust for doing evil (Isa. ix. 18; Jas. iii. 6).
The fire which burned these bricks was the intense desire
for power over men's souls, which produces zeal for self,
not for God. It is amazing with what ardor the lust of
spiritual dominion will work. It will compass sea and
land to make a proselyte. It will both do and suffer much
more than true religion requires, to accomplish its insane
ends.

"When truths are the stones, the love of truth is the
cement which unites them firmly together. Truths without love are like stones without mortar, loose and devoid
of strength. However much a man knows, if he lacks the
love of the truth, he has no saving strength in the sight
of Heaven. But the uniting principle among Babel-
builders is merely the lust of being worshipped by others,
and is therefore described by slime. Nothing is so unclean
as the love of self in its varied forms. It spurns the chaste
delights of marriage, and longs to wallow in the impurities
of adultery. Out of the evil heart comes all that really
defiles a man. His dreams even reek with defilement.
From such a state the Psalmist rejoiced to be delivered:
'He brought me up also out of a horrible pit, out of the
miry clay, and set my feet upon a rock, and established my
goings' (Ps. xl. 2). The wall, like the tower, is a system
of falsehood; the untempered mortar, like the slime, means
the impure affections which sustain it.

"How diligently the laborers work at their tower!
They teach, they preach, they indoctrinate, they counsel.
They parade their mysterious powers, they decry reason,
they insinuate that science is of very doubtful character.
Religion is an awful mystery, and they are its only ex-
pounders. The people would certainly destroy themselves,
if they ventured to investigate and decide for themselves.
Pray and pay, are enough for the people. Happily, how-

ever, He who keepeth Israel never sleeps, and He comes down to see the city and the tower.

"The Lord is said to see, when He makes it manifest to His creatures that He sees. Undoubtedly, He who fills heaven and earth is present everywhere, and knows all things. But, when He manifests Himself to man, He seems to come down to him, and when He shows that He knows, it appears to us that He then first observes. It is in this way the Lord is said to have come down to see the city and the tower which the children of men builded.

"He is divinely careful of human freedom and human progress. And when a system, fraught with peril to both, has proceeded so far as fully to unfold its noxious character, then is the time for infinite goodness to act. Midnight has come over the mind, and it is time to commence the morning. Man's necessity is God's opportunity. The trumpet of judgment sounds. God reveals His light to some minds capable of better things, and His truth flashes conviction. The tower of superstition totters. Men feel that God is there. He has come down to their states, and they see, as it were, His lightning striking their lofty structures, and hurling them to the dust.

"The confounding of the languages represents the different doctrines which arise when a spiritual despotism is exposed and overthrown. The system in which men have apathetically trusted, having been shown to be fictitious, and hurled down, its former adherents know scarcely what to do. They are thrown upon their own resources, and those resources are most scanty. They have been trained in lies, and the rational faculty, the true servant and representative of divine truth in the soul, has been systematically neglected, or crushed. The unregenerate heart, the most fruitful source of malignant error, has been unpurified by the sacred streams of heavenly wisdom, and it mixes itself largely in the general turmoil, and the result is confusion, which the word Babel in Hebrew means. They do not understand each other's doctrines, they oppose and fly from each other. They are no longer united for despotism, nor are they united at all. The tyranny of the priesthood is broken; and innumerable sects are formed. In the turmoil of the universal fray, different nations seize upon different dogmas, and form them into separate churches. The wildest notions are taken up, some by one party, some by another. The whole structure is broken down into fragments, each land holding a language, a doctrine of its own, and excommunicating the others. Such was the Babel of modern times, and such was that of the ancients, represented in the Babel before us."

XVIII.

Sun Worship and Idolatry.

THE origin of Idolatry has been a mystery, but the writings of Swedenborg have thrown a flood of light upon this subject. The science of correspondences between natural and spiritual things, revealed by the Lord therein, is the key which unlocks the mysteries not only of the Word, but also of the World, enabling us to read its past history and view its present state in a new light. Let us remember, then, that this science was once understood by all men who were living upon the earth, and it will be seen that remains of it must be found everywhere among all nations now, either handed down by tradition, or embodied in their religious ideas, and even in their every-day language.

Swedenborg, in his work on "The Sacred Scriptures," says: "The reason why the idolatries of the Gentiles of old took their rise from the science of correspondences was because all things that appear on the face of the earth have correspondence; consequently, not only trees and vegetables, but also beasts and birds of every kind, with fishes and all other things. The ancients, who were versed in the science of correspondences, made themselves images which corresponded with heavenly things, and were greatly delighted with them by reason of their *signification*, and because they could discern in them what related to heaven and the church. They therefore placed those images not only in their temples, but also in their houses; *not with any intention to worship them*, but to serve as means of recollecting the heavenly things *signified by them*. Hence in Egypt, and in other places, they made images of calves, oxen and serpents, and also of children, old men, and virgins; because calves and oxen signified the affections and powers of the natural man," etc.

"Succeeding ages, when the science of correspondences was obliterated, began to adore as holy, and at length to worship as deities, the images and resemblances set up by their forefathers, because they found them in and about their temples."—*Sac. Scr.* (p. 23.)

"How deep, how full of wonder," exclaims the Rev. George Field, "are our feelings, when we contemplate the past; in passing with telescopic vision through the intermediate darkness, to see presented to our astonished gaze the glorious pages of a remote antiquity; to behold again that wisdom so long lost to man, and esteemed by the ancients as the science of all sciences, of which the ' key of knowledge' opens and unfolds arcana which have been sealed for ages; *removes the veil of Isis*, and passing the Sphynxes, enters the portals of the temple, over which may now be seen the changed inscription, ' *Nunc licet*' (now it is allowable).

"Without this golden key, in vain are the memories of the past, or the records and traditions of primeval ages; for though we possessed all the writings of antiquity, we could not read them."

Speaking of the constellations of the zodiac he says:

"Any one might know that there are not literally any such images in the heavens as are marked on the celestial globe; neither do the stars really, by any effort of imagination, look any more like the forms in which they are

pictured, than they do like the letters which spell their
names.   Originally the natural heavens were no more
thought of than we think of the state of the atmosphere
when we tell an angry man that he is too *warm*, and
had better keep *cool;* or than we think of a man's *feet*,
when we advise him to *walk* in the way of the Lord.
Natural images were *borrowed* as symbolical of spiritual
ideas, from their correspondences, not because we think
about, or mean the letters or types, but those things
which the types are used to represent.   But in process of
time, as men descended into more exterior states, this
knowledge began to decline, and at last, instead of seeing
it intuitively, it was studied as a *science;* and thus, even-
tually, instead of the stars and constellations being used as
pure symbols, men thought that they were *literally meant*.
Thus the stars (which correspond to the *knowledge* of
goodness and truth) were invested with a zone, or golden
girdle, symbolical of the band of charity which united
heavenly with earthly sciences, in the harmony of universal truth and goodness, the music of the spheres; and
in their relation to *heavenly knowledges* it is that,

> ' In Reason's ear they all rejoice,
> And utter forth a glorious voice.' "

SUN WORSHIP.

"He who looks," says Swedenborg, "at things internal,
from those that are external, when he views the heavens
or sky, does not think at all of the starry heaven, but of
the angelic heaven; when he beholds the Sun, he does
not think of the Sun, but of the Lord, as being the Sun
of Heaven. * * * *   The reason why all and single
things in the heavens or sky, and on the earth, are representative, is because they existed, and do continually
exist, that is subsist, from an influx of the Lord through
heaven."   Consequently, "there is not a single object
existing in the sky or in the earth, which is beautiful and

agreeable, but what is in some way representative of the Lord's kingdom." (*A. C.* 1807.)

The natural sun corresponds to the Lord, the spiritual sun; its light and heat, correspond to the divine wisdom and love which are spiritual light and heat to our souls. The natural sun has been created from the spiritual sun, and there is a constant influx into it from the latter, which sustains its natural light and heat; therefore the sun's rays are perpetual—forever. It will never fail.

"The SUN, as we have seen, is representatively an image of the LORD, and is not only the centre, but, as it were, the creator, sustainer, vivifier and illuminator of its system: thus the sun is, in its degree to the earth, what the Lord is to man. The heat and light proceeding from the Sun, are representative of the Love and Wisdom emanating from the Lord, the Sun of the heavenly world. As 'God is a consuming fire,' and the fountain of light, so is the Sun in Nature. No one can see the face of Jehovah in His unveiled glory, without being consumed, or perishing in the intensity of that Infinite and uncreated celestial heat and light; so neither can any one behold the face of the Sun of nature, but through an attempering medium; and then it is only in its outward brightness that the Sun is seen, which is but the glory of its radiant orb. So to angelic vision, the Lord appears, not as He is in Himself, but in His effluent glory; so ardent is the radiance of the Divine Love and Wisdom that its proximate sphere, or first proceeding emanation from the Lord, appears as a Sun, as the Sun shining in His strength."—*Rev. G. Field.*

It will be seen that the Ancients did not worship the Sun, and only bowed to the natural as representing the spiritual, and through it worshipped the Lord. Nor has this idea fully perished at this day. The most sacred oath of the Mexican commenced with, "I swear by *the life of the Sun.*" The Indian tribes of North America paid their religious devotions to "the great, beneficent, supreme, holy, *spirit of* FIRE" (the "Great Sun"), which, says Mr.

5

Schoolcraft, they regard "as the mysterious element of the universe, typifying Divinity."

And Prescott, in his "Conquest of Peru," thus describes the great Temple of the Sun: "The most renowned of the Peruvian temples, the pride of the capital, and the wonder of the empire, was at Cuzco, where, under the munificence of successive sovereigns, it had become so enriched that it received the name of *Coricancha,* or the 'Place of Gold.' It consisted of a principal building, and several chapels and inferior edifices, covering a large extent of ground in the heart of the city, and completely encompassed by a wall, which, with the edifices, was all constructed of stone. * * * The interior was literally a mine of gold. On the western wall was emblazoned a representation of the Deity, consisting of a human countenance, looking forth from amidst innumerable rays of light, which emanate from it in every direction, in the same manner as the Sun is often personified with us."

The wise men from the East who followed the Star, and visited the new-born child at Bethlehem, were, without much doubt, from among those denominated Sun-worshippers. But did they worship the material sun? According to Herodotus, the Persians, who pre-eminently are supposed to have been Sun-worshippers, worshipped on the tops of mountains, and were not permitted to pray for themselves alone, but were bound to offer their supplications for all others, but especially for the Persians and their king. Herodotus continues: "When the person who offers the sacrifice has cut the victim into small pieces, and boiled the flesh, he lays it on a bed of tender grass, especially on trefoil, and after all things are disposed, one of their *Magi,* or wise men, standing up, sings an ode addressed to Deity; which last ceremony they consider as an indispensable rite of their worship, and it is never omitted." Herodotus says they sacrificed to the Sun. "It is but fair to state this," says a recent writer, "because, in the letter, it affords some ground for the assertion that they adored material objects; but other proof will be given—and is also fairly deducible from the language of Herodotus, as expressed above—that the Persians, from the highest point of their mountain-worship, elevated their thoughts and their affections, or prayers, to the *Only God;* that they looked upward through the sun of earth, as the highest created type of the Sun of heaven; thus to their Creator and Preserver, to whom the wise and holy men who conducted the worship, directly addressed their worship and sung their ode."

Joseph von Hammer, one of the first Orientalists of our later times, declares that the ancient Persians were neither Sun nor Fire-worshippers, but believers and adorers of a Supreme Being; that they regarded the sun of this world merely as the highest emblem of the Divinity; through which emblem, or type, they addressed their devotions to the God of Heaven, in whom they believed, and in whom they trusted.

Jacob Bryant, the author of a work entitled "A New System, or an Analysis of Ancient Mythology," first published in 1774–1776, treats very fully of the religious character of the ancient nations; and some of his declarations go far to establish the belief, which we cannot avoid considering as most just, that the religion taught by the Zoroasters and accepted by the Persians and Parsees was neither materialistic nor idolatrous, but that it inculcated, for thousands of years, the belief in a *Supreme Being,* the Source of life and Author of all things made or created. There are strong reasons for the belief that the Persians were the last people who became idolatrous. Mr. Bryant, in his "immortal work," quotes Otanas as saying that there had been a true notion of the Deity transmitted by Zoroaster, and maintained by the *Magi,* after the rest of the world had become shrouded in moral darkness.

The more fully we come to understand and carefully examine the religions of all nations, the more evident it is that in them we have the remains of a once true religion—

a knowledge of the Lord and of the life which leads to happiness and heaven—and the remains of a once universal science, or that of the correspondence between natural and spiritual things, in accordance with which Divine revelations have been given to man. The men of the Golden Age, or of the Most Ancient or Adamic Church, which existed before the fall and deluge of falses and evils, as we have heretofore stated, according to the revelations made through Swedenborg, had direct revelation from the Lord, open vision into the spiritual world, and perceived the correspondence between spiritual and natural things. All natural objects represented things pertaining to the mind of man, and had a spiritual signification, and manifested the wisdom and love of their Creator. Nor has this knowledge entirely perished at this day from the language and perceptions of men, however little they may realize its wonderful significance.

A distinct moral character is possessed by every animal. "So distinct is this," says a recent writer, "that their very names have become expressive of their characters, and are used as adjectives. Lion-like, fox-like, bearish, lamb-like, wolfish, dogged, suggest distinct ideas from the distinct characteristic of each of these animals. We use such adjectives to describe the characters of men, because we perceive the inevitable analogy existing between animals and men. Man's moral nature is seen to include *all* these dispositions; and as any one of them acquires an undue predominance, so the man is described. The animals are each a distinct incarnation of *one* human quality. Man is the embodiment of *all* animal qualities and characteristics. He is the comprehensive aggregate of *all*. *They* are the incarnated integers. Ferocity, possible to man, is the very nature of the wolf. Cunning, possible to man, is the very nature of the fox. Innocence, possible to man, is the very nature of the lamb. Imitation, possible to man, is the very nature of the monkey. Poetry has made such analogies familiar to every one, and universal perception has confirmed and adopted them. Birds have, in like manner, furnished similar analogies to man's *mental* nature. All the world has seen the analogy between keen perception and the hawk, vain-show and the peacock, soaring intellect and the eagle; nor have men been slow to admit the exquisite correspondence of turtle-doves, nor the image of selfish shrewdness in the cuckoo. Languages have been formed of, and records conveyed by, such analogies, and the wisdom of centuries has been communicated by such inscriptions. Such a doctrine of analogy it is, that alone explains the origin, or accounts for the dissemination, of divination, magic, witchcraft, astrology, the prevalence of charms or the universality of sacrifices.

"The analogy between our natural senses and spiritual faculties has been long observed. We *see* truth, we *hear* laws, we *weigh* arguments, we have mental *tastes.* Truth is mental *light,* love is spiritual *heat.* We are *inflamed* with passion and *chilled* by antipathy, we *warm* to a subject, and we *freeze* towards individuals. Natural qualities are analogous to spiritual qualities. Reproaches are *stabbing,* couched in *cutting* words, pangs are *bitter,* and oppression is *grinding;* feelings are *lacerated* by *stinging* sarcasms, and we are *melted* into tenderness by *soft* compassion."—*Rev. John Hyde.*

But with the decline of our race, when men began to love themselves supremely instead of the Lord and their neighbor, the perception of truth and of correspondences faded gradually; then especially, during the days of the church of Noah, the wise men began, for the sake of preserving a knowledge of the Lord, true ideas concerning Him, and of a true life, to study and store up in their memories the spiritual significations of natural things, and to teach them to their children, and to write them down; and finally to form images to remind them of spiritual things, not with any thought of worshipping such images, for such worship only resulted when the true spiritual signification was lost. Thus has originated sun-worship and all forms of Idolatry, and this is the reason why they are so universal. The mysteries, rites and ceremonies of Masonry have had a similar origin. It was long anterior to the days of Solomon that wise men cultivated a knowledge of correspondences, and of the one God, and a good life; and for the sake of preserving this knowledge as pure as possible, they transmitted it secretly to their successors.

Mythology has had the same origin; that is, it has arisen from the science of correspondences, and can only be interpreted correctly in accordance therewith, although more or less perverted and superficial, like all the writings and works of man, when compared with the Word and works of God. In the better and early ages of the world men regarded spiritual knowledge as being far more important than natural knowledge; therefore they were disposed to talk and write in correspondential or allegorical language. It is for this reason that the earliest writings are allegorical; even the history of Rome, traced back, ends in a myth.

But the question will doubtless arise with many: "If the first chapters of Genesis, the book of Revelation, the parables of the Lord, and other portions of the Word, are allegorical, or composed and not real histories, bearing a resemblance, to say the least, to the mythological writings of the ancients, how are we to distinguish between what writings are Divine revelations and what are merely human productions?" On a very superficial, and without a somewhat careful examination, this might be as difficult as it would be to distinguish at a distance, and on such an examination, between either a nicely painted and dressed manikin or a mere figure of a man and a real living man; certainly not more difficult than it is to distinguish between a selfish, sensual man, whose chief delight is his own gratification, and the true God-serving man, who delights in doing good to others, and conscientiously does what is just and right. We distinguish a real man from the most careful man-made image, by discovering evidences of life in the one, and in every part, even the most minute, and all parts connected, and acting harmoniously, which we do not find in the other. So, to distinguish between the bad and good man, we must read the real life of each as manifested in looks, speech_ and acts. The Lord when on earth declared: "It is the spirit that quickeneth, the flesh profiteth nothing; the words that I speak unto you, they are spirit and they are life." Here then lies the grand distinction between the Word of God and the words of man; the one is living, having a spiritual sense running throughout containing infinite treasure of spiritual wisdom; there are no real contradictions, no conflict, no jar in the spiritual sense—it is one woven from the top throughout; whereas in the mythological writings of men, there is no connected spiritual sense—no infinite treasures of wisdom; there is a lack of Divine harmony and unity—they are man-made. The reader has only to carefully read the writings of Swedenborg, to see how wonderfully clear is the distinction between the sacred Scriptures and the writings of men, and to be able to perceive clearly that the former are indeed Divine, special revelations given for the good of man, and even angels, for we read, "Thy Word, O Lord, is established forever in the heavens."

That there were other sacred writings or revelations given to the ancients, besides those contained in our Bible, is manifest from the quotations contained in the Scriptures from such works; and it is certain that some of them, at least, were prophetical and composed histories or were allegorical, similar to the first chapters of Genesis.

Thus says Swedenborg: "The saying that the sun stood still upon Gibeon and the moon in the valley of Ajalon, signified that the church was entirely vastated as to all good and truth. For a battle was then fought against the king of Jerusalem and the kings of the Amorites; and by the king of Jerusalem the truth of the church entirely vastated by falsities is signified, and by the kings of the

Amorites is signified the good of the church vastated by
evils.   Therefore those kings were smitten with hail-
stones, by which are signified the horrible falsities of evil.
It is said that the sun stood still and the moon stayed, that
is, in the sight of the children of Israel, that they might
see their enemies; but this was prophetical, although
historically related, as may appear from the circumstance
that it is said, '*Is not this written in the book of Jasher?*'
which was a prophetical book out of which these words
were taken.   From this same book therefore it is said too,
'*Until the nation was avenged upon its enemies,*' and not
until the children of Israel were avenged upon their
enemies, for the word 'nation' is said prophetically.
The same is evident moreover from the consideration that
this miracle, if it had been just so accomplished, would
have inverted the whole order of nature; which the other
miracles in the Word would not have done."

We fancy that the reader will be a little better able to
understand how the Divine love and wisdom, denoted in
correspondential language by the sun, which combine infinite mercy, and a true faith signified by the moon, ceased
to progress in the hearts and intellects of these cruel, bar-
barous men who were relentlessly killing each other, even
killing their helpless captives in cold blood, than how the
natural sun and moon stood still, or the earth stopped
turning on its axis.   There ever flow down to man from
the Lord, love, mercy, and truth; it is man that perverts
these heavenly influences into hatred and falsehood, until
at length he becomes so vastated of all goodness and truth,
by a life of evil, that he sees falsehood as truth, and acts
of cruelty, when they gratify his selfishness, as good.

In regard to these ancient revelations not embodied in
our Bible, Swedenborg says:

CONCERNING THE ANCIENT WORD WHICH IS LOST.

"The religious systems of many nations are derived
from that Word, and were conveyed from the land of

Canaan, and from many parts of Asia into Greece, and
thence into Italy, and through Ethiopia and Egypt into
certain kingdoms of Africa; but in Greece they converted
the correspondences into fables, and the divine attributes
into so many gods, the chief of which they called Jove,
from Jehovah."

´ XIX.

Spiritualism.

WE must either deny the truth of the many relations
of spiritual vision contained in the sacred Scriptures, and the reports and traditions of such visions existing among all nations, or we must admit the possibility of
man's having intercourse with spirits; and if men have
ever had such intercourse in the past, it would certainly
seem possible for them to have such at this day; therefore
we feel no disposition to deny any of the well attested facts
of modern Spiritualism, although we must use our reason,
enlightened by the revelations which the Lord has given
us, to judge of its phenomena, as we have done in the case
of the standing still of the sun and staying of the moon at
the command of Joshua; for we know that the world is
full of truths which are only apparent, and not real truths,
like the apparent passage of the sun around the earth;
and many of these apparent truths can only be distinguished from real truths by enlightened reason, and not a
few of them by the aid of Divine revelation alone. Admit-
ting, then, the possible reality of modern Spiritualism,
after sifting out all deceptions and frauds, we know that
all things are not as they seem to its advocates; and if
Spiritualists will but read the writings of Emanuel Swedenborg, they will find that there are many apparent
truths in their philosophy, and they will also find a
science which fairly underlies Spiritualism, written long
before its phenomena commenced.

But it is one thing to admit that it is possible at this

day to hold intercourse with spirits, but it is quite another thing to admit that it is either well, safe, or desirable to do so.

Let us see what the Bible, that glorious volume which has come down to us from our fathers, which not only claims to be, but, as we have seen, is the Word of God, has to say on the subject of Spiritualism? From this book we learn that there is a spiritual world, and that it is possible to see and converse with spirits, and that man has guardian spirits, and that there are evil or unclean spirits; and numerous examples or instances are given of open vision and spiritual communication, and even of men being possessed by spirits, so that Spiritualism is not new.

But we hear from the sacred volume that there are two kinds of Spiritualism—if you please; one by Divine permission, protection, and guidance, in which the Lord and His angels manifest themselves to men, and reveal important truths, and permit men to see the inhabitants of the spiritual world, as was the case with the prophets and disciples, and especially with John the Revelator; the individual man not having sought such intercourse, but seeming to have been chosen for his office, and only when some important knowledge or information for the good of his race was to be imparted by or through him. The second class of communications and spiritual phenomena would seem to be disorderly and evil, from the fact that they are prohibited by the Lord in the Old Testament, and that the Lord when on earth cast out the possessing spirits, in one instance permitting them to enter a herd of swine, the latter being among the lowest and most filthy of all animals, these possessing spirits choosing them for a habitation; but it seems no good came to the poor swine, for according to the record it would appear that the whole herd ran down a steep place and perished in the sea. In the Old Testament we read : "Regard not them that have familiar spirits, neither seek after wizards to be defiled by

t:.m. I am the Lord your God" (Leviticus xix. 31).
"And the soul that turneth after such as have familiar
spirits and after wizards, to go a whoring after them, I
will even set my face against that soul, and will cut him
off from among his people' (Lev. xx. 6). "There shall
not be found among you any one that maketh his son or
his daughter to pass through the fire, or that useth divination, or an observer of times, or an enchanter, or a witch, or
a charmer, or a consulter with familiar spirits, or a wizard,
or a necromancer. For all that do these things are an
abomination to the Lord, and because of these abominations the Lord thy God doth drive them out from before
thee" (Deut. xviii. 10–12). "And when they shall say
unto you, Seek unto them that have familiar spirits, and
unto wizards that peep and that mutter; should not a
people seek unto their God? for the living to the dead?
to the law and to the testimony? if they speak not according to this word, it is because there is no light in them"
(Isaiah viii. 19, 20). Can it be that the Word of the Lord
would so pointedly condemn seeking communications from
spirits, even to the driving of nations out of their lands
and cutting them off, if it were a harmless practice? If it
was an evil, and such a deadly one, to seek intercourse with
spirits several thousands of years ago, is it any the less
wrong now? If obsession was so objectionable that the
Lord, when on earth, drove out possessing spirits, and
gave His disciples power over such spirits, should men and
women to-day allow spirits to take possession of their
bodies, and perhaps souls, and speak and write through
them? And should we, as rational beings, seek com- '
munications either through mediums, or directly from
spirits, in defiance of the above warnings of Divine revelation? These are questions well worthy of our most serious
consideration, for our eternal welfare may depend, more
than we imagine, on our decision, and consequent action.

Is there any good reason why the Lord prohibited,
under the most fearful penalties, the consulting with

familiar spirits, or even with those who have such spirits?
What real objection can there be to our seeking open intercourse with spirits, and consulting and regarding those
who can see and converse with spirits? Surely, if it is
wrong, there must be some good reason why it is so,
which would appeal to our understandings. A great
many intelligent men at this day, and who are not among
the worst of men, have in a great measure outgrown
authority; and, perhaps to a greater extent than they
should have done, reverence for ancient dogmas. If
Spiritualism, for instance, is objectionable and wrong, as
the Bible plainly teaches, they want to understand the why
and the wherefore.

Let us then carefully examine this subject in the light
of revelation and of reason. In the first Epistle of John we
are directed to "believe not every spirit, but try the spirits
whether they are of God;" and the following is the crite-
rion: "Hereby know ye the spirit of God; every spirit
that confesseth that Jesus Christ is come in the flesh is
of God;" and we are told that every spirit that confesseth
not this doctrine is not of God. Now, how many spiritual
mediums and communicating spirits are of God, according
to this test? In First Timothy we have a prediction; the
reader can judge whether it is being fulfilled at this day
or not. We read: "That in the latter times some shall
depart from the faith, giving heed to seducing spirits and
doctrines of devils." The divinely commissioned seer for
the New Jerusalem dispensation, which is now being
established on earth, Emanuel Swedenborg, assures us
from actual observation in the spiritual world, and from a
most intimate knowledge of the laws of that world, and
of spiritual intercourse with and influx into this world,
"that to speak with angels of heaven is granted to none
but such as are grounded in truths originating in good,
especially in the acknowledgment of the Lord and of the
divinity in His humanity; this being the truth in which
the heavens are established. For the Lord is the God of

heaven; the Lord's divine sphere constitutes heaven, and the Lord's divine sphere in heaven is love to Him and charity towards the neighbor derived from Him." It will here be noticed that Swedenborg's testimony is in strict agreement with the apostle John's statement.

Swedenborg found in the spiritual world, and described carefully, three heavens, all the inhabitants of which acknowledged the Lord Jesus Christ as God, the sacred Scriptures as revelations from God, and were actuated in all they·did and said by either love to the Lord, charity to the neighbor, or love of obedience to the Divine commandments. He also found three other societies opposite the heavens, which he denominates hell, all the inhabitants of which deny the divinity of the Lord Jesus Christ, deny that the sacred Scriptures are the Word of God, and are actuated in all that they do by some form of selfishness, and deny the possibility of any one acting from any higher motive than a selfish motive. He found intermediate between heaven and hell what he calls the world of spirits, which is the common receptacle for all men when they leave this world, where their ruling loves are developed and they are prepared to enter either heaven or hell. He assures us that the world of spirits is like this world, from which it is constantly being peopled, to a great extent, filled with lying and deceiving inhabitants, or spirits, who deny the Lord, the necessity for regeneration and heavenly truths. Unless guided and protected by the Lord and His angels, for a special purpose, a man, in open intercourse, simply comes in contact with his associate spirits, or those like himself, in a similar faith and life; consequently, when a man is believing false doctrines, and actuated by evil loves or perverted affections, if he has intercourse with spirits, he necessarily comes in contact with evil spirits. Therefore, says Swedenborg, "to speak with spirits is at this day rarely granted, because it is dangerous; for the spirits then know that they are present with man, which otherwise they do not know, and evil spirits are of such a nature that they regard man with deadly hatred, and desire nothing more than to destroy him." Especially do they strive to destroy all heavenly truths and affections in his soul. Such destruction is spiritual death—not annihilation, but the death which was pronounced in Eden.

Again, Swedenborg says: "It is believed by many that man may be taught of the Lord by spirits speaking with him; but they who believe and desire this do not know that it is connected with danger to their souls. 'So long as man lives in the world, he is as to his spirit in the midst of spirits, and yet the spirits do not know that they are with man, nor does a man know that he is with spirits. The reason is that they are conjoined immediately as to affections of the will, and mediately as to the thoughts of the understanding. For man thinks naturally, and spirits think spiritually; and natural and spiritual thought do not make one otherwise than by correspondences—and unity by correspondences causes that one knows nothing of the other. But as soon as spirits begin to speak with a man they come out of their spiritual state into the natural state of the man; and then they know that they are with the man, and conjoin themselves with the thoughts of his affections, and from these speak with him. They cannot enter into anything else; for a similar affection and consequent thought conjoins all, and a dissimilar separates. It is owing to this that the spirit speaking is in the same principles as the man, be they truths or be they falsities; and also that he excites them, and by his affection conjoined to the man's affection strongly confirms them. * * * From these considerations it is evident to what danger a man is exposed who speaks with spirits, or manifestly feels their operation. Man is ignorant of the quality of his own affection, whether it be good or evil, and with what other beings he is conjoined; and if he has a conceit of his own intelligence the spirits favor every thought that comes from it. So it is if any one, inflamed with a sort of fire, has a leaning to certain principles; which is the case with those who are not in truths from a genuine affection. When a spirit favors a man's thoughts or principles, from a similar affection, the one leads the other as the blind leads the blind, until both fall into the pit. Such were the Pythonic (diviners) of old; and also the magicians in Egypt and in Babylon, who on account of their converse with spirits, and on account of the operation of them upon themselves, manifestly felt, were called wise. But the worship of God was thereby converted into the worship of demons, and the church perished. For' this reason such communications were forbidden to the children of Israel under penalty of death."

Not only the church but those mighty nations perished also; where are Egypt and Babylon to-day?

The first sentence of the following quotation from Swedenborg's "Heaven and Hell" throws a flood of light on the subject of modern Spiritualism, the want of reliability and identity of spirits, etc., etc.

"It is not lawful for any angel or spirit to converse with man from his own memory, but only from that of the man. For angels and spirits have memory as well as men; and if a spirit were to speak with a man from his own memory, the man would not know but that the things which then became the subject of his thoughts belonged to himself, although they belonged to the spirit. This is like remembering a thing which, nevertheless, the man had never heard of or seen. That such is the fact has been given me to know by experience. This is the origin of the opinion held by some of the ancients, that after some thousands of years they should return into their former life, and into all its transactions, and that they actually had so returned. They drew this conclusion from the circumstance, that there sometimes occurred to them what seemed to be a remembrance of things which, nevertheless, they had never seen or heard. This appearance was produced by an influx of spirits, from their own memory, into their ideas of thought."

If we bear the above statement of Swedenborg in mind, we shall be the better able to appreciate and comprehend the following quotations from his writings; and the reader will please remember that Swedenborg wrote about a century before "Modern Spiritualism" commenced; and we here acknowledge that we are either directly or indirectly indebted to his writings, or to the Lord through his instrumentality, not only for the quotations, but also for all the ideas contained in this section on Spiritualism, which have not been drawn from the sacred Scriptures.

One of Swedenborg's immediate friends and followers suggested to him, or inquired of him, if it would not be well to omit his "memorable relations" of things seen and heard in the spiritual world, which are interspersed throughout his writings, as they tended to prejudice people against the doctrines of the New Jerusalem. His reply was, simply, that he was commanded to write them. We think it is not difficult to-day to understand why the Lord required him to write them, and the notes of instruction and warning which they contain to us. Nor is it difficult to understand why he was permitted to experience and detail many things for our enlightenment and warning which, to his acquaintances, must have seemed very strange and incomprehensible; among which may be named: spirits writing through his hand, without his being conscious of what they wrote while they were writing; but he informs us that he was commanded to destroy all such writings, and not a line remains—only the suggestion which his statement conveys, which is a caution to us, if we are wise.

Swedenborg informs us that spirits which have intercourse with man " know all the thoughts which the man himself knows, *and also the smallest minutiæ of the thoughts and affections, which the man doth not know ; yea, such things as it is impossible for him to know in the life of the body."* And again, "They enter into all his memory, and into all the sciences of memory which man possesses; thus they put on all things which are man's, insomuch that they know no other than that those things are theirs; spirits have this prerogative above men; hence it is that all things which man thinks, they think, and that all things which man wills, they will; and vice versa, all things which those spirits think, man thinks, and all things which those spirits will, man wills; for they act in unity by conjunction. Yet it is supposed by both parties that such things are in themselves, so spirits suppose, and so men; but this is a fallacy." (*A. C.* 5853.)

Again he says: "When similar things are called up in the memory of man, and are thus represented to them [spirits], they think they are the same person; then all the things are called forth from the memory which represent those persons, both the words, the speech, the tone, the gesture, and other things." "It has many times been shown to me that the spirits speaking with me did not know otherwise than that they were the men who were the subject of thought; and neither did other spirits know otherwise; as yesterday and to-day, some one known to me in life (was represented by one), who was so like him in all things which belong to him, so far as they were known to me, that nothing was more like. Wherefore, let those who speak with spirits beware lest they be deceived, when they say that they are those whom they know, and that they are dead."

"For there are genera and species of spirits of a like faculty; and when similar things are called up in the memory of man, and are thus represented to them, they think that they are the same person: then all things are called forth from the memory which represent those persons, the words, the speech, the tone, the gesture, and other things; besides that, they are induced to think thus when other spirits inspire them, for then they are in the phantasy of those, and think they are the same."

Again Swedenborg says: "Sometimes it was shown to me by experience, that spirits were induced to believe that they were those persons about whose life and manners I was able to have some knowledge, and from this knowledge in my mind they induced other spirits to believe that they were these persons; they spoke in the same manner, had the same disposition, and many other like things. They were endeavoring even to make me believe that they were these persons; but because I had learned that other persons may be personified thus perfectly by spirits, they could not impose upon me.

"Wherefore let those be careful to whom it is granted to speak with spirits lest they believe that the spirits are those whom they pretend to be; for they are able to assume the likeness of any man which they find in the memory of the man with whom they are. That this is so may also appear from this circumstance, because such spirits are associated with men as are like them; and when they are with men they do not know otherwise but that they are they." (*Spirit. Diary*, 2686, 2687.)

"The spirits attendant on those who are in Heresies, in Fallacies, and Illusions, as to the truths of faith, and in falses, are in the like, without the slightest difference. *The reason of this is, that man may be in his freedom, and may not be disturbed by any propriety of a spirit.*" (*A.C.* 5860.)

The above statements are worthy of our most serious consideration; for, in their light, it is not difficult to understand why we should not seek open intercourse with spirits, if we would preserve our mental freedom, and retain our rational faculties unimpaired, and avoid being misled by presumptuous spirits.

It will be seen that, according to the above statements, any spirit, if he can get access to our memory, either directly, or through a medium, can not only give us the names of our friends in the spirit world, but also personate them in every respect, even as to looks, handwriting, etc., etc.

Again Swedenborg says: "*That the things which I*

*learned in representations and visions, and from discourses
with spirits and angels, are from the Lord alone.* Whenever there was any representation, vision, and discourse,
I was kept interiorly and most interiorly in reflection
upon it, as to what thence was useful and good, thus what
I might learn therefrom; which reflection was not thus
attended to by those who presented the representations
and visions, and who were speaking; *yea, sometimes they
were indignant when they perceived that I was reflecting.*
Thus have I been instructed; consequently by no spirit, nor
by any angel, but by the Lord alone, from whom is all truth
and good; yea, when they wished to instruct me concerning various things, there was scarcely anything but what
was false; wherefore I was prohibited from believing anything that they spake; nor was I permitted to infer any
such thing as was proper to them. Besides, when they
wished to persuade me, I perceived an interior or most
interior persuasion that the thing was such, and not as
they wished; which also they wondered at; the perception
was manifest, but cannot be easily described to the apprehension." (*Sp. Diary,* 1647.)

He says, "That spirits relate things exceedingly fictitious, and lie. When spirits begin to speak with man, he
must beware lest he believe them in anything; for they
say almost anything; things are fabricated by them, and
they lie; for if they were permitted to relate what heaven
is, and how things are in the heavens, they would tell so
many lies, and indeed with solemn affirmation, that man
would be astonished; wherefore, when spirits were speaking, I was not permitted to have faith in the things which
they related. For they are extremely fond of fabricating."

In regard to the desirability of speaking with spirits and
its influence on men, Swedenborg says: "Speaking with
the dead would produce a like effect, as miracles, concerning which just above; namely, that man would be persuaded and driven to worship for a little time; but
because this deprives man of rationality, and at the same

time shuts in evils as was said above, this enchantment or internal bond is loosed, and the evils shut in burst forth, with blasphemy and profanation; but this takes place only when the spirits induce some dogma of religion, which is never done by any good spirit, still less by any angel of heaven." (*D. P.*, 134.)

Swedenborg makes one statement which every man and woman will do well to heed, in order to keep out of danger, which is: If a man hears a spirit speaking to him it is not lawful for him to reply; for if he does then the spirit knows that he is with man in this world, which otherwise he would not know, and could not injure the man. How important then that we never give the consent of our will by voluntarily attending "circles," "séances," the lectures of "trance speakers," etc., etc. Or if we have already done this, that we shun doing it again, lest we be led by evil spirits to doubt and deny the Divinity of the Lord Jesus Christ, and the Holiness of the sacred Scriptures; and the necessity of regeneration, if we would enter the kingdom of heaven.

XX.

In What Degree a Mediate Revelation, which is Effected by Means of the Word, is Preferable to an Immediate Revelation, which is Effected by Means of Spirits.

SWEDENBORG says: "It is generally believed that man might be more enlightened and become more wise if an immediate revelation was granted him by means of converse with spirits and angels; but the reverse is the case. Illustration by means of the Word is effected by an interior way, whereas illustration by means of an immediate revelation is effected by an exterior way. The interior way is by the will into the understanding, the exterior way is by the hearing into the understanding. Man, by means of the Word, is illustrated by the Lord in proportion as his will is in good; but man by hearing may be instructed, and as it were illustrated, although his will is in evil, and what enters into the understanding in a man whose will is in evil, is not within the man but without him, and is only in his memory and not in his life; and what is without man and not in his life is gradually separated, if not before, nevertheless after death; for the will which is in evil either casts it out or suffocates it, or falsifies and profanes it; for the will constitutes the life of man, and continually acts upon the understanding, and regards as extraneous what is derived into the understanding from the memory.   On the contrary, the understanding does not act on the will, but it only teaches in what manner the will should act; wherefore if a man knew from heaven whatever is known to the angels, or if he knew whatever is contained in the Word, and moreover all that is contained in the doctrines of the church, which the fathers have written and councils declared, and his will remains in evil, nevertheless after death such a man would be regarded as one who knows nothing, because he does not will what he knows; and whereas evil hates truth in this case, the man himself casts out truths, and in the room thereof adopts such falses as are in agreement with the evil of his will. Moreover, permission is not granted to any spirit nor to any angel to teach any man on this earth in divine truths, but the Lord himself teaches every one by means of the Word, and man is taught in proportion as he receives good from the Lord in his will, and he receives good in the same proportion as he flees evils as sins; every man also is in a society of spirits as to his affections and as to his thoughts thence derived, in which society his mind is as it were present with them; wherefore spirits speaking with man, speak from his affections and according to them.

"A man *cannot converse with other spirits unless the societies in which he is be first removed, which cannot be done except by a reformation of his will;* because every man is in society with spirits who are in the same religion with himself; wherefore when the spirits converse with him, they confirm whatever a man has made a part of his religion; consequently enthusiastic spirits confirm whatever is of enthusiasm with man; Quaker spirits confirm whatever is of Quakerism; Moravian spirits whatever is of Moravianism, and so forth. Hence proceed confirmations of the false which can never be extirpated. From this it appears that mediate revelation, which is effected by means of the Word, is preferable to immediate revelation, which is effected by means of spirits. As to what regards myself, it was not allowed to take anything from the dictate of any spirit, or from the dictate of any angel, but from the dictate of the Lord alone."

Spiritualists generally recognize and acknowledge most distinctly and clearly, in their conversation and writings, the great law of spiritual association or affinity; that like dwell with like, and that like attract like, which Swedenborg so fully illustrates in all his writings; consequently, that man, while here, attracts to himself spirits like himself, both as to principles and life; therefore, in open intercourse he only comes in contact with his like. Now, if they will stop and use the reason to which they appeal in the case of the Bible, they can but see the impropriety and danger of seeking intercourse with spirits. Let us look at this subject for a moment from their own standpoint, or the law of affinity, the truth of which they admit, in the light of reason; for we fully agree with them that the sacred Scriptures even, in order that they may retain their hold upon an enlightened age as special revelations from God to man, must stand the severest tests of reason; and we know that, when interpreted in accordance with the grand science of correspondences between natural and spiritual things revealed through Swedenborg, they will stand the test, and shine brighter and brighter as the ages roll on; for the thoughts and affections of the Creator are manifested alike in His Word and works, and can never conflict when correctly interpreted.

Can modern Spiritualism stand the tests of enlightened reason ?   Let us see.

If this life is but the beginning of an endless life, it is manifest that doctrines, thoughts, words, and acts, which tend to subdue our evil inclinations, and to lead us to love the Lord and our neighbor supremely are of first importance, for they tend to unity and peace, happiness and heaven.   But with multitudes to-day, selfishness and sensualism rule, and they must be born again, or put away their supreme selfishness, and come to act from higher motives, or it is manifest that they can never enter the kingdom of heaven ; for heaven is not a pen or place into which a man can be let as a matter of favor.   Heavenly principles must rule us before we can enter the gates of the celestial city.   Now, let the man who is ruled by either the selfish love of power or money, or who is vain, licentious, or given to drunkenness, jealousy, or envy, seek communications from spirits, and what is the inevitable result?   Please remember, like attracts like.   Being swayed by evil motives, his associate spirits are necessarily evil, and evil spirits are in false doctrines, therefore they deny the divinity of the Lord Jesus Christ, for they hate him; they deny the necessity for regeneration, in fact deny that man can live from any higher motive than selfishness; and, if the man hearkens to them, they will use every effort and art to hold him in his present state of life, and to destroy all reverence for the Lord, and the sacred Scriptures as special revelations from Him ; for, if the man changes for the better, they are repelled and will have to leave him.   Thus by seeking and hearkening to spiritual communications, the evil or unregenerate man confirms himself in his evil loves ; his spirits justifying him by every seductive argument imaginable, and thus even the prospect of his future regeneration is materially lessened, if not actually destroyed.   Could a greater misfortune befall an evil man here below, than this ?   Again, supposing a man has commenced living a new life, the work of regeneration is not accomplished in a day; but regeneration results from the warfare of a lifetime. Little by little are his evil inclinations and thoughts put away; evil inclinations and thoughts are prompted by evil spirits, and supposing while temporarily harboring such, the man seeks and heeds communications from spirits, these evil spirits will necessarily use every art to destroy the new resolutions for a better life by, as rapidly as he will bear it, denying all heavenly doctrines, and confirming him, if possible, in his evil states. Could a greater misfortune befall him? Once more, there are three heavens, seen and carefully described by Swedenborg, within the reach of men, and whether a good man shall reach the lowest, middle or highest, depends upon the progress made here in the regenerate life. Supposing a good man, in a good state, seeks communications from spirits. His associate spirits are no better than he is, and open vision with them or communicating with them will tend to fix him in his present state of life, and prevent his progress towards a higher life; thus checking the great work of regeneration. How serious the injury to the man!

But there is another view in the case of good men, or of those who reverence the Lord and His Word and who are striving to lead a good life in accordance with the Divine commands, seeking such communications. They have the Divine warnings sounding in their ears, and are consequently reasonably sure to have conscientious scruples when they seek such communications; and if so, they are, it would seem, almost necessarily brought in contact with evil spirits. The Christian, therefore, who, from the stand-point of a distinct recognition of the Lord and of Divine revelation, goes away into Spiritualism, and seeks communications from spirits, must run a fearful risk; and have we not good reason to fear, that he will fall to rise no more forever? Whilst for those who have little or no reverence for the Lord Jesus Christ, and for the sacred Scriptures, there may be far less danger and comparatively little harm from their seeking such inter-course, as they do not profane holy things. In fact, thousands of skeptics and naturalists have been convinced that they are to live after death, by the phenomena of Spiritualism; and finding the communications entirely unreliable and unsatisfactory, have turned to Divine revelation, and to the Lord, and thus have been led into the Lord's church. Here then is a use which Spiritualism is performing for many earnest seekers after truth; and perhaps this may be one of the reasons why it is permitted by the Lord. But, oh, how unwise is the man who rests satisfied with the phenomena and revelations of Spiritualism, when they should lead him up to the feast of fat things, and wine on the lees, or to the spiritual good and truths revealed by our Heavenly Father in the Divine Word, and in the writings for the New Jerusalem !

The following statements by Swedenborg appeal to our highest reason: "Good spirits and angels," he says, never induce any dogmatic principle of religion, "for the Lord alone teaches a man, though mediately, through the Word in illumination." "Nor do they say anything which takes away the freedom of reason," such as dictating or attempting to control his actions, for this would impair his manhood if he were to obey such dictations; only evil spirits attempt such interferences with man's freedom and reason.

In conclusion, we will ask the reader if enlightened reason, and even the common sense with which God has endowed man, do not condemn in the most earnest and positive manner the seeking of open intercourse with spirits, or the obtaining communications from them? The sacred Scriptures, as interpreted in the writings of Swedenborg, reveal to us a knowledge of a higher and nobler life than it is possible for our associate spirits to comprehend or unfold to us; and if any one is anxious or curious for a knowledge of the spiritual world, or of spirits, or even of modern Spiritualism, according to the

6

best of our judgment, after a careful examination of the whole subject, he can only obtain reliable information by reading the writings of the Swedish seer. For him the Lord had a special mission; he sought it not, but he was called to it by the Lord Himself, and he cheerfully forsook his scientific and worldly pursuits, and, guided by the Lord and His angels, he devoted his life and means to writing and circulating his works. How important was his mission, if a reverence for the Lord Jesus Christ, or even for a personal God and His Word, is to remain with men, Spiritualism is now making manifest in one direction, and Naturalism or Scientism in another.

In a small work on "Intercourse between the Soul and Body," Swedenborg says: "That there is a spiritual world in which are spirits and angels, distinct from the natural world in which men are, has hitherto been deeply hidden, even in the Christian world. The reason is, because no angel has descended and declared it, and no man has ascended and seen it. Lest, therefore, from ignorance concerning that world, and the uncertain faith concerning Heaven and Hell that results from such ignorance, man should be infatuated to such a degree as to become an atheistic naturalist, it has pleased the Lord to open the sight of my spirit, and to elevate it into Heaven, and also to let it down into Hell, and to exhibit to its view the quality of each. It is thence manifest to me that there are two worlds which are distinct from each other; one in which all things are spiritual, which is thence called the spiritual world, and another in which all things are natural, which is thence called the natural world; and spirits and angels live in their own world, and men in theirs; and also that every man passes by death from his own world into the other, and lives therein to eternity."

Writing within a few years after the opening of his spiritual sight, he said: "For several years I have now almost continuously conversed with spirits and angels, and they with me. In this manner I have been instructed respecting the state of souls after death; respecting the divers sorts of spirits who seduce man; respecting Hell, and its various and cruel afflictions and punishments; respecting the heavens and the felicity of the souls which are there; respecting true faith and the interior senses."

The Lord punishes no one, but evil carries with it its own punishment in that world as it does in this. From the doing of evil suffering inevitably results—evil the cause, suffering the effect. Hell-fire is self-love perverted.

XXI.

An Appeal to Spiritualists in behalf of the Writings of Emanuel Swedenborg.

(A LARGE PORTION OF THIS SECTION WAS FIRST WRITTEN FOR AND PUBLISHED IN "THE BANNER OF LIGHT.")

WE ask of you, fellow-citizens, children of the same Heavenly Father, journeying toward the mansions of the spiritual world, to lay aside for a few moments— if you are troubled with any such infirmities—prejudice, preconceived opinions, and the spirit of sect or party—a very difficult thing, we know, for most men to do—and to consider for a short time the claims of the Swedish seer to your attention, and compare them with those of modern seers and mediums, and then judge for yourselves. For the truth we should all seek, for the truth alone can make us free from the mistakes of ignorance, the snares of bigotry and sectarianism, and the dominion of evil. It is of no moment to us that we should be able to confirm ourselves in our present views; for, although it should gratify our vanity, it might do us great harm; but it is of vast moment that we should seek and find the truth, and be able to see truth in the light of truth, and to live in accordance with it. Those truths and that system of truth are the most important to us which will lead us to the best and highest life. It is a glorious maxim which Swedenborg proclaimed when he declared that "All religion has relation to life, and the life of religion is to do good." It is not to arouse the spirit of controversy, which is latent in every man, that we write these pages, for such a spirit judges and condemns opposite views before it understands them; no seeker after truth should do this, and no truly wise man will do it.

Emanuel Swedenborg, the seer, a native of Sweden, lived and wrote the wonderful revelations contained in his writings about a century ago. He was one of the most celebrated philosophers of his day; well and thoroughly educated in his youth, he devoted his life and best energies to philosophical pursuits, and the application of scientific principles to the mining and business affairs of his native land. He wrote extensively on the economy of the animal kingdom, and the animal and mineral kingdoms, and a goodly number of his philosophical works have within a few years been translated into English, and are found to contain the germs of many of the discoveries of a later date. His writings show that he was accustomed to observe closely and watch patiently and carefully, and to draw rational conclusions from the operations of Nature. With a mind thus trained and disciplined by study, and an active life of usefulness, at the age of fifty-seven years he commenced his spiritual writings; and for over twenty-seven years he claimed to have open intercourse with the spiritual world; to see and converse with spirits and angels face to face, as man converses with his fellow-man here, and that daily, not in a state of sleep, but of most perfect wakefulness; claims which, when we consider their length, breadth and duration, no other man does or ever has made, or can make with any show of justice. Although written a century ago, long before the appearance of modern Spiritualism, there is scarcely a phase of the latter which is not noticed and described in his writings, and of much of it, the underlying philosophy is given; yes, far more than this, the most wonderful events, even revolutionary changes, are carefully described as they occurred in the spiritual world, and were witnessed by him at the time he wrote; and whole kingdoms in the spiritual world are described, of which modern mediums as a general rule evidently know little and have apparently seen less. He declares that he witnessed the Last Judgment in the world of spirits in the year 1757, and he has given us a careful description of the same. What has astonished us more than anything else, is the apathy and neglect with which the writings of this grand old seer have been regarded by the great mass of Spiritualists; and affectionately and earnestly to call their attention to them, is our sole object in writing this section.

Even the sectarian enemies of Swedenborg have never questioned his intelligence, his honesty or truthfulness, for his life was blameless; with them he was insane, or a visionary, who was himself deceived by his imagination. No intelligent Spiritualist should or can for a moment justly harbor such objections without first reading his writings, for to do so would be to condemn his own faith, and justify the blind opponents of that faith in their opposition to it. A man should not oppose without being able to give a reason.

In one respect—to which we desire especially to call the attention of the reader at this point—Swedenborg stands out boldly as the prince of seers. The son of a clergyman, reared and educated in an orthodox church, busy with literary and scientific pursuits up to the very hour of the opening of his spiritual vision, we would reasonably have expected that the faith of his fathers, and preconceived ideas, would have colored his writings and revelations; but in many respects his doctrines are not in harmony with those in which he was educated, or with those which prevailed at the time he wrote in the religious world around him. The doctrines inculcated in his writings do not agree with those in very many particulars, and Swe-

denborg expressly teaches that the First Christian Church
had come to its end through evils of life and a falsification
of doctrines.   How wonderful that a man should be able
to so perfectly lay aside his preconceived ideas, and to sink
himself, as it were !   And although he spent his time and
money freely in writing, printing, and circulating his
works, he did it anonymously until near the close of his
life, when, at the earnest solicitation of his friends, his
name was published on the title-page of the " True Christian Religion," simply : " By Emanuel Swedenborg, servant
of the Lord Jesus Christ."   He did not desire men to
receive the revelations made through and by him on his
authority, but they were to be received because they are
perceived to be true.   Such were his views.

No man who has ever read Swedenborg's writings can,
for a moment, question but that, if there is any truth in
Spiritualism, or if any man has ever had intercourse with
spirits and the spiritual world, either recently or in the
Bible days, Swedenborg surely had; and it would seem
that his writings are entitled to a respectful consideration
from every one, especially from Spiritualists.   A philoso-
pher by nature and long practice in the natural sciences,
even his spiritual writings are philosophical and beautiful beyond comparison ; order and system reign supreme.
The laws of the spiritual world; the resurrection from the
dead; the state of man after death; the association of
spirits with men; spiritual vision and conversing with
spirits; the relation which the deeds of this life have to
the state of man after the death of the body; spiritual influx, and the correspondence between natural and spiritual
things—are all explained, illustrated, and demonstrated
with a power and force which, it is safe to say, have never
been surpassed or even equalled in any particular; and
which have in the past carried, and are to-day carrying,
conviction to the minds of thousands who have never witnessed any of the spiritual manifestations.   No attentive
reader of his writings doubts the possibility of spiritual in-

tercourse, or that many of the present manifestations are from spirits, for they most wonderfully confirm his statements of the laws of the spiritual world, and of spiritual intercourse.

Many of you, at first sight, may be disappointed at the ideas which he proclaimed; but you will find many of them new, and all of them worthy of the most serious consideration. With Swedenborg a personal God is the centre, and special revelations from Him, or the sacred Scriptures, are the ladder let down from Heaven to earth, on which the angels ascend and descend to man. Modern Spiritualists too frequently ignore a personal God, and all special revelations from God.

In the science of correspondences, revealed through Swedenborg, we have the key for the rational interpretation of the sacred Scriptures, so that we can know that they are revelatious from God, for we can intellectually see that the interpretation is true. In the light of this newly revealed science the skeptic is disarmed, and revelation and reason, the Bible and science, are reunited; and God is shown or clearly manifested in the person of our Lord Jesus Christ, the Father in the Son. As we have already intimated, in a previous section, the day is not far distant when the Bible will be reverenced as it never has been before, as men begin more and more clearly to see. that the letter, which to-day killeth,' is but the covering or clouds for the spirit which giveth life, and that God's Word differs as much from the words of man, as God's works do from the works of men.

Even Nature can never be fully understood, so long as this "science of all sciences" is not recognized. Our scientific men are too many of them wandering on in the dark, ignoring the world of causes, or the spiritual side of nature; but it will not always be so.

In the writings of Swedenborg we are taught that love to the Lord and neighbor constitute heaven, and love of self and the world constitute hell; therefore, man being

c

born into selfish natural affections, must be born again
before he can enter Heaven; in other words, by shunning
evils as sins against God, and living a life according to
His commandments, the old ruling selfish loves must be
subdued, and heavenly affections take their place.   Spiritualism generally teaches progression instead of spiritual
regeneration; and too many of its advocates deny the
necessity for regeneration.   With Swedenborg the Lord
Jesus Christ is the chief corner-stone of the New Jerusalem, and a special providence is clearly and beautifully
taught, whereas Spiritualists, with but few exceptions,
deny the divinity of the Lord, and all special providence.

If Spiritualists would either understand the signs of the
times, or obtain reliable knowledge of the spiritual world,
let them read Swedenborg's writings; and there is no
reason why all men should not read them, as increasing
thousands are doing.   God's truth, like the light of the
natural sun, is free to all.   The idea of a new revelation
from the Lord sounds strangely to the man steeped in
naturalism, and to the bigot, although the Lord promised
a second coming in the clouds of heaven—not of earth;
but it should not to Spiritualists.   Was there ever a greater
need of a revelation of genuine spiritual truth than at this
day, when the simple precepts of the Gospels have been
made of non-effect by the doctrines and traditions of men,
until multitudes are expecting to escape the consequences
of an evil life by a simple act of faith or belief, instead of
expecting to reap what they have sown?   Has the Lord
forgotten His children?   Lo! He comes to the Christian
world in an unexpected hour and manner, as he came at
the end of the Jewish dispensation.   Does He find faith
on earth?   Let those who are watching for the morning,
judge.

In concluding this appeal we will say, that if you will
carefully read the writings of Swedenborg, we can but feel
that you will be satisfied that he was selected by the Lord,

as a man through whom he could reveal to men the science of correspondences, the spiritual sense of His Word in accordance with this science, true doctrines; or the truths of His Second Coming in the clouds of heaven; together with the actual state of man in the spiritual world.   And you will be further satisfied that Swedenborg was permitted by the Lord to enjoy privileges such as no other man has ever enjoyed, and such as we have good reason to expect that no other man will enjoy for many centuries to come, at least.

You can hardly fail to be satisfied that the revelations made through Swedenborg are immeasurably better calculated to benefit man, and elevate our race, than are the revelations and phenomena of modern Spiritualism.

XXII.

Doctrines of the New Jerusalem.—God.

THAT there is but one God, in one Divine person, is clearly taught in the first commandment, and throughout the sacred Scriptures, when they are correctly understood.   When the Divine declaration was made: "Hear, O Israel, Jehovah our God is *one* Jehovah," it was not a truth then for the first time revealed; for it was well known by the Most Ancient or Adamic Church, and also by the Ancient or Noachian Church, that there is but one God; and, as all the inhabitants of the world have descended from the members of those ancient churches, some knowledge of this grand central truth, more or less obscured by the doctrines of men, is to be found in the earliest religious or sacred writings and traditions of all nations.

This one God is thus described in the Vedahs: "'Perfect truth; perfect happiness; without equal; immortal; absolute unity; whom neither speech can describe, nor mind comprehend; all-pervading; all-transcending;   * * *   understanding all.   Without cause, the first of all causes; all-ruling; all-powerful; the Creator, Preserver, Transformer of all things; such is the Great One, BRAHM.' This is in reality no other than a paraphrase of the 'I AM;' but, says Mr. Squier, 'The supreme God of Gods of the Hindus was less frequently expressed by the name BRAHM than by the mystical syllable O'M, which corresponds to the Hebrew JEHOVAH' (or AM). The same Divine Being, as to His infinite and eternal essence, is described on Egyptian monuments, and in the Hermetic books, as KNEPH, 'the first [or inmost quality of] God, immovable in the solitude of His Unity, the fountain of all things, the root of all primary, intelligible, existing forms, the God of Gods.' The same idea prevailed among all the Scandinavian nations; and in the ancient Icelandic mythology He is called 'the author of everything that existeth; the Eternal, the Ancient, the Living, the Awful Being, the Searcher into concealed things, the Being that never changeth.' By the ancient Mexicans He is called the 'Creator of Light,' the 'Giver of Life,' the God of battles or 'God of Hosts,' the 'Almighty,' etc. Also as the 'Supreme Lord of the Universe; the Disposer, and Ordainer of all things; the Confounder of His enemies, the Bestower of Wisdom, the Father of mankind,'" etc.

The Ancient Druids taught that "There is but One Supreme Being, the Creator and Governor of the Universe, of an eternal, mysterious, and immaterial nature, which pervades all space. In Him consists the plenitude of life, knowledge, power, and love, which are sources of all His actions and dispensations. These being in themselves most beneficial and harmonious, necessarily tend to annihilate the power of evil, and bring man to everlasting happiness."

With the North American Indian are found the remains of this doctrine, for he worships the Great Spirit, the Creator of all things on earth, and the "beautiful hunting-grounds" to which his fathers have gone.

We have already alluded to the fact, that all this knowl-

edge of God has come from revelations from God, made in
the early ages of the world, and is not of human invention
or discovery. "Revelation," says Rev. John Hyde, "must
reveal God and explain man. Nature does not teach the
existence of God. That is, the origin of the idea is not
attributable to the nature of the universe, or the nature of
man. Nature is the plane of effects, not of causes. The
consideration of effects can carry us no higher than effects,
the first effect and the final *natural* cause. The idea of
God's existence being known, nature can abundantly furnish man with illustrations of Divine operation, and
proofs of the Divine continuance. Atheists assert themselves careful students of nature, and in spite of the existence and predominance of the idea among men, they
testify that nature does not teach or communicate it. Yet
it is. The idea exists. If nature taught it, they say
nature taught a lie. If nature did not teach it, and could
not teach it, it must have been taught · of revelation.
Admit their testimony, and we must deny their conclusion. But all will admit that if God communicates a
revelation, he must reveal HIMSELF. Nature does not
teach the object or the destiny of man's existence. The
cradle and the grave are its limitations, the twin bounda-
ries that circumscribe our being. If a revelation be given,
it must transcend external and visible nature, and teach
us wisdom on *super*-natural subjects. These must be the
themes which it will treat, and subordinate to these
themes must every statement, every precept, every narrative be. If God has given a revelation of Himself, of
man's nature, and of man's destiny, this Revelation must ·
as evidently be the *Word* of God, as external nature is the
Work of God."

If now we return to the sacred Scriptures, we shall find
the unity of God most clearly and beautifully taught; and
also that He is our Saviour, and the Being whom we are
to love supremely; for the following command is given by
this one God: "Thou shalt have none other gods before

me;" and again in the sixth chapter and fifth verse of
Deuteronomy: "And thou shalt love the Lord thy God
with all thine heart, and with all thy soul, and with all
thy might." That this one God is our Saviour, is abundantly taught in almost innumerable passages in the Old
Testament, as in the following, in the forty-third chapter
of Isaiah: ".Thus saith the Lord that created thee, O
Jacob, and He that formed thee, O Israel, fear not; for I
have redeemed thee." "For I am the Lord thy God, the
Holy One of Israel, thy Saviour." "Before me there was
no God formed, neither shall there be after me. I, even I,
am the Lord; and beside me there is no Saviour.". In
the forty-ninth chapter of Isaiah we read, "That all flesh
may know that I Jehovah am thy Saviour, and thy Redeemer, the Holy One of Jacob." Also in the forty-fifth
chapter: "There is no God else beside me, a just God and
a Saviour, there is none beside me. Look unto me, and
be ye saved, all the ends of the earth: for I am God, and
there is none else." In the third chapter of Second Samuel, we read: "The Lord is my rock, and my fortress, and
my deliverer; the God of my rock; in Him will I trust;
He is my shield, and the horn of my salvation, my high
tower, and my refuge, my Saviour." In the nineteenth
Psalm will be found the following: "Let the words of my
mouth, and the meditation of my heart be acceptable in
thy sight, O Lord, my strength and my Redeemer;" and
in the one hundred and thirtieth Psalm we read: "Let
Israel hope in the Lord; for with the Lord there is mercy,
and with Him is plenteous redemption, and he shall
redeem Israel from all his iniquities;" and in the thir-
teenth chapter of Hosea: "Yet am I the Lord thy God
from the land of Egypt, and thou shalt know no God but
me, for there is no Saviour beside me."

We have quoted comparatively few of the numerous
passages which clearly teach us that there is but one God,
and that He is our Saviour, and that there is no other
Saviour. And in the eighth verse of the forty-second

chapter of Isaiah, He distinctly declares: "I am the Lord: that is my name: and my glory will I not give to another."

But we have predictions in the Old Testament of the coming of a Saviour, and all Christians acknowledge, that in the person of the Lord Jesus Christ those predictions were fulfilled. Let us inquire then, whether the Jehovah, or Lord and Saviour, of the Old Testament is the Saviour of the New Testament, or whether He has given His glory to another, contrary to His express declaration. In order to settle satisfactorily this point we shall need to examine the prophecies in regard to the coming of the Saviour into the world.

XXIII.

The Incarnation.

"BUT," say some, "it is contrary to the laws of Nature for a child to be born without a natural father," and thus, without further consideration, they decide the question. If it were certain that they understood all the laws of nature, their conclusion would be reasonable, and undoubtedly correct; for we do not for a moment suppose that the Lord violates His own laws. But, in the light of known and acknowledged facts, let us examine this question. Science shows conclusively that the time has been when no man or animal lived on this earth, and now it is peopled with men of various races, and there are also a great variety of animals. It follows that not only man, but a pair—a male and a female—(and perhaps several of them) were actually created without either a natural father or mother: now, if the above objection to the idea of the Incarnation holds good, what a tremendous violation of the laws of nature there was in the creation of the first pair—four times as great at least as the incarnation of the Lord by a natural mother. It matters not whether man was originally created in the human form, or was gradually developed from the lower forms of animal life, the creation of the first pair of animals, however low in the scale, without natural parents, was as much a violation of the laws of nature, as the creation of the human body in the present form. But, for ourselves, we can see no good reason why man was not created in the human form; for it is not in accordance with what we know of "the Laws of Nature" to suppose that either men or animals were created full grown; and man commences from a point or cell as small as many of the animals. But the origin of man, or how he was created, is a question foreign to our present inquiry; and as the Lord has not revealed to us the ultimate truths of Natural Science, we shall .eave this question to scientists to investigate and specu-.ate over to their hearts' content, and if they ever deter-:nine it to the satisfaction of our reason, we shall accept their conclusions without any hesitation, for we shall ever strive not to let preconceived ideas stand between us and the truth.

That a son should have been born of Jewish parents— and illegitimate at that, and thus inheriting·specially a tendency to the violation of the most sacred relation of life—who, at the age of about thirty years, should be able to proclaim such precepts of life as the Lord Jesus Christ did, and set such an example of meekness, for-bearance, and good-will, would certainly have been a far greater violation of the laws of nature, or of hereditary transmission of inclinations, than was the Incarnation of the Lord.

We think, then, we may safely and absolutely dismiss the objection, that the Incarnation was a violation of the laws of nature, as not worthy of further consideration; but in doing this we cheerfully admit that there certainly are some laws of nature which we do not fully understand, and others of which we know very little.

WHY THE LORD CAME TO THIS EARTH.

The second objection which we hear against the doctrine of the Incarnation, is: "When we behold the boundless extent of creation, the innumerable worlds which exist, many of which at least we have every reason to think are peopled by human beings, is it reasonable to suppose that the Lord selected and came down to this little insignificant world of ours to be Incarnated, to the neglect of all others?" This at first sight would seem to be a serious objection, but it is very satisfactorily answered in the revelations made by the Lord through Emanuel Swedenborg, as follows:

"There are many reasons why it pleased the Lord to be born and to assume the Human on our earth and not on another, concerning which I have been informed from heaven. The principal reason was for the sake of the Word, that this might be written in our earth, and being written might be published throughout the whole earth, and once published might be preserved to all posterity; and that thus it might be made manifest, even to all in the other life, that God was made Man. That the principal reason was for the sake of the Word, was because the Word is the very Divine truth, which teaches man that there is a God, that there is a heaven, that there is a hell, and that there is a life after death; and teaches, moreover, how he ought to live and believe that he may come into heaven and thus be happy to eternity. All these things without revelation—thus on this earth without the Word—would have been entirely unknown; and yet man is so created that as to his internal man he cannot die. The Word could be written on our earth, because from a very ancient time the art of writing has existed here, first on tablets of wood, then on parchments, afterwards on paper, and finally (writing came) to be published by types. This was provided of the Lord for the sake of the Word. * * * The Word once written could be preserved to all posterity, even for thousands and thousands of years; and it is known that it has been so preserved. It could thus be made known that God became Man; for this is the first and most essential thing for which the Word was given. For no one can believe in a God, and love a God, whom he cannot have a conception of under some form; wherefore they who acknowledge what is incomprehensible glide in thought into nature, and so believe in no God. For this reason it pleased the Lord to be born here, and to make this evident by the Word; in order not only that it might be made known on this globe, but also that thereby it might be made manifest to all in the universe who from any other earth whatsoever come into heaven; for in heaven there is a communication of all things. It should be known that the Word on our earth, given through heaven by the Lord, is the union of heaven and the world—for which end there is a correspondence of all things in the letter of the Word with Divine things in heaven; and that the Word in its highest and inmost sense treats of the Lord, of His kingdom in the heavens and on the earths, and of love and faith from Him and in Him, therefore of life from Him and in Him. Such things are presented to the angels in heaven, from whatsoever earth they are, when the Word of our earth is read and preached. * * * It should be known that the Lord acknowledges and receives all, from whatsoever earth they are, who acknowledge and worship God under the human form; since God under the human form is the Lord. And as the Lord appears to the inhabitants of the earths in an angelic form, which is the human form, therefore when spirits and angels from those earths hear from the spirits and angels of our earth that God is actually man, they receive the Word, acknowledge it, and rejoice that it is so. To the reasons which have been already adduced it may be added, that the inhabitants, the spirits, and the angels of our earth relate to the external and corporeal sense in the Greatest Man; and the external and corporeal sense is the ultimate, in which the interiors of life end, and in which they rest as in their (receptacle). So is truth Divine (in its ultimates) in the letter which is called the Word; and on this account too it was given on this earth and not on another. And because the Lord is the Word, and its first and last, that all things might exist according to order He was willing to be born on this earth, and to become the Word—according to these words in John: 'In the beginning was the Word, and the Word was with God, and God was the Word. The same was in the beginning with God: all things were made by Him, and without Him was not anything made that was made. . . . And the Word was made flesh and dwelt among us, and we beheld His glory, the glory as of the only begotten of the Father. . . . No man hath seen God at any time; the only begotten Son, who is in the bosom of the Father, He hath brought Him forth to view.' The Word here is Divine truth."— (*A. C.* 9250–9360.)

It was, then, not because the inhabitants of our earth were better than those of other earths, or more spiritual, but because they had descended lower into naturalism and sensualism; and by the Lord's coming to this earth, the First became Last, and He could thus redeem the inhabitants, and benefit the spirits and angels of all earths, by bringing or accommodating the Divine truth to their wants, and presenting Himself as a Divine Man for them to reverence, love and worship. We think the reader will join with us in hoping that the inhabitants of no other earth have sunken lower than those of our earth have, spiritually; or into selfishness, love of rule, and perverted sensualism. It is difficult to see how they could sink much lower without being annihilated by their evils.

The third objection which is often made to the doctrine of the Incarnation, and one which is quite apt to trouble the novitiate student, is: "What became of the universe when the Lord was dwelling on earth—who took care of that?" -

If we bear in mind that man is but a recipient of life, that he has no life of himself, but constantly receives it from the Lord, and that the beginning of man's life is but the beginning of a receptacle for life to flow into, and that even the physical body can only exist by constantly receiving physical substances into it, it will help us the better to understand this subject. The conception without a natural father in the case of the virgin, was simply the formation of a receptacle for receiving the Divine life, as well as human life; whereas, in the case of ordinary men, they having a natural father as well as mother, receive only created life. While evil is not transmitted, and no child is to blame or responsible for the deeds of his parents, still an inclination to the evils which not only his parents but also his ancestors have voluntarily made their own, by indulging in them, is transmitted from both father and mother. The child born, then, in the manger, inherited from the mother the inclinations to evil of the Jewish race, one of the most selfish and sensual of the races of men on earth, and also the frailties and peculiarities of the race of men before them, or their ancestors. It was, then, by assuming these inclinations, that the Lord came down to the level of fallen humanity, and became subject to temptations, like other men. The Divine could never be tempted, but the human could be; and it was from the maternal side that He was subject to temptations, but from the Divine within, that He was able to overcome in temptations, and therefore was without sin. Of course, the whole of the Divine love and wisdom were not manifested in the child, nor was it possible for it to be, until the inclinations inherited from the mother were overcome; and while this manifestation of the Lord on earth was taking place, he was none the less present in heaven, and controlling the universe than previously; in fact, we should remember that heaven is not far distant, only from the evil. The Lord says it is actually within the good man; and of little children He says, "their

angels do always behold the face of our Father in heaven."
Little children are innocent, and are consequently near to,
and under the protection of the Lord and His angels; and
the Divine Father manifesting Himself in the Son born of
Mary, was in the midst of heaven, the very life thereof.
The child born, possessed a dual nature, inheriting inclinations and capacities from both father and mother like
all other children, and it was only after many years of
conflict with the inherited tendencies, which were derived
from the mother, and victories achieved, that the Father
was so far manifested in the Son, that our Saviour was
able to say: "I and my Father are one; whoso hath seen
me, hath seen the Father;" and it was only after the last
temptation of the cross that he was able to exclaim, "It is
finished," and that IIe ascended to His Father and our
Father, His God and our God, having made God manifest
to man.

The idea that our heavenly Father, who has created the
world and the boundless universe for the sake of creating
man, and all for his use, should so love us as to bow the
heavens and come down to us in our low estate, for the
sake of redeeming and saving mankind from falsehood and
evil, is one of the most sublime, beautiful, and reasonable
ideas of all the ages; and it is beautiful because it is true:
and this glorious truth, so human, so like what God has
implanted in the heart of His earthly children to strive to
do for their children, has made the anniversary of the
birth of our Saviour a season of joy and gladness, and it
will remain so forever.

The first prophetical intimation or announcement of
the coming of the Lord was made in the Garden of Eden,
when it was declared that the seed of the woman should
bruise the serpent's head. The woman signified man's
proprium or selfhood; the serpent, man's sensual nature;
the seed of the serpent, infidelity which has resulted
from evil of every kind. "The serpent's head," says
Swedenborg, "is self-love; the seed of the woman is the

Lord ; the enmity which is put, is between the love of
man's proprium and the Lord, thus between man's own
prudence and the Divine Providence of the Lord." This
Divine allegory was understood by the descendants of the
Most Ancient or Adamic Church, and also of the Noachian
or Ancient Church, from which have sprung all the
inhabitants of the world. For in those early days, as we
have already shown, they understood the science of correspondences. It will be readily seen that such an important
idea as the Incarnation of the Lord, existing among all
men at any one period, could hardly be lost; but would
be transmitted either by tradition, or by writing, among
all nations ; or, to say the least, low and degraded must
be that nation or race where some traces of this cheerful
and hopeful belief is not to be found.

"And such revelations," says Rev. G. Field in his
work entitled 'The Two Great Books of Nature and
Revelation,' "have never been wanting, and have always
been adapted to the state of human reception. Thus we
find that in the earlier days of the world, in the time of
the gold and silver ages (when natural images were used
to represent spiritual ideas), the coming of the Lord had
been variously foretold and symbolized, and was by tradition preserved among all nations, and couched under
various personifications, on the earth, and in the heavens;
thus we find the same or similar predictions among the
heathen, as are in the Sacred Books, and these originally
obtained from earlier Divine revelations, all relating to
the coming of Jehovah.

HERCULES.	ESCULAPIUS.	JESUS CHRIST.
'The lay records the la-bors and the praise, And all the immortal acts of Hercules. First, how the mighty babe when swathed in bands, The serpents strangled with his infant hands;	'Once as the sacred in-fant she surveyed, The God was kindled in the raving maid; And thus she uttered her prophetic tale :	'Ye nymphs of Solyma begin the song ! O thou, my voice in-spire, That touched Isaiah's hallowed lips with fire ; Rapt into future times, the bard began ;

Then as in years and matchless force he grew,
The Œchalian walls, and Trojan, overthrew.
Besides a thousand hazards they relate,
Procured by Juno's and Euristheus' hate.
Thy hands, unconquer'd hero, could subdue .
The cloud-born Centaurs and the monster crew;
Nor thy resistless arm the Bull withstood;
Nor he, the roaring terror of the wood.
The triple porter of the Stygian seat,
With lolling tongue lay fawning at thy feet,
And, seized with fear, forgot the mangled meat.
The infernal waters trembled at thy sight;
Thee, God, no face of danger could affright,
Nor huge Typheus, nor the unnumbered snake,
Increased with hissing heads in Lerna's lake.'

Virgil's Æneid, Bk. 8.

Hail, great physician* of the world, all hail!
Hail, mighty infant, who in years to come
Shall heal the nations, and defraud the tomb!
Swift be thy growth, thy triumphs unconfined;
Make kingdoms thicker, and increase mankind.
Thy daring art shall animate the dead,
And draw the thunder on thy guilty head;
Then shalt thou die, but from thy dark abode
Shalt rise victorious, and be twice a God.'

Ovid's Metamorp. Bk. 2.

* Esculapius, as well as Hercules, was but a personification, prefiguring the advent of Jehovah (when the full time should be come), either as the 'mighty Hero,' or the great Therapeuta, or the healer of the soul, and thus as the 'great physician of the world,' or God incarnate.

A virgin shall conceive, a virgin bear a son.
Swift fly the years, and rise the expected morn,
O spring to light! auspicious babe, be born.
He from thick films shall purge the visual ray,
And on the sightless eyeball pour the day;
'Tis he the obstructed paths of sound shall clear,
And bid new music charm the unfolding ear.
The dumb shall sing, the lame his crutch forego,
And leap exulting like the bounding roe.'

Pope.

"The avatars, incarnations, and transmigrations of the ancients, do not mean, as now generally understood, actual physical descents, or embodiments, but typical ones, having reference to this great final act, in the coming of the Great Redeemer into the world, when the state of humanity should call for its accomplishment. Long before that grand prophecy was fulfilled in outward nature, festivals were held throughout the eastern world, by the Pagans, in honor of the Virgin *Paritura.* And the Apocalyptic Divine, even after this event had been literally fulfilled, speaks of it as future, or rather as *independent of all time;* because it is a principle which always *spiritually* takes place, when the mind of man is in a proper, receptive state. Thus on the theatre of the spiritual world, a woman representatively brings forth a man child, and they are pursued by the Dragon, etc. The Revelator describes the same mental phenomena in allegorical or symbolical language, as is described in the Gospels, in the sense of the letter, by the Virgin bringing forth a Son, and being pursued by Herod, fleeing into Egypt, etc., only that in the Gospel this state was actually ultimated in the plane of the natural world, that thus there might also be a base upon which all things above might repose or rest."

" *Brahma* is prophetically described, in a period of remote antiquity, long before the days of Abraham, as becoming incarnate, and bringing down the Divine Law to man, for his restoration and salvation. *Prometheus* in like manner is a personification of a similar Theophany, or a revelation of the love of God through the spiritual perceptions of a chosen instrument. It was thus also, says Milman, that the Divine Truth was successively brought down to the apprehensions of man, as the *Memra*, or *Divine Word;* and the 'appellation is found in the Indian, the Persian, the Platonic, and the Alexandrian systems.' Which term is also applied to the Messiah by the Targumists, or earliest Jewish commentators on the Scriptures. — *History of Christianity.*

"And not only is that prophetic descent of the great Deliverer, and Saviour, thus written upon the tablets of all nations, in His passage through the spiritual heavens, by the assumption of an angel's body, by Shekinahs, Theophanies, and Avatars, but even the then far-off event of His own actual advent—down to the earthly senses, and tabernacling in the flesh—was also predicted and typified in the most definite manner. In some of the ancient Chinese books which have been brought into Europe, (The Books *Yking, Likiyki,* etc.) it is foretold that a time would come 'when everything is to be restored to its first splendor, by the coming of a Hero called *Kiunts⁴,* which signifies *Shepherd* and *Prince,* to whom they give likewise the names of *The Most Holy,* the *Universal Teacher,* and the *Supreme Truth.* He answers exactly to the *Mythras* of the Persians, the *Orus* of the Egyptians, the *Mercury* of the Greeks, and the *Brahma* of the Indians. The Chinese Books speak likewise of the sufferings and conflicts of Kiuntsé just as the Syrians do of the death of *Adonis,* who was to rise again to make men happy; and as the Greeks do of the labors and painful exploits of the son of Jupiter who was to come down upon earth. It looks as if the source of all these allegories was only an ancient tradition common to all nations."— *Theology and Mythology of the Ancients.*

" The Persian sphere, cited by Aben Ezra, 'represents a beautiful Virgin, with flowing hair, sitting in a chair, with two ears of corn in her hand, and suckling an infant, called Jesus by some nations, and Christ in Greek.' The Arabian astronomer, Alboazar (or Abulmazar), has this passage quoted by Kirker Selden, and R. Bacon, and Dupuis: 'In the first decan of the sign of the Virgin, following the most ancient tradition of the Persians, the Chaldeans, the Egyptians, Hermes, and Esculapius, a young woman, called in the Persic language Seclenidos de Darzama; in the Arabic, Adrenedefa, that is to say, *a chaste, pure and immaculate Virgin, suckling an infant,* which some nations call *Jesus,* but which we in Greek call *Christ.*'

" And 'To this day Egypt has consecrated the pregnancy of a Virgin, and the nativity of her son, whom they annually present in a cradle to the adoration of the people, and when King Ptolemy, 350 years before the Christian era, demanded of the priests the signification of this religious ceremony, they told him that it was a mystery that had been taught to their forefathers by a respectable prophet.'

" Thus in the ancient Books of China they have a record of the coming or 'incarnation of the great Hero, his birth by a Virgin, his low estate, his teaching for three years, his suffering for the sins of the whole world, resurrection, ascent into heaven, and coming to judgment, the eternal happiness of the good, and the eternal misery of the wicked."—*N. J. Magazine*, 1848.

" The Jesuits in China were appalled at finding in the Mythology of that country, the counterpart of the 'Virgo Deipara.'" For further information on this subject, see Milman's "History of Christianity," also Volney, Taylor, Field, and others.

We turn now to the predictions of the Incarnation of the Lord contained in the sacred Scriptures.

In the seventh chapter of Isaiah we read: "Therefore the Lord Himself shall give you a sign: Behold, a virgin shall conceive, and bear a son, and shall call his name Immanuel, or God with us;" and in the ninth chapter we read: "Unto us a child is born, unto us a son is given; and the government shall be upon his shoulders; and his name shall be called Wonderful, Counsellor, the Mighty God, the Everlasting Father, the Prince of Peace." And in the twenty-fifth chapter: "It shall be said in that day, Lo, this is our God, we have waited for Him, and He will save us'; this is the Lord, we have waited for him, we will be glad and rejoice in his salvation." In the fortieth chapter of Isaiah we read: "The voice of him that crieth in the wilderness, Prepare ye the way of the Lord, make straight in the desert a highway for our God." "And the glory of the Lord shall be revealed, and all flesh shall see it together, for the mouth of the Lord hath spoken it." " Behold, the Lord God will come with a strong hand, and his arm shall rule for him: behold, his reward is with him, and his work before him." "He shall feed his flock like a shepherd."

In the twenty-third chapter of Jeremiah, is the following: "Behold, the days come, saith the Lord, that I will raise unto David a righteous branch, and a king shall reign and prosper, and shall execute judgment and justice in the earth. * * * And this is the name whereby he shall be called, the Lord our Righteousness." In Zechariah, second chapter, we read: "Sing and rejoice, O daughter of Zion: for, lo, I come, and I will dwell in the midst of thee, saith the Lord. And many nations shall be joined to the Lord in that day, and shall be my people: and I will dwell in the midst of thee, and thou shalt know that the Lord of hosts hath sent me unto thee." In the fifth chapter of Micah, we read, "But thou, Bethlehem Ephratah, though thou be little among the thousands of Judah, yet out of thee shall come forth unto me that is to be Ruler of Israel; whose goings forth have been from of old, from everlasting, He shall stand and feed in the strength of the Lord, in the majesty of the name of the Lord his God." And in the third and fourth chapters of Malachi, we read: "Behold, I will send my messenger, and he shall prepare the way before me; and the Lord whom ye seek, shall suddenly come into his temple, even the messenger of the covenant, whom ye delight in; behold, he shall come, saith the Lord of hosts. But who may abide the day of his coming? or who shall stand when he appeareth? for he is like a refiner's fire." "Behold, I will send you Elijah the prophet, before the coming of the great and dreadful day of the Lord."

The Prophet Daniel declares that he "Saw in the night visions, and, behold, one like the Son of man came with the clouds of heaven, and came to the ancient of days, and they brought him near before him. And there was given him dominion, and glory, and a kingdom, that all people, nations, and languages, should serve him; his dominion is an everlasting dominion, and shall not pass away, and his kingdom that which shall not be destroyed. * * * And all dominions shall serve and obey him." Seventh chapter.

We have cited but a few of the passages to be found in the Prophets which teach more or less clearly that the Lord, or Jehovah Himself, was to assume humanity, or manifest Himself in the flesh for the salvation of our race. Let every one who reverences the sacred Scriptures, as the

7

Word of God, search the Old Testament from beginning
to end, and see if they do not testify to this great truth—
that the Jehovah and Saviour of the Old Testament and
the God manifest and Saviour of the New Testament are
the same.   We have shown how wonderfully the predictions of the Prophets in the Holy Word, are sustained by
the traditions and "sacred writings" which are to be
found among Gentile nations, and which have come down
from the earliest churches established by the Lord on
earth—even from the Adamic and Noachian churches.

We know full well that many sincere Christians in
every church, in whom the Word of the Lord has not
been made of none effect by the traditions and doctrines
of men, and who have not confirmed themselves in false
doctrines, know of the Lord because they strive to keep
His commandments and sayings, and think of and worship
no other God than the Lord Jesus Christ.   But to those
who have either framed for themselves, or embraced false
doctrines, which permit them to hope for heaven, short of
a constant living effort to keep the Divine commandments,
or those who have pinned their faith upon the sleeves of
blind leaders, instead of searching the Scriptures for the
truth, and have confirmed themselves in errors, the First
or Second coming of the Lord is a day of darkness and not
of light.   Truly to such does the Prophet Amos predict
by inquiring: "Shall not the day of the Lord be darkness
and not light? even thick darkness and no brightness."
Fifth chapter.   "Wo unto you that desire the day of the
Lord! to what end is it for you?   The day of the Lord
is darkness and not light," is the prophetical language
addressed by the Lord through the prophet Amos to the
makers of false doctrines, and worshippers of false gods of
all ages; to the man who is in the pride of his own intelligence, bigoted, intolerant, lover of ruling in spiritual
things—the blind leader.   It is addressed to the worshippers of mammon and of self in every form; to the lovers of
rule, or of approbation, for the sake of self; the worship-

pers of nature, and of the spirits of the dead. For all such in this world there is little hope of their seeing the dawning light of this new day, unless in the kind providence of the Lord, their selfish and worldly expectations and hopes are restrained by afflictions, losses, or disappointments, which shall lead them from their selfish schemes, to seek the only true and living God as He is revealed in His Divine Word.

But sincere seekers after truth, who reverence the Word of the Lord, and are striving to lead a good life according to its precepts, of all religious denominations, and those of no sect, who are without prejudice, will be able to see this grand central doctrine, in the light of the descending New Jerusalem, in all its beauty and splendor. That God is one, and that the Lord Jesus Christ is that one God, is the corner-stone of the New Jerusalem, and upon this rock the church of the future is being founded and is to be built. This doctrine, as we shall see when we come to examine the New Testament, is clearly taught in the *letter* of the Scriptures, but it is most beautifully illuminated and illustrated by the science of correspondences, revealed by the Lord through Emanuel Swedenborg for the benefit of the men of this new age. In the spiritual sense all the sacred Scriptures treat of the Lord, the assumption of the humanity on earth, the glorification of that humanity, and of the regeneration of man. The long-predicted day when there shall be but one God and His name one in all the earth, is at hand. The Christian church is yet to be reunited and built up in the bonds of charity on this rock ; and with a correct knowledge of the Lord, a host of conflicting and false doctrines will disappear from view, as do the birds of night at the rising of the natural sun.

Rev. Abiel Silver, in his excellent work on the "Symbolic Character of the Sacred Scriptures," says truly : "It is therefore from false, and not from true views of the Word, that men are divided. Truths are eternal verities.

They are ever and unchangeably the same; and all truths are in harmony, and sustain each other. About them, when seen, men cannot differ. It is about falsities, altogether, that the Christian world is contending. Falsities are all dark, unstable, deceptive, and mysterious; fit grounds for contention and strife, and for the proud display of self-wisdom; and constant changes of opinion are and must be taking place among those who build upon such grounds; while those who build on the 'Rock of ages,' the spiritual truth of the Word, rationally seen in the light of analogy, never can change their views, nor disagree in their doctrines, unless by sin they lose their language. When this light is seen in the study of the Holy Word, it will as inevitably lead all sincere students of divinity to the same conclusions in every jot and tittle of the Word, so far as it is seen, as the light leads to the sun from which it flows. The reason is, the investigation is carried on by a scientific law, and that law is divine. The reason, therefore, why men who read the Word in the science of correspondences, differ not in its doctrines, is the very reason why men differ not in mathematics; it is because, in both instances, the truths are indisputable. If, as we believe, there are no two persons who, without the light of this science, agree as to the doctrines of the Word, and no two, who have it, that disagree, the question, as to its truth, becomes a startling one.

"Now we wish it distinctly understood, that this language or science was once universal; that it has been lost, and is now revealed; that the revelation has been made by the Lord himself in fulfilment of prophecy, and not by any man; that 'The Lion of the tribe of Judah ... hath prevailed to open the book, and to loose the seven seals thereof,' and has evolved this science from nature and the Holy Word, and not from the mind of any man; and has caused its general elements and rules to be recorded in the works entitled the 'Arcana Cœlestia,' the 'Apocalypse Revealed,' and the 'Apocalypse Explained,' written by

Emanuel Swedenborg; and that when we read these works, and learn this science, and behold its light, we obtain both the science and the light from the Holy Word and from nature, and not from those works except as the light shines in them from the Word.

"As we read .those wonderful books with an humble and teachable disposition the Holy Word comes up constantly before us with newly shining pages, which grow brighter and brighter as we progress, until the heavenly harmony and beauty of the Word become so absorbing to the mind that we lose all sight of the writings we are reading, and the Word itself becomes its own interpreter—its own revealer of the divine law in which it is written. One passage throws its light upon another, and receives back the other's lustre in blending beauty, and their united blaze is responded to by a third, and all these are embraced by a fourth, and so on, till every sacred text we see becomes an evidence of the truth of all the rest, and the whole blessed Word, so far as we behold it, stands before us in symmetrical glory and beauty, a perfect whole, in an infinitude of parts, all in harmony. And though we are lost in the depth and immensity of its wisdom, yet, we are lost in light and not in darkness. And every advance we make in the regenerate life enables us to drink still deeper at this inexhaustible fountain of the water of life."

We will turn now to the testimony concerning the Lord to be found in the New Testament.

In the first chapter of Matthew we are told that the angel of the Lord appeared unto the husband of Mary in a dream, saying, "Joseph, thou son of David, fear not to take unto thee Mary thy wife: for that which is conceived in her is of the Holy Ghost. And she shall bring forth a son, and thou shalt call his name Jesus; for he shall save his people from their sins. Now all this was done that it might be fulfilled which was spoken of the Lord by the prophet, saying, Behold a virgin shall be with child, and shall bring forth a son, and they shall call his name Immanuel; which being interpreted is, God with us."

In the first chapter of John we read, " In the beginning was the Word, and the Word was with God, and the Word was God. The same was in the beginning with God. All things were made by Him; and without Him was not anything made that was made. In Him was life; and the life was the light of men. And the light shineth in darkness, and the darkness comprehendeth it not."

In the second chapter of Luke we read that " there were in the same country shepherds abiding in the field, keeping watch over their flocks by night. And lo, the angel of the Lord came upon them, and the glory of the Lord shone round about them; and they were sore afraid. And the angel said unto them, Fear not: for behold, I bring you good tidings of great joy, which shall be for all people. For unto you is born this day in the city of David a Saviour, which is Christ the Lord."

The first chapter of Mark commences thus: " The beginning of the gospel of Jesus Christ the Son of God; as it is written in the prophets, behold I send my messenger before thy face, which shall prepare thy way before thee. The voice of one crying in the wilderness, Prepare ye the way of the Lord, make his paths straight."

Thus we see that both the Angel of the Lord and the Evangelists declare, that in the person of the Lord Jesus Christ was fulfilled the prophetical annunciation of the prophets of the Old Testament in regard to the Messiah, and that they all declare that He was God with us.

Let us turn now to the testimony of the Lord Himself, as recorded in the gospels, as to His true character.

In the fourteenth chapter of John he says, " Let not your heart be troubled; ye believe in God, believe also in me. * * * Thomas said unto him, Lord, we know not whither thou goest; and how can we know the way? Jesus said unto him, I am the way, the truth, and the life: no man cometh unto the Father, but by me. If ye had known me, ye should have known my Father also: and from henceforth ye know Him and have seen Him. Philip said unto him, Lord, show us the Father, and it sufficeth us. Jesus said unto him, Have I been so long time with you, and yet hast thou not known me, Philip? He that hath seen me, hath seen the Father, and how sayest thou then, show us the Father? Believest thou not that I am in the Father and the Father in me? The words that I speak unto you, I speak not of myself; but the Father that dwelleth in me, He doeth the works. Believe me, that I am in the Father, and the Father in me."

In the twelfth chapter of John we read, "Jesus cried and said, He that believeth on me, believeth not on me, but on him that sent me. And he that seeth me, seeth him that sent me." In the first chapter we are told, "No man hath seen God at any time; the only begotten son, which is in the bosom of the Father, he hath declared him." And in the tenth chapter of John we read, "My Father, which gave them me, is greater than all; and no man is able to pluck them out of my Father's hand. I and my Father are one."

Such then is the testimony of the Lord Jesus Christ Himself. Could language be plainer? Is it possible that any being should proclaim such beautiful, useful, and heavenly doctrines—the very doctrines of spiritual life—and set such an example to men as did the Lord Jesus Christ, and yet represent Himself as being one with the Father, and that he that had seen Him had seen the Father, when it was not true?

We will now glance at the testimony of the Apostles in the Epistles.

In the second chapter of Colossians, St. Paul declares that in Christ "dwelleth all the fulness of the Godhead bodily." In the first chapter we are told that Jesus Christ "is the image of the invisible God, the first-born of every creature; for by Him were all things created that are in heaven, and that are in earth, visible and invisible, whether they be thrones, or dominions, or principalities, or powers. All things were created by Him and for Him; and He is before all things, and by Him all things consist."

James calls him the Lord of Glory; and Jude closes his Epistle with these words: "To the only wise God our Saviour be glory and majesty, dominion and power, both now and forever. Amen."

Let us now turn to the book of Revelation, the last book of the Divine Word, and see if the testimony therein contained is in harmony with the Old Testament, the Gospels, and the Epistles, in regard to the Lord.

In the first chapter of Revelation, John the revelator declares that he was in the Spirit on the Lord's day, and heard behind him a great voice as of a trumpet saying, I am Alpha and Omega, the first and the last. And, turning to see from whom the voice came, he "saw one like unto the Son of Man," and when John had fallen at his feet as dead, this same person lays his right hand upon him, and says: "Fear not, I am the first and the last. I am he that liveth, and was dead, and behold, I am alive for evermore." Thus leaving no doubt that the Lord Jesus Christ, or the Son of Man, was the being whose voice the revelator heard behind him. Again, in the last chapter of Revelation, where the Second Coming of the Lord Jesus is spoken of, He says: "And behold, I come quickly; and my reward is with me to give every man according as his work shall be; I am Alpha and Omega, the beginning and the end, the first and the last."

"In the Old Testament, Jehovah," says Rev. B. F. Barrett, (from whose excellent work on "The New Dispensation," and other works, we intend taking several extracts for this section and the one on the Trinity,) "repeatedly declares Himself to be the First and the Last; and since there evidently cannot be two firsts and lasts, in the sense in which these words are here used, therefore the Lord Jesus Christ must be the same, as to person, as Jehovah. But

there are other passages in the book of Revelation, which
render the identity of Jesus and Jehovah, as to person,
evident beyond doubt;" for in the seventeenth chapter we
read: "'These shall make war with the Lamb, and the
Lamb shall overcome them; for he is Lord of lords, and
King of kings." That the Lamb denotes the Lord Jesus
Christ is manifest from many passages; as in the following in the fifth chapter, where we are told that John
heard the voice of ten thousand times ten thousand,
and thousands of thousands of angels round about the
throne: "Saying with a loud voice, Worthy is the Lamb
that was slain to receive power, and honor, and glory, and
blessing." In the same chapter we are told that "the four
and twenty elders fell down before the Lamb," and they
sung a new song, saying, "Thou art worthy to take the
book, and to open the seals thereof; for thou wast slain
and hast redeemed us, etc."

We have now taken a hasty glance at the abundant
testimony which the Divine Word from beginning to end
bears to the truth of this doctrine—that the Lord Jesus
Christ is the Supreme and only God of heaven and earth.
We find that the same titles are applied to Him as to
Jehovah God, the same attributes of eternity and self-
existence predicated of Him by myriads of angels, that is
proper to be given to the Lord alone.

XXIV.

The Divine Trinity.

THAT the Lord is a Triune being is not a new doctrine, nor is a knowledge of the Trinity which existed
previous to the Incarnation, confined to the sacred Scriptures, but it is also to be found among the traditions and
"sacred writings" of many Gentile nations, having been
transmitted to them from the Noachian or Ancient
Church.

Says the Rev. G. Field, in his work on "The Two Great Books": "Not only was there given to man from the most ancient time the truths of this universal religion, in relation to One God, One Glorious and Infinite Divine Man, as the Creator, Preserver, Saviour, and Redeemer; as the 'Eternally Ancient One,' the essential substance of all being in whom, according to the testimony of the Druids and the unperverted teaching of all the oldest traditions of the eastern nations (and from remnants found in the western world), there was a triad of essential perfections, 'infinite Love, infinite wisdom, and infinite power;' but He is also constantly presented as our Saviour, Redeemer, and Deliverer. Thus, says Milman, the infinite and eternal Father was the *Bythos* (or the Divine LOVE), together with 'His own first conception,' or its existing *form*, 'His *Ennoia*' (or the Divine WISDOM). This is the divine *substance and form* of the *first degree*, the JEHOVAH ELOHIM of the Old Testament, which in its 'development, or self-manifestation, was *mind* (*Nous*), whose appropriate consort was *Aletheia*, or TRUTH;' or the JESUS CHRIST of the New Testament, from whom proceeded the third degree, 'the LOGOS and ZOE,' the WORD OF TRUTH, and the HOLY SPIRIT; or God, as He is in Himself, above the heavens, as He became (or was to become) manifest in the flesh on earth, and as His Holy Spirit, or proceeding life which was to be stamped upon the 'Anthropos and Ecclesia,' or upon man and the church."

The Druid Triads declare that:

"*Three* things evince what God has done, and will do: Infinite Power, Infinite Wisdom, and Infinite Love; for there is nothing that these attributes want, of power, of knowledge, or of will to perform."

"The *three* regulations of God towards giving existence to everything: to annihilate the power of evil, to assist all that is good, and to make discrimination manifest that it might be known what should and what should not be."

" *Three* things will infallibly be done: all that is possible for the *power*, for the *wisdom*, and for the *love* of God to perform."

" *Three* things it is impossible that God should not perform: what is most beneficial, what all most need, and what is the most beautiful of all things."

" *Three* things proceed from the primeval Unities: all of life, all that is good, and all power."

" God consists necessarily of three things: the greatest of life, the greatest of knowledge, and the greatest of power, and of what is the greatest there can be no more than one of anything."

" Is not the Christian doctrine of the Trinity in the Godhead foreshadowed, in the foregoing, in a light which is consistent with rationality? It would appear to be."— *Rev. C. A. Dunham's Letters from Wales.*

The New Testament treats of the Father, Son, and Holy Ghost; and doubtless some of our readers will inquire: " If these names do not signify three persons, what do they mean ? "

In both Matthew and Luke we are distinctly taught, that our Lord Jesus Christ had no human father. In the Gospel of Luke we read that the Angel Gabriel was sent unto a virgin named Mary: " and said unto her, the Holy Ghost shall come upon thee, and the power of the Highest shall overshadow thee; therefore also that holy thing which shall be born of thee shall be called the Son of God."

The skeptic, and the denier of Divine revelation, make light of the idea that our Saviour had no human father, and declare such a birth a violation of the laws of nature and therefore impossible. We have already fully considered this objection; but as it is often heard, at the risk of repeating in substance a few lines, we will inquire: If it could have been more difficult, or more of a violation of the laws of nature for our Heavenly Father to create a human form by the aid of a natural mother, than it was

for Him to create the first man and woman who existed on
earth without either natural father or mother? Geology
teaches that man has not always existed upon the earth;
and his creation, whether he was created a man, as most
Christians believe, or from development from the lower
orders of the animal kingdom, as some believe, was unmis-
takably a special effort of creative energy. And it would
seem almost self-evident, that few things are more unreasonable, and contrary to acknowledged, even manifest
facts, than such objections against the Divinity of our
Saviour. With him whose reverence for the Divine
Word has not been impaired, and who delights in the
Law of the Lord, such objections do not weigh, but he
decides this question by its merits.

The power of the Highest shall overshadow thee, was
the prophetic annunciation of the angel. There can be
but one Highest, and that is Jehovah. Jehovah, then, is
the Father of the Humanity born of the Virgin Mary,
according to the testimony of the angel Gabriel. The
Son, then, was that humanity born in time.

The words which are sometimes translated " Holy
Ghost," properly signify a holy breathing, or exhalation,
and is a going forth of the Divine through the humanity.
Therefore we read that our Lord, after His resurrection,
breathed on His disciples, and said unto them, " Receive
ye the Holy Ghost" (John xx. 22).

We are taught by the herald of the New Dispensation,
Emanuel Swedenborg, that in our Lord Jesus Christ there
is a Divine Trinity, consisting of the all-begetting Divinity
which is called the Father, the Humanity which is called
the Son, and the proceeding Divine, which is called the
Holy Spirit. (*A. R.* 962.)

Thus the stone which sectarian builders have too frequently rejected, has indeed become the head of the
corner; even the corner-stone of the New Jerusalem,
which is now descending from God out of heaven. And
the man of this new age, in paying supreme homage to the

Lord Jesus Christ, worships all the adorable Trinity, for he worships the Father in the Son; and the Holy Spirit is the Divine proceeding sphere of the Son from the Father operating upon man.

That we may understand more clearly the Divine Trinity, let us examine the trinity in man; for we read that man was created in the image of God. If this be true, and in God exists a trinity, in man must exist a finite image of that trinity. In man exists a will, or a receptacle for love or affections; an understanding, or a receptacle for wisdom or truth; and through the latter the affections flow forth into thoughts, words, and acts; clothed as it were in the understanding—a manifestation of our affections to others, and by which they are affected for good or evil. So in the Lord, the giver of all that man receives, we have the Divine Love or the Father, the Divine Wisdom or the truth as the Son, and the goings forth of the Divine Love or affections through the Divine wisdom or truth, clothed by the latter as Divine thoughts and words, and Providential rulings descending as the Holy Ghost to influence and bless men.

How beautiful and sublimely true then are the first few verses of St. John's Gospel. "In the beginning was the Word, (or Divine Truth) and the Word was with God, and the Word was God. The same was in the beginning with God. All things were made by him, and without him was not anything made that was made. In him was life, and the life was the light of men." It is manifest that the Divine Truth is light to man's spirit.

But let us examine this great doctrine of the Trinity in a still lower, or more external plane; for we read that "The Word was made flesh, and dwelt among us (and we beheld His glory, the glory as of the only begotten of the Father) full of grace and truth." That we may the more readily comprehend the subject, let us turn again to the trinity in man. Man has a soul and body, and through his body goes forth his spirit into words and acts. Jeho-

vah or the Father, as we have seen, was the indwelling
soul of our Lord Jesus Christ, for the latter had no human
father; the body or Son was from Mary, and through this
body the Divine flowed down in words of wisdom and acts
of goodness and mercy to man. Truth is the form of love,
and it alone can manifest a good affection. Therefore the
Lord was manifested to men by the truth, or the Father
in the Son, or "God in Christ reconciling the world unto
Himself."

How mystery disappears, or vanishes, from the Divine
Trinity when, without preconceived opinions or prejudice,
it is viewed in the light of the Holy Word in its literal
sense, we hope to be able to show to the satisfaction of
many; but if the reader would be able to see this doctrine
in all of its fullness and beauty, he must read the writings
of Swedenborg, and study the spiritual sense as unfolded
by the science of correspondences; for it is the spirit that
giveth life to the letter, and God in His great mercy to us
has at this day revealed to us the true meaning of the
Holy Word, and the law in accordance with which it was
written, so that he who runneth may read.

Man not only inherits a material body from the mother,
but he also inherits an inclination to pervert his passions,
appetites, and desires; for we see in the hereditary inclinations and capacity of the child, both as to the affections
and intellect, the mother as well as the father represented.
So our Saviour not only possessed a Divine nature from
the Father, but He also inherited, as has already been intimated, from the mother, Mary, human affections, and even
inclinations to those evils in which the Jewish race were
sunken; therefore we read that He was subject to like
passions with other men. Had He not inherited an inclination to evils from the mother, He could not have
been tempted, for it is evident the Divine could not be
tempted to do evil; nor can there be any temptations
where neither active nor passive inclinations to evil exist.
No one is to blame for his hereditary inclinations—

original sin is a myth—therefore the Lord was without sin, for He overcame His hereditary inclinations to evil.

Man receives from the Lord conscience, and the capacity to elevate his thoughts into, or so as to see, the truths of the Divine Word, which teach him the life of regeneration; and when man wills to lead such a life, the Lord enables him to overcome both his hereditary and acquired inclinations; not in a day, for it is the work of a lifetime. The Lord's glorification was typical of man's regeneration; and as the former was only perfected when the humanity had passed through the various temptations of which we read in the Gospels, even to the last great temptation on the cross, when in agony the humanity cried to the Divine within: "My God, my God, why hast thou forsaken me?" "It is finished," He cried, and gave up the ghost. As the final hour approached before His crucifixion, in the garden, we read that "He fell on his face, and prayed, saying. O my Father, if it be possible, let this cup pass from me;" but He is given the strength to respond: "Nevertheless, not as I will, but as thou wilt;" and in His next prayer He prayed, saying, "O my Father, if this cup may not pass away from me, except I drink it, thy will be done."

So with man; the Lord tempers the winds to the shorn lamb, and it is only as the Christian gains strength to overcome, that he is permitted to encounter the most fearful temptations, and the last hours of a long life may arrive before he is able to bear the last great temptation; if in fact he is ever able to withstand it in this world. Almost constantly, from the very beginning of regeneration, is there a warfare between the new will, which the Lord has given the Christian, and the unlawful selfish desires and sensual appetites of the natural man.

"There are in man," says Swedenborg, "two minds, the one superior or interior, which is called the spiritual mind, and the other inferior or exterior, which is called the natural mind. The natural mind in man is first opened and cultivated, because this is proximately extant to the world (or in contact with it). The spiritual mind is opened and cultivated afterward, but only in proportion as man in life receives the knowledges of truth from the Word, or from doctrine derived from the Word; wherefore it is not opened with those who do not apply those knowledges to life." We here see the reason why evil men are not troubled like other men.

But the man in whom the life of regeneration has commenced, has, as it were, two wills or two minds, one willing to do good and the other evil. The Apostle manifestly alludes to this double nature when he says: "I find then a law, that when I would do good, evil is present with me. For I delight in the law of God after the inward man; but I see another law in my members, warring against the law of my mind, and bringing me into captivity to the law of sin" (Rom. vii. 21 to 23). In another place, Paul says: "For the flesh lusteth against the spirit, and the spirit against the flesh; and these are contrary the one to the other" (Gal. v. 17).

Rev. Mr. Barrett says truly: "Now that the Apostle does not here mean by the *flesh* man's material body, but the external or natural mind, in contradistinction to what he calls 'the inward man,' is manifest from some of the things which he afterwards mentions as 'the works of the flesh;' such as hatreds, emulations, wrath, strife, envyings, etc., all of which proceed not from the material body, but evidently from the natural unregenerate mind."

Every man who is earnestly trying to lead a good and true life feels that he has a higher and lower nature, and that he must look to the higher to guide and not to the lower, as the human of the Lord looked to the Divine within, before that human was fully united, or made one with the Divine; but because of these two conflicting states or minds, of which a man is conscious within himself, he is not two persons, nor has he two separate souls, or consciousnesses; nor had the Psalmist when he addressed his soul in the following sublime language: "Why

art thou cast down, O my soul? and why art thou dis-
quieted within me? hope thou in God; for I shall yet
praise Him who is the health of my countenance, and my
God " (Psalms xlii. 11).   Nor are such appeals to the soul,
as though it were a distinct person, uncommon in the
Holy Word.   The Psalmist exclaims: " Bless the Lord, O
my soul."   " Praise ye the Lord.   Praise the Lord, O my
soul."

We are taught in the writings of Swedenborg that:
" Because the Lord had from the beginning a human from
the mother, and successively put off this, therefore, while
he was in the world, He had two states, which are called
the state of humiliation and the state of glorification or
union with the Divine, which is called the Father.   The
state of humiliation was in the time and in the degree
that He was in the human from the mother; and the
state of glorification, at 'the time and in the degree that
He was in the human from the Father.   In the state of
humiliation He prayed to the Father, as to one different
from himself; but in the state of glorification He spoke
with the Father as with himself.   In this state He said
that the Father was in Him and He in the Father, and
that the Father and He were one; but in the state of
humiliation He underwent temptations and suffered the
cross, and prayed that the Father might not forsake Him;
for the Divine could not be tempted, and still less suffer
the cross.   From these things now it is manifest, that by
temptations, and continued victories over them, and by
the passion of the cross, which was the last of the temptations, He fully conquered the hells and fully glorified the
human." (D. L. 35.)

After His resurrection the Lord appeared unto His disciples and spake unto them saying: " All power is given
unto me in heaven and in earth " (Matt. xxviii. 18).   How
clearly is this great doctrine taught in this passage, that
the Father is in the Son, and that it is through the glorified Divine humanity that thenceforth all power is to be

exercised both in heaven and in earth. So that being "baptized in the name of the Father, and of the Son, and of the Holy Ghost" does not signify in the name of three Gods, or of three Divine persons, but in the name of the three essentials of the one God—the Divine Love or Father, the Divine Humanity or Son, and the Divine proceeding from the Lord, or the Holy Ghost or Holy Spirit.

It is impossible for us to worship a being of whom we can form no image, and to attempt it is to worship an unknown God. How then can we worship the Father except as He has manifested Himself in the Son? "Ye have not heard the voice of the Father at any time, nor seen His shape" (John v. 37). "No man hath seen God at any time: the only begotten Son, who is in the bosom of the Father, He hath declared Him."

"Jesus said unto him (Thomas), I am the way and the truth and the life: no man cometh to the Father, but by me" (John xiv. 6). And again in the tenth chapter of John we read : "Verily, verily, I say unto you, he that entereth not by the door into the sheepfold, but climbeth up some other way, the same is a thief and a robber." * * * But when "they understood not what things they were which He spake unto them" (6th verse), Jesus said "unto them again, Verily, verily, I say unto you, I am the door of the sheep" (7). "I am the door; by me if any man shall enter in, he shall be saved" (9). "Come unto me, all ye that labor and are heavy laden, and I will give you rest" (Matt. xi. 28).

"Jesus Christ, then, is plainly the only true object of religious worship, for He is the God of Revelation—the only God revealed to men. He is, as we have seen, the manifested Jehovah— Immanuel, or God with us. He is God come down to us in our low estate, in order that He might raise us up towards heaven and Himself: in order that He might in His own assumed Human, clearly reveal to us how the principles of infinite truth and love operate in the redemption and salvation of men, and that He might give to these principles their fullest power and effect. This is the greatest, most important, and most comprehensive of all truths."—*Barrett.*

The Scriptures declare, as we have seen, that He is Immanuel, or God with us, and that He is our Saviour. In the Old Testament, as we have already shown, we are repeatedly told that Jehovah is our Saviour, and that beside Him there is no Saviour; and Jehovah assures us that He will not give His glory to another.

Jesus Christ says: " I am the good shepherd: the good shepherd giveth his life for the sheep—my sheep hear my voice, and I know them, and they follow me; and I give unto them eternal life" (John x.). The Psalmist says: "Jehovah is my shepherd; I shall not therefore want: He maketh me to lie down in green pastures, He leadeth me beside the still waters."

In the fortieth chapter of Isaiah we read: " Say unto the cities of Judah, behold your God. Behold, the Lord God will come with a strong hand, and His arm shall rule for Him; behold, His reward is with Him, and His work before Him. He shall feed His flock like a shepherd: He shall gather the lambs with His arm, and carry them in His bosom, and shall gently lead those that are with young." Could language be plainer than this?—the Saviour of the Old Testament the same person as the predicted and risen Saviour of the New Testament—God manifest.

In the fifty-fourth chapter of Isaiah, we read: " Thy Maker is thy husband; Jehovah of Hosts is His name." In the New Testament, Jesus Christ is called the Husband and Bridegroom, and the Church His Wife and Bride.

In the Old Testament we read that " Jehovah is a God of Truth; He is a living God, and an everlasting King" (Jer. x. 10). In the prophetical annunciations of the Lord's coming, and in the New Testament, Christ is called King, Zion's King, the King of Israel, and also

King of Kings, and Lord of Lords. Again, God is called
a Rock, as in the eighteenth Psalm, "For who is God,
save Jehovah, or who is a Rock, save our God?" St. Paul
declares that Christ was a rock, and that He is a stone
laid for a foundation in Zion, "a tried stone, a precious
corner-stone, a sure foundation." Again, Jehovah calls
Himself I Am, as in Exodus iii. 14. "God said unto
Moses, I Am that I Am; and He said, Thus shalt thou
say unto the children of Israel, I Am hath sent me unto
you." Jesus calls Himself by the same name in the
eighth chapter of John, for He declares: "Before Abraham was, I Am." And again He says, "If ye believe not
that I am, ye shall die in your sins." "Then said Jesus
unto them, when ye have lifted up the Son of Man, then
shall ye know that I Am."

Again, Jehovah God calls himself the First and Last.
"Thus saith Jehovah, king of Israel, and His Redeemer
Jehovah of Hosts; I am the First, and I am the Last;
and beside me there is no God" (Isaiah xliv. 6). Jesus
Christ applies the same language to himself in Revelation:
"I am Alpha and Omega, the First and the Last. I am
He that liveth, and was dead; and behold I am alive for
evermore; Amen: and have the keys of hell and of death"
(first chapter).

In the Old Testament God is called the Light. The
Prophet Isaiah, addressing the church, says: "Jehovah
shall be unto thee an everlasting light, and thy God thy
glory" (lx. 19). John says that "God is Light, and in
Him is no darkness at all;" and he also says that the
Word which was made flesh, and dwelt among men, "was
the true light which lighteth every man that cometh into
the world." Jesus declares that "He is the Light of the
world; he that followeth Me," he says, "shall not walk in
darkness, but shall have the light of life."

When Paul was journeying toward Damascus, he says:
"I saw in the way a light from heaven, above the brightness of the sun, shining round about me, and them that

journeyed with me." And it is important to observe that, when in reply to the voice which he heard, he inquired, " Who art thou, Lord?" the answer was, " I am Jesus, whom thou persecutest."

The Psalmist says : " Forever, O Jehovah, thy Word is established in heaven " (cxix. 89); and in the fortieth chapter of Isaiah we are told that this " Word of our God shall stand forever." Jesus said, " Heaven and earth shall pass away, but my Word shall not pass away" (Matt. xxiv. 35). In Deuteronomy viii. 3, we read that " man doth not live by bread only, but by every word that proceedeth out of the mouth of the Lord doth man live." Jesus said, " I am the living bread that came down from heaven, if any man eat of this bread, he shall live forever; and the bread that I shall give is my flesh, which I will give for the life of the world." ·Again, " It is the spirit that quickeneth; the flesh profiteth nothing; the words that I speak unto you are spirit and are life " (John vi.).

In Second Chronicles we read: " O Judah, and ye inhabitants of Jerusalem, believe in Jehovah your God, so shall ye be established." Jesus Christ says: "I am the resurrection and the life ; he that believeth in me, though he were dead, yet shall he live, and whosoever liveth and believeth in me shall never die " (John xi. 25 and 26).

In Isaiah xlv. 22, we read: "Look unto me and be ye saved, all the ends of the earth ; for I am God, and there is none else"; "a just God and Saviour, there is none beside me." Jesus saith: " Come unto me, all ye who labor and are heavy laden, and I will give you rest" (Matt. xi. 28).

We find, then, that the same attributes are predicated of Jesus Chrst as of Jehovah. He is therefore, in the language of Peter, our "God and Saviour Jesus Christ." "To Him be glory both now and forever" (1 Peter xi. and last chapter). Truly, in the language of Simon Peter, we may exclaim: " Lord, to whom shall we go? thou hast the words of eternal life " (John vi. 68).

A knowledge of the Lord was possessed in the Christian church at its commencement. In the Apocryphal New Testament (a work which, says a distinguished writer, is valuable on account of its reflecting to us the opinions of some of the early Christians), Nicodemus says: "And I know now that He is Almighty God, and mighty in His human nature, who is the Saviour of mankind " (xv. 19). Again he says: "And so it appears that Jesus, whom we crucified, is Jesus Christ the Son of God, and the true and Almighty God" (xxii. 20).   Clement says: "Brethren, we ought so to think of Jesus Christ, as of God, as of the Judge of the living and the dead " (2 Cor. i. 1). Ignatius repeatedly speaks of our Lord Jesus Christ, and says that "God Himself appeared in the form of a man, for the renewal of eternal life" (Eph. iv. 13).

But, alas! until the dawning light of the descending New Jerusalem began to dispel the darkness, the Sun has been darkened for many centuries throughout the Christian world; or, in other words, the Supreme, sole and exclusive Divinity of the Lord Jesus Christ, has been denied by too many creed builders, and thus they have rejected the chief corner-stone.   No wonder then that all has been confusion in the Christian world, and that the cry is Lo here, and Lo there, among hundreds of conflicting sects—all claiming to be right.   The prophetic annunciation has been fulfilled: "Verily I say unto you, there shall not be left here one stone (truth) upon another, that shall not be thrown down" (Matt. xxiv. 2).   When the chief corner-stone, or the doctrine that the Lord Jesus Christ is God alone, or God manifest in the flesh, is rejected in the church, the doctrines built on other foundations are built upon sandy foundations, "for," says the Apostle, "other foundations can no man lay than that is laid, which is Jesus Christ."

The Unitarian, in the past more frequently than at this day, denied the Divinity of the Lord Jesus Christ, and sustained his views by quoting some of the passages which refer to the Lord before His glorification, or before His Humanity was made Divine.

The Trinitarian has also, in the past more frequently than to-day, divided God into three persons, and upon this foundation has built a system of doctrines entirely inconsistent with the strict personal unity of God. If the various churches were all to acknowledge that there is but one God, and that the Lord Jesus Christ is that one God, many of the prevailing doctrines would all vanish speedily, for they would have no foundation—not even a sandy one—for all men would see that faith separate from charity is dead, and that all genuine religion has relation to life—must be lived. With one known God there can be unity in the church, for there is a centre; and as this grand central doctrine is gradually dawning in the world, a spirit of charity and brotherly love toward other denominations is slowly but surely taking the place, among religious teachers and laymen, of the old, cold, harsh, sectarian spirit.

If Jesus Christ is God, and in Him dwelleth all the fullness of the Divinity, it is plain that He is our Father in heaven, and that we ought to go directly to Him, and to acknowledge no other, and to try to think of no other, and to pray to no other God besides Him. But, alas! how is it in the Christian world, even to-day? are prayers always or even generally addressed to the manifested Jehovah, or to Jesus Christ? Let every man answer this question for himself; we would barely suggest that it would always be well to remember the Lord's words: "No one cometh to the Father but by me." How many are there in the Christian world that fully realize that the Father dwells in the Son, and that they are one—the one known God?

Was there no need then of the Lord's Second Coming, when He was so generally denied, as He was over a century ago, at the time Swedenborg wrote the things revealed to him by the Lord?

In the writings of Emanuel Swedenborg we have re-

vealed to us the glorious truths of the Lord's Second
Coming in the clouds of heaven, not of earth—a coming
in power and great glory; coming down to man's intellectual perceptions, and satisfying all the highest demands
of his reason.

The sacred Scriptures are opened by the revealed science
of correspondences—the correspondence of all natural
things to spiritual things. "That there is a relation of
some sort," says a recent writer, " existing between the
visible creation and the invisible, between the objects of
the natural universe and the subjects of the spiritual universe, the things seen by man and the thoughts and affections of man, is evident. Of this, the least reflecting must
be convinced. The language of the people proves this perception. Poetry confirms this perception more abundantly.
That there must be such a relation is evident from the fact
that all things were created with a distinct reference to
man, and that man was created with a definite relation
to God—His image. There must be an orderly law of
sequence from the lowest things up to man, and from man
up to the Divine Humanity of God. All created things
bear some relation and possess some resemblance to the
Creator. Outbirths from God, they must be to a certain
extent mirrors in which God is made visible. St. Paul
expresses it: 'For the invisible things of Him [God] from
the creation of the world are *clearly seen*, being understood
by the things which are made, *even* His eternal power and
Godhead' (Rom. i. 20). In the visible we behold the
symbols or representatives or correspondences of the invisible things of God.

"Man's relation to God may be clearly seen. He was
formed to be 'an image and likeness' of his august Creator. In him were, therefore, made receptacles, as we have
already intimated, into which the essentials of the Divine
Nature might *finitely* flow. A marred image, yet a finite
miniature of God! The Divine Love might flow into his
capacity to love, or his *will :* the Divine Wisdom might

flow into his capacity to be wise, or his *understanding.* The Infinite Power of God is finitely imaged in his power. In man, then, is therefore a beautiful finite image of the Divine Trinity. The things of God may be received by and finitely seen in man. All the dispensations of God's Providence have this one great end—that man may become an agent under the Lord, inspired by His Love, directed by His Wisdom. Not that man's will and understanding should become absorbed into, but infilled by, the Divine Love and Wisdom. That thus man might to all eternity become more and more fully the child of his Divine Father; a free being, yet freely choosing to be led and taught by his august Creator."

Now is being fulfilled the prophecies in regard to the descent of the New Jerusalem, "Behold I make all things new." Under the figure of the New Jerusalem a New Dispensation—not a new sect—is being established, in which there shall be no mental night or darkness, "for the Lord God giveth them light." St. John declares that he saw no temple therein, for the Lord God Almighty and the Lamb are the temple of it. "By the Lord God Almighty," says Swedenborg, "is meant the Lord from eternity, who is Jehovah Himself; and by the Lamb is signified His Divine Humanity." Two beings are no more signified in this and similar passages in the New Testament than there are in the following from Isaiah xliv. 6: "Thus saith the Lord the King of Israel, and His Redeemer the Lord of Hosts, I am the First and I am the Last, and besides Me there is no God."

Is it of little or no moment whether we acknowledge or reject the Lord Jesus Christ at His Second Coming, or that we say, that we have Moses and the Prophets, the Gospels and the Epistles, what need we of Him? Were the Jews guiltless who rejected the Lord at His First Coming? Shall it be said of any of us, having eyes ye will see not, ears have ye but you hear not? Or shall we prove all things and hold fast that which is good? that it be not said that it shall be more tolerable for Sodom and Gomorrah than for us, in the day of Judgment.

We have dwelt thus at length on the doctrine of the Lord and the Trinity, for they are, as has already been stated, fundamental. No man can reasonably be expected to rise in life superior to the idea which he cherishes of the God whom he worships. If his God in his estimation is cruel, harsh, unforgiving, actuated by hatred, envy, jealousy, requiring to be appeased before He can forgive, and punishes his enemies, the man is reasonably sure to indulge in such passions and actions to a greater or less extent. How important to all such is the law of correspondences, which shows conclusively that all such language, when applied to the Lord in the sacred Scriptures, is but the language of appearances, the real truth being that God is love, and unchangeably so, and that He never hates and never punishes; but sin carries with it its own consequences, or punishment, if you please, as causes always produce their effects in the spiritual as well as in the natural plane.

XXV.

Sacrificial Worship.

THAT sacrifices have been offered in worship by men of widely different nations and races, even long before the Jewish or Israelitish Church was established, is well known. The science of correspondences, once understood by all men on earth, which has long been lost, but has now been restored by the Lord through Swedenborg, alone can furnish us with a key which will unlock the mysteries which attend this subject and show us their origin, and their original and true design.

" But, it is asked, ' What is the strongest and most conclusive evidence which you have to offer in proof of the truth and certainty of this new science?' We answer, No evidence can be sufficiently clear and full to satisfy a mind that will not look at it, or that has no taste nor desire for things beyond the gift of this world. But if even such a person were entirely unacquainted with the Chinese language, and should remove to China, and there learn to speak and write that language, so as to read their books and understand them, and should find that they contained a rational and consecutive chain of ideas and history of events, he certainly would be convinced that they had a language, and that he had learned it. It is precisely so with the language of analogy. It must be examined and learned, and tested by the reading of analogical language, before it can be understood.

" Now man, in true order, is in the general image and likeness of God. Any other created thing in true order is only an image of some principle or principles in God or in man.

" The order of the outward creation of the world was, from lower things to higher, first minerals, then vegetables, then animals, and finally man; thus orderly and gradually approximating by higher and purer organizations the real divine image, until God finally crowned the creation with man, as the sum total and embodiment of all things below him. When all but man was created, and everything was in readiness to produce man, the vast variety of things scattered all over and throughout the universe, were but humanity in fragments; every single thing was an image of some principle which was to be in man; and it took them all, combined, to make up the full man. Man could not exist until these things were created; for upon them his body must subsist; and through them his mind is to be educated.

" But when in the process of the creation all things were in readiness for the production of man; when the vast variety of human principles lay scattered throughout the mineral, the vegetable and the animal kingdoms, in living, speaking forms; when all nature was a beautiful page of mental symbols in physical robes, without an

admirer on earth; with no created rational being to read
the expressive characters of that wonderful book, and to
love and worship the Author; then it is that we behold
Man, making his appearance—Man, the sum total of the
creation, the connecting link between God above him and
nature below him, and thus, the crowning act of the creation.   And when all these materials were brought harmoniously together, in man, and all was pronounced good,
the vast universe corresponded to man, and man to his
Maker."—*Rev. A. Silver.*

"The animals of the earth," says Swedenborg, "in
general, correspond to affections; the tame and useful
animals correspond to good affections, and the fierce and
useless kinds to evil affections.   In particular, oxen and
bullocks correspond to the affections of the natural mind;
sheep and lambs to the affections of the spiritual mind;
and birds or other winged creatures, according to their
species, correspond to the intellectual faculties and exercises of both minds.   Hence it is that various animals,
as oxen, bullocks, rams, sheep, she-goats, he-goats, and
male and female lambs, also pigeons and doves, were
employed in the Israelitish Church, which was a representative one, for holy uses, it being of them that the sacrifices and burnt offerings consisted; for when so employed,
they correspond to certain spiritual things and were
understood in heaven according to their correspondences.
Animals, also, according to their genera and species, actually are affections; the reason of which is because they
live; and nothing can have life except from affection, and
according to it.   Hence, likewise, it is that every animal
possesses an innate knowledge according to the affection
of its life.   Man, too, as to his natural man, is like the
animals; wherefore, also, it is usual to compare him to
them in common discourse.   Thus a man of a mild disposition is called a sheep or lamb; a man of rough or fierce
temper is called a bear or wolf; a crafty person is termed
a fox or a serpent, and so in other instances."

The Rev. Samuel Noble, from whose "Appeal" to the Christian world in behalf of the writings and disclosures of Emanuel Swedenborg, we have selected most of what follows in this section, says: "The sacrifices of the Mosaic law are generally allowed to have been of a typical nature; and the doctrines of the New Jerusalem bring the antitypes of these types to view in the most clear and satisfactory manner.

"*First*, then, it shall be shown that the sacrifices of the Mosaic law were not meant to represent the punishment of sin, but the hallowing of every affection and principle of the mind, and thus of the whole man, to the Lord. *Secondly*, that the sacrifice of Jesus Christ did not consist in His suffering the punishment due to sin, but in His hallowing every principle of His Human Nature to the Godhead, till at length His Human Nature became a living sacrifice, or fully consecrated, sanctified, and hallowed, by perfect union with His Divinity. *Thirdly*, that the Lord is called a Mediator in respect to His Humanity, because in this He has opened to us a new and living way of access, or medium of approach to His Divinity.

"The prevailing opinion in regard to the Levitical sacrifices is, that the slaying of an animal, and the burning of it, or of part of it, on the altar, represented the punishment due to the offerer, and that, in sacrificing the animal, the offerer was considered as entreating that the suffering inflicted upon it might be accepted in lieu of the punishment deserved by himself. This is the notion which the Jewish Rabbins have of the subject; who say also, that a confession of sins was made over the victim, when the offerer laid his hand upon its head, and thus that the sins were considered as transferred to the animal, and punished in it instead of the offerer. It is, however, certain, that this is merely one of the traditions of the Jews, by which, as in so many other instances, they have perverted the divine law; for although the offerer was commanded to lay his hand upon the head of the victim, *not one word is*

*said in the Scriptures of any confession of sins to be then
made.* The only instance in which a confession 'of sins
accompanied the laying on of the hand, is that of the
scape-goat; respecting which Moses commanded that
'Aaron should lay both his hands upon the head of the
live-goat, and confess over it all the iniquities of the
children of Israel, and all their transgressions in all their
sins, putting them upon the head of the goat' (Lev. xvi.
21). But this goat being thus representatively loaded
with sins, was considered as unclean, and instead of being
sacrificed, was sent away into the wilderness: even the
man that was employed to send it away was considered as
contaminated by the operation, and rendered unclean also,
so that he was required to wash his clothes and bathe his
flesh in water, before he was allowed to return into the
camp (verse 26). Seeing then, when it was intended that
a confession of sins should be made over a victim, the
command for it is so expressly given, can it be supposed
that a similar confession was intended to be made over all
the victims, when it is never commanded at all? And
when the representative effect of this confession of sins
over an animal was to render it unclean, so that to have
offered it up in sacrifice would have been an abomination,
and the only orderly way of disposing of it was to send it
away into the wilderness, to denote the rejection of man's
sins, separated from himself, to hell from whence they
came; can it be supposed that the animals actually sacrificed were in like manner rendered unclean, by a similar
confession of sins being made over them, and thus a similar representative transfer of sins to them? The idea is
monstrous in the extreme.

"The reason then why, in all sacrifices, he that offered
the sacrifice was directed to put his hand upon the head of
the victim, was, not by that act representatively to transfer his sins—for to do this the sins were also to be confessed over it, and that by positive command, as in the
case of the scape-goat—but to express communication be-

tween the offerer and his sacrifice, which was necessary to give the animal its representative efficacy. The animals offered in sacrifice represented the good affections of various kinds from which the Lord is to be worshipped; but without this symbol of communication between the offerer and the animal, the latter would not represent any good affection presented by him; to imply that the offerer himself wished to worship the Lord by and from the good affection which the animal represented, it was necessary that he should perform the representative rite of putting his hand upon its head; after which the animal represented a good affection cherished by him and presented by him to the Lord, from a sincere acknowledgment that everything good is from the Lord alone.

" Now, that this is the true idea of sacrificial worship, is evident from many parts of Scripture; we will just select one which is completely conclusive. That the putting of the animal to death and burning of it upon the altar, does not represent the punishment due to the offerer, is clear from this circumstance, that the altar, on which the sacrifices were offered, is called, in various places, 'the table of the Lord.' Thus the Lord says by the prophet to the priests, 'Ye have profaned it (that is, the name of the Lord) in that ye say, The *table* of the Lord is polluted, and the fruit thereof, even His *meat* (the *meat*, observe, of the Lord) is contemptible.' Again: 'Ye offer polluted *bread* upon Mine *altar :* and ye say, Wherein have we polluted Thee?' The answer is, 'In that ye say, The *table* of the Lord is contemptible.' Nothing can be more clear, from these and numerous other instances, than that the things offered in sacrifice, and burnt upon the altar, were considered as constituting a *feast*—were presented as upon a *table* for the Lord to *eat ;* which He was considered to do when they were consumed by fire. This is the reason why it is so often said in Leviticus, that they were to be burnt 'for a sweet-smelling savour to the Lord.' They are expressly called the Lord's *bread*, and

His *meat.* Can that, then, which He is considered to accept as food, be the punishment and torment of sinners?

"What then are the viands of which the Lord can partake in reality ? When any allusion is made in Scripture to His hunger, it means, His intense desire that His goodness and love should be received by mankind. On the occasion of His temptation in the wilderness it is said, that 'when He had fasted forty days He was afterwards *a hungered;*' where His fasting refers to the depraved state of mankind, and of the church in its entire desolation, and His hungering, to His intense desire for man's salvation. The hunger of the Lord then is satisfied, when His love and goodness are received by mankind; and this is done, when man receives affections of goodness and truth, or spiritual graces, from Him, and returns them to Him in sincere adoration, with the heartfelt acknowledgment that they are from Him alone.

"Here then we have a clear idea of the purport of the sacrifices in use in the representative or Israelitish Church, and also among the Gentile nations—an idea which explains the whole system, and banishes obscurity from every part ; whereas, on the supposition that they represent the punishment due to sinners, and transferred from them to the Lord Jesus Christ, we find ourselves stumbling amid difficulties and inconsistencies at every step.

"But it may perhaps be thought that this view of the subject excludes all reference of the sacrifices to the Lord Jesus Christ. The direct contrary, however, is the fact. All the Mosaic law of sacrifices was fulfilled in, and by, the Lord Jesus Christ, in a super-eminent manner, and thus in its highest sense, it has reference to Him; it is only in a subordinate sense, and as we are followers of Him, that it has a spiritual fulfillment in us. We, in our subordinate degree, as walking after Him, are to be sacrifices too; but He is the great sacrifice of all.

"When man continually receives from the Lord the graces of which He is the author, and ascribes all to Him, in the manner represented by the sacrificial worship of the Mosaic law; when every affection and perception of his heart and mind, of. which the various kinds of sacrifices were representative, or himself in regard to such affections and perceptions, is thus continually hallowed to the Lord; it follows, that his entire sanctification will at length be completed, when the whole man will thus be devoutly consecrated to his God. This is the state which the Apostle exhorts us to attain, when he says, 'I beseech you, brethren, that ye present your bodies *a living sacri-* *fice,* holy, acceptable unto God; which is your reasonable service' (Rom. xii. 1). The Apostle calls this our *reasonable service* in allusion to the *carnal service* of the Levitical law; meaning, that he who thus presents himself *a living sacrifice* truly performs that of which the *animal sacrifices* were types. Such a *living sacrifice* is a man wholly devoted to the Lord, who is wholly renewed by the reception of new principles of love, thought, and action, from Him; whose selfish life is extinct, whilst he lives by a new life, which is life indeed."

We are now enabled to see the truth of our second proposition: that the sacrifice of Jesus Christ did not consist in His suffering the punishment due to sin—for if, as we have seen, nothing relating to punishment is included in the Scripture idea of sacrifices, nothing of this could be included in the sacrifice of Jesus Christ. The Lord came into the world to save men from sin, and not from the penalty of sin, for the evil-doer shall not go unpunished—only as he ceases from sin—sin is the cause; suffering, the effect.

"All things," says a great authority, "are of God, who hath reconciled us to Himself by Jesus Christ, and hath committed unto us the ministry of reconciliation; to wit, that God was in Christ reconciling the world unto Himself, not imputing their trespasses unto them" (2 Cor. v. 18, 19.)

"The Apostle here delivers, in one single sentence, the
whole doctrine of the Atonement; and to call attention
to it he propounds it in the most express and formal manner. '*God hath reconciled us to Himself by Jesus Christ:*'
and the ministry of this reconciliation, committed to the
Apostles, was, to declare this truth : '*to wit, that God was
in Christ reconciling the world unto Himself*, not imputing
their trespasses unto them.' The word here translated
reconciliation, is the same as is elsewhere rendered *atonement :* it cannot then be denied, that the Atonement of
Scripture is nothing else but our reconciliation with God,
effected by the dwelling of God in the person of Jesus Christ.

"That the Lord is called a Mediator in respect to His
Humanity, because in this He has opened a new and living
way of access to His Divinity, must now, one would appre-
hend, be so evident, that it is needless to employ many
words in its proof.

"The Apostle says of Jesus, that 'He ever liveth to
make intercession for us' (Heb. vii. 25).   But by inter-
ceding he does not here mean *soliciting* or *entreating*, as a
supplicant to a sovereign ; nor is there anything in the
context to sanction such a gross, external idea ; but *acting
as a medium*, or as *that which goes between*, which is the
strict literal meaning of the word *to intercede*.   Such intercession is the proper office of the Divine Humanity, for
this receives into Itself the unmitigated fulness of the Divine Essence, and dispenses it to man in a form adapted to
his capacities of receiving it; just as a man's body receives
into itself the whole of the powers of his soul, and dispenses its energies, in the manner adapted to make them
efficient, on persons and things around it.   How exactly
does the Lord Himself describe His action in this inter-
ceding or mediatorial character, when He says, respecting
the Comforter or Holy Spirit,—'whom *I* will send unto
you *from the Father*' (John xv. 26); teaching, that the
Divine Essence is the origin of the Divine Influencing
Power, but that the Divine Humanity in which it abides

in all its infinite fulness, is the Medium of dispensing its agency on mankind.

"Now, how precisely is the true doctrine on this subject expressed by the Apostle Paul! 'There is one God,' says he, 'and one Mediator between God and men, the Man Christ Jesus.' He expressly affirms, that it is the *Man* Christ Jesus who is the Mediator. But Jesus is generally allowed to be God as well as man; yet the Apostle takes care to guard us from supposing that His Divinity mediates between us and some other Divinity, by thus expressly restricting the office of mediation to His Humanity; hence, also, he never uses the title, ' the Man Christ Jesus,' on any other occasion whatsoever. How plainly does this instruct us, that the Human Nature of the Lord Jesus Christ is the only Medium by which we can have access to His Divine Essence; and that His Divine Essence is not distinct from that of the Father, but is the Father Himself! His essential Divine Nature is what the Apostle calls God, and which he declares to be One; His glorified Human Nature is what he calls *the Man* Christ Jesus, and which he also declares to be one, to intimate that the Human Nature in Him is essentially different from what it is in all other beings, and is as His Divine, being the adequate organ of conveying to man the divine communications.

"The Lord when on earth said, ' I say not unto you, *that I will pray the Father for you :* for the Father Himself loveth you, because ye have loved Me, and have believed that I came out from God.' Thus, instead of engaging to make prayer and supplication to the Father in behalf of those who believe in Him, He expressly assures . them that He will *not* do so. Rightly to believe in Him, also, is, He declares, to believe that He *came out from God;* which means, to believe that His Humanity is an immediate evolution from His Divine Essence.

"Hence again we see that the Lord's Humanity is the Medium by which we gain access to His Divinity, and are brought into communication with it, just as by the medium of a man's body we gain access to, and have communication with his soul. The Lord teaches the same truth in the most direct form when He says, 'I am the door: by Me, if any man enter in, he shall be saved, and shall go in and out and find pasture' (John x. 9). What is the door but the medium of access? And that, to obtain such access, we are not to address the naked Divinity immediately, but the Lord Jesus Christ as the Divine Person of the Father, He again teaches when He says, 'Verily, verily, I say unto you, He that entereth not by the door into the sheepfold, but climbeth up some other way, the same is a thief and a robber' (ver. 1).

"Altogether it seems abundantly evident, that the Mediatorship of Jesus Christ does not consist in His introducing us, by entreaty or any other means, to the favor of a God out of and separate from Himself; but in His having assumed and glorified a Humanity to afford a Medium of access to the Divinity which dwells in fulness in it. Let us then, instead of thinking to climb up some other way, enter in 'by a new and living way which He hath consecrated for us through the veil, that is to say, His *flesh*' (Heb. x. 20)—that Humanity, which He has deified and united to Deity to be for men the Medium of approach to God!'"

XXVI.

The Cross.

"NOR does the doctrine of the *Cross* owe its origin to the Christian era, but is as ancient, perhaps, as the knowledge of *immortality* of which it is the symbol. The *Crux ansata* is indeed one of the most ancient relics of a true religion, and is found among the sculptures of the Egyptians of the most remote antiquity, with whom it denoted *eternal life*. Mr. Gliddon, in one of his lectures, says he 'had seen in a remote quarry in middle Egypt, a figure designed to represent the Saviour, drawn as if appended, not to a *Cross*, but to this symbol of immortality. The

Cross had therefore the same meaning with them as with us; it was the type of the life everlasting beyond the tomb.' In the destruction of the temple of Serapis (at Alexandria) by the Christians, the Cross was found in. many parts of the building; and Sozomenes, in writing the history of the Church, speaking of the temple of Serapis, says: 'It is reported that when this temple was destroyed, there appeared some of those characters called hieroglyphics, surrounding *the sign of the Cross*, in engraven stones; and that by the skillful in these matters, these hieroglyphics were held to have signified this inscription: 'THE LIFE TO COME.' Socrates (the historian) makes the statement, and says, the words were found to indicate, 'SALVATION AND LIFE TO COME.' The two principal Pagodas of India (Benares and Mathura), are also built in the form of *Crosses.* In China, the Cross is one of the most ancient relics of their worship, and in one of the sacred books of that country, has lately been deciphered from their enigmatical writings, the following sentence: 'La croix devant les yeux règle le cœur des hommes;' or *The Cross before the eyes governs the heart of man.* This Cross, says Mr. Squier, which is similar to the sacred *Tau,* and not unlike the Mexican *Tree of Life* (which undoubtedly is its origin), is not only discovered in the hands of Egyptian and Assyrian Divinities as the sign of life, but is sometimes dependant from the necks of their deified Serpents. 'Pontiffs and prelates (says Volney), that crucifix of which you boast the mystery, without comprehending it, is the Cross of Serapis, traced by the hands of Egyptian priests on the plan of the figurative world, which, passing through the equinoxes and the tropics, became the emblem of *future life and resurrection*, because it touched the gates of ivory and horn, through which the soul was to pass on its way to heaven.'—*The Two Great Books.*

"But the Cross did not then, as now, mean a *penal crucifixion*, nor were any painful ideas ever associated with this emblem; on the contrary, all its associations were

joyful and pleasant. Milman, in his 'History of Christianity,' says the Cross was the symbol of Christianity, or
of a true faith, 'many centuries before the *Crucifix*. It
was rather a cheerful and consolatory, than a depressing
and melancholy sign; it was adorned with flowers, with
crowns and precious stones, a pledge of the *resurrection*,
rather than a memorial of the passion. The catacombs of
Rome, faithful to their general character, offer no instance
of a crucifixion, nor does any allusion to such a subject of
art occur in any early writers. Cardinal Bona gives the
following as the progress of the gradual change: 1st, The
simple Cross; 2d, The Cross, with the Lamb at the foot of
it; 3d, Christ clothed on the Cross, with hands uplifted in
prayer, but not nailed to it; 4th, Christ fastened to the
Cross, with four nails, still living, and with open eyes. He
was not represented as dead, till the tenth or eleventh
century. There is some reason to believe that the bust of
the Saviour first appeared on the Cross, and afterwards the
whole person. The head was at first erect, with some
expression of Divinity; by degrees it drooped with the
agony of pain, the face was wan and furrowed, and death,
with all its anguish, was imitated by the utmost power of
coarse art; mere corporeal suffering without sublimity, all
that was painful in truth, with nothing that was tender
and affecting. This change took place among monkish
artists of the lower empire. Those of the order of St. Basil
introduced it into the West, and from that time these
painful images, with those of martyrdom, and every scene
of suffering which could be imagined by the gloomy fancy
of anchorites, who could not be moved by less violent
excitement, spread throughout Christendom.' Thus it is
only in these latter days that the true meaning of the
Cross is lost; its pure and genuine symbolism was coeval
with the revelation to man of the joys of the world beyond
the grave."—*Rev. G. Field.*

That a meaning is attached to the cross in the sacred
Scriptures very different from the literal idea at present

so generally entertained, must be manifest to every attentive reader. Our Saviour says not unfrequently, that he who would be His disciple, must take up his cross and follow Him. "I am crucified with Christ: nevertheless, I live; yet not I, but Christ liveth in me," says the Apostle.

"The cross," says Swedenborg, "signifies temptations;" and "to take up the cross is to fight against our inclinations to evil, and to follow the Lord is to acknowledge Him to be God." To acknowledge the Lord and to resist and overcome in temptations is the way which leads to eternal life, of which the cross has ever been emblematical. The Lord, by the passion of the cross, did not take away sins, but He bore them. "The Lord Jesus," says Rev. John Hyde, "speaking of the law upon which David is so eloquent, declares that, 'I am not come to destroy the law and the prophets, but to fulfil' (Matt. v. 17). Not to fulfil in the sense of *abolishing*, but in the sense of *filling-full*, as Johnson defines the word, 'to fill till there is room for no more.' The Lord's meaning is illustrated in the context. The law against murder is *filled-full* so as to include hatred and enmity. The law against adultery is *filled-full* so as to embrace all sinful desire and lust. The law is not only applied to external acts, but also to internal wishes and thoughts; thus showing that the law has a spiritual pertinence, and therefore a spiritual signification."

Eternal life is a life of genuine love to the Lord and the neighbor, and it is only by taking up our cross, suffering, resisting, and overcoming in temptations, and following the Lord in the regeneration, that this heavenly state can be reached. To fall in temptations, and yield to our hereditary or acquired inclinations to evil, is to die spiritually: and when we come to a state in which we are ruled exclusively by that which is false and evil, as we shall, if we do not repent and follow the Lord, then all heavenly life will have perished in our souls; for we will

have no love for that which is really good and true—only
selfishness.

But the reader, to understand fully this grand doctrine
of the cross and its spiritual signification, must read the
writings of Swedenborg, for it is impossible in a few words
to even begin to do justice to it. If we shall be successful
in seriously calling the attention of the reader to the vast
treasures of spiritual knowledge revealed by the Lord
through him for the special benefit of the men of this age,
we shall have accomplished all that we could reasonably
expect. We do not expect in this short treatise to answer
satisfactorily all the questions of the honest inquirer after
truth, nor to silence the skeptical scoffer; but the earnest
inquirer will be abundantly, and more than satisfied, if he
will read diligently the writings of the Swedish seer.

XXVII.

A True and Heavenly Life.

THAT a man should lead a good and true life, repent,
shun evils as sins against God, and do good to his
fellow-man, in order to reach happiness and heaven, was
not unknown to the ancients long before the days of
Moses; nor is this knowledge confined at this day to
Christian nations, but is to be found, more or less perverted, among all nations on earth; having descended
either by tradition or in a written form from the ancient
or Church of Noah.

The following precepts were among the accepted teachings of the ancient Druids:

"Believe nothing without examination; but when
reason and evidence will warrant the conclusion, believe
everything; and let prejudice be unknown. Search for
truth on all occasions, and espouse it in opposition to the
world."

"Light is the emblem of purity, holiness and truth—
the emblem of the source of all good, and of all mental (or

spiritual) illumination. Every act of the Bard (or the inspired instructor or teacher of the people) must be done *in the eye of the light*."

" Pride is that passion by which a person assumes more than the laws of nature (the laws of nature are the laws of God) allow him ; for all persons are equal, though differently stationed in the state of humanity, for the common good. Whoever assumes such a superiority is an usurper, and he attaches himself thereby to evil to such a degree that his soul falls at death into the lowest point of existence."

"One infallible rule of duty is, not to do anything, or desire to do it, but what can eternally be done, and obtained in the celestial state where no evil can exist. The good and happiness of one being must not arise from the evil or misery of another."

In Johnson's "Rambler" is given the following translation of a prayer of the pagan *Simplicius,* which is full of fervent and genuine piety:

> " O Thou, whose pow'r o'er moving worlds presides,
> Whose voice created, and whose wisdom guides !
> On darkling man in pure effulgence shine,
> And cheer the clouded mind with light Divine.
> 'Tis Thine alone to calm the pious breast,
> With silent confidence and holy rest ;
> From Thee, great Jove, we spring, to Thee we tend,
> Path, motive, guide, Original, and end."

Plato, Pythagoras, and other "ancient heathens," breathe the same spirit, and look to the same Infinite and eternal One, who is thus addressed on behalf of the sinner: "Great Jove! Father of man! O free them from those evils, or discover to them the demon they employ!" And, addressing man : "Consider all things well, governing thyself by reason, and setting it in the uppermost place. And when thou art divested of thy mortal body, and arrived in the most pure ether, thou shalt be exalted among the immortal gods (angels), be incorruptible and never more know death." The Prayer of Pythagoras, as thus versified by Mr. Adams, is also full of vital and practical religion:

> " Let not soft slumber close thine eyes,
> Before thou recollectest thrice
> The train of actions through the day:
> Where have my feet found out their way?
> What have I learned where'er I've been,
> From all I've heard, from all I've seen?
> What know I more that's worth the knowing?
> What have I done that's worth the doing?
> What have I sought that I should shun?
> What duty have I left undone?
> Or, into what new follies run?
> These self enquiries are the road
> That leads to virtue, and to God."

"Indeed," says the Rev. George Field, "it is abundantly evident that, both as to faith and life, there never has been but one religion, however much it may have been perverted, lost, or prostituted to improper purposes, for that 'which is now called the Christian religion (says St. Augustine) really was known to the ancients, nor was wanting at any time from the beginning of the human race, until the time when Christ came into the flesh; from whence the true religion, which had previously existed, began to be called Christian; and this in our days is the Christian religion, not as having been wanting in former times, but as having in latter times received this name.'"

In the revelations made by the Lord through Emanuel Swedenborg, on the "Doctrine of Life for the New Jerusalem," we read: "That all religion has relation to life, and that the life of religion is to do good. Every one, who has any religion, knows and acknowledges, that whosoever lives well will be saved, and that whosoever lives wickedly will be condemned; for he knows and acknowledges, that whosoever lives well, thinks well, not only concerning God, but also concerning his neighbor, whereas it is otherwise with him who lives wickedly. The life of man is his love, and what a man loves, he not only does willingly, but also thinks willingly."

This accords strictly with the Lord's teaching when on earth. "If any man will do his will he shall know of the doctrine whether it be of God." The Psalmist declares that "a good understanding have all they that do His commandments."

The more earnestly, then, we strive to ultimate in external life the truth we already have, the more clearly shall we be able to see the truth. Man is not saved by faith or truth alone for it becomes no part of him—it does not enter his life until he strives to live in accordance with it, and thus unites it with goodness. The Lord's commandments are simply Laws of Spiritual Life, which we must earnestly strive to keep, if we would enter into eternal life—or a life of love to the Lord and neighbor, which alone is genuine life, or heavenly life. How clearly and beautifully the Lord teaches this great doctrine of Life. "If ye love me, keep my commandments." "If thou wilt enter into life, keep the commandments."

The Lord when on earth declared that He came "not to destroy the Law but to fulfil;" and we must strive to follow His blessed example, not only as to external acts, but also as to the thoughts of the understanding and affections of the will. St. Paul declares truly that "by the works of the law shall no flesh be justified." While it is quite evident that he referred more especially to the ceremonial laws of the Jewish Church, and not to the Ten Commandments, still there is a sense in which it is true, that by the works of the law man is not justified; for good external acts done from purely selfish motives, such as love of money, power, or glory, have not heavenly life within them; and when the evils we are commanded by the Lord not to do, are shunned simply through worldly fear, or from selfish motives, and not shunned because they are sins against God, or a violation of His laws, and will affect our spiritual well-being in this world and the next, our motives or hearts are not changed. Faith in the Lord is essential, but faith without works, says St. James, is dead, being alone. "But wilt thou know, O vain man, that faith without works is dead?" "Seest thou how faith wrought with his works, and by works was faith made perfect?" "Ye see then how that by works a man is justified, and not by faith only?" "For as the body without the spirit is dead, so faith without works is dead also."

In the New Jerusalem now descending out of Heaven, faith and charity will be reunited; for, in its teachings, the Lord's dealings with His children have again been clearly revealed, not for the first or second time, but as distinctly as they were to Jeremiah, Isaiah, Ezekiel and the Jewish people of old, and the disciples of our Lord when He was on earth. Whenever faith, or Cain, destroys charity, or Abel, in the Lord's church on earth, the church has reached its end, for the Word of the Lord is rendered of none effect by the doctrines and traditions of men, and nothing but a new revelation of Divine truth can rescue our race from destruction—or preserve heavenly life on earth. The Lord provides that a remnant shall be left in the expiring church who are ready to hearken anew to the word of the Lord in its integrity.

When, at the command of the Lord, Jeremiah went down to the potter's house, how clear was the message: "O house of Israel, cannot I do with you as this potter? saith the Lord. Behold, as the clay is in the potter's hand, so are ye in mine hand, O house of Israel. At what instant I shall speak concerning a nation, and concerning a kingdom, to pluck up, and to pull down, and to destroy it; if that nation, against whom I have pronounced, turn from their evil, I will repent of the evil that I thought to do unto them. And at what instant I shall speak concerning a nation, and concerning a kingdom, to build and to plant it; if it do evil in my sight, that it obey not my voice, then I will repent of the good, wherewith I said I would benefit them" (Jer. xviii.).

And so in Ezekiel, "The soul that sinneth, it shall die. The son shall not bear the iniquity of the father, neither shall the father bear the iniquity of the son; the righteousness of the righteous shall be upon him, and the wickedness of the wicked shall be upon him. But if the wicked will turn from all his sins that he hath committed, and keep all my statutes, and do that which is lawful and right, he shall surely live, he shall not die. All his transgressions that he hath committed, they shall not be mentioned unto him: in his righteousness that he hath done he shall live. Have I any pleasure at all that the wicked should die? saith the Lord God: and not that he should return from his ways and live? But when the righteous turneth away from his righteousness, and committeth iniquity, and doeth according to all the abominations that the wicked man doeth, shall he live? All his righteousness that he hath done shall not be mentioned: in his trespass that he hath trespassed, and in his sin that he hath sinned, in them shall he die" (Ezek. xviii.).

But in the same chapter, after declaring that He will judge every one according to his ways, the Lord calls most affectionately and earnestly upon all sinners to repent and turn from all their transgressions; so that iniquity shall not be their ruin. In great mercy He exclaims: "Cast away from you all your transgressions, whereby ye have transgressed; and make you a new heart and a new spirit; for why will ye die, O house of Israel? For I have no pleasure in the death of him that dieth, saith the Lord God: wherefore turn yourselves, and live ye;" and this call is to every sinner—to even the worst—it is the call of Divine love.

How plain, how simple is the Bible scheme of salvation! No unwillingness on our Heavenly Father's part to forgive and receive the returning sinner. He even beholds him when afar off; yes, and stands at the door of his heart, and knocks, and cries unto him, "Seek, and ye shall find; knock, and it shall be opened unto you." There is no intimation of either any vicarious punishment or a substitute being required.   Our heavenly Father, the Lord Jesus Christ—or God in Christ—is to-day reconciling the world unto Himself, and does not require being reconciled unto the sinner, for He is more ready to forgive the repentant sinner than any earthly parent is to forgive his erring but repentant child; so He has assured us.   The way of Life, as unveiled by Divine Revelation, although straight and narrow, is so plain that the wayfaring man, though a fool, need not err therein.   The sinner has but to turn his course and stop sinning, or violating the Divine commands, in the acts of his every-day life; and by thus seeking the Lord he opens his understanding and heart to the Divine Truth and love; and he will find strength gradually to banish evil thoughts and inclinations, and thus to become a new creature—"a man "— "an angel." Man has simply to open the door of his spirit, and co-operate with the Lord by striving to do as He requires, and the Lord will create in him a new heart, and renew in him a right spirit.

Regeneration is not the work of a day, and of course is not instantaneous; in fact, as we have seen in considering the first chapters of Genesis, it is the work of a Lifetime, and at this day is rarely completed in this world.   The Lord likens it to a birth, and says we must be born again. When we repent and acknowledge the Lord, and, looking to Him, sincerely resolve to stop sinning, and set about it, then is the beginning of a new life in us—a bare beginning, and day by day, as we strive to shun evils and do right, is the new resolve or will strengthened; but many a day of conflict is before us—yes, many a year before the old man is put off, and the new man put on, and we reach the stature of a renewed man.   All heavenly life is from the Lord, and if we live according to the laws of such life —the Commandments—spiritual health and heavenly life, which is real life, will as surely flow in, as natural life and health will, when we live according to natural laws. Cause and effect are as operative in the one case as in the other; —God is the bountiful giver in both cases, man is simply a recipient, he has no life of himself; without Divine aid he can do nothing, but he has only to ask aright to receive the aid he needs.

When the young man declared that "all these have I observed from my youth, then Jesus beholding him loved him, and said unto him, One thing thou lackest: go thy way, sell whatsoever thou hast, and give to the poor, and thou shalt have treasure in heaven; and come, take up the cross, and follow me." By this, in the spiritual sense, is understood that he should reject the falses which were the doctrine of the Jewish nation, and receive the doctrine of truth from the Lord; and that he was to undergo conflicts and temptations from falses, signified by taking up the cross and following the Lord, without which there could be no salvation. It is not enough to keep the commandments from selfish motives, but we must acknowledge the Lord in all things.

Turn we now to the last and closing chapter of the Divine Word, and we find the following sublime language: "Behold I come quickly, and my reward is with me, to give every man according as his work shall be. I am Alpha and Omega, the beginning and the end, the first and the last. Blessed are they that do his commandments, that they may have right to the tree of life, and may enter in through the gates into the city." Amen. Even so come Lord Jesus, into every understanding and every heart.

XXVIII.

The End of the World and the Second Coming of the Lord.

"AND as He sat upon the Mount of Olives, the disciples came unto Him privately, saying, Tell us, when shall these things be? and what shall be the sign of Thy coming, and of the end of the world?" (Matt. xxiv. 3.)

"The 'End of the World,'" says the Rev. Wm. B. Hayden, from whose excellent work for new readers, "Light on Last Things," we have selected a large portion of the contents of this section, "is a subject which has attracted considerable attention. That such an event is to take place has long been a doctrine in the Christian world. It has been supposed that this habitable globe will be destroyed, the ground or earth be consumed by fire, the stars fall from the visible heavens overhead, the heavens themselves being rolled together like a scroll, be swept from existence, the history of nations cease, and the birth or propagation of mankind come to an end.

"These views have been drawn from the sacred Scripture. Two classes of passages in the Bible have been supposed to teach or imply them, viz.: first, those in which, as in the above, the end of the world is distinctly spoken of, and secondly, those others in which the sun, moon, and stars are spoken of as falling from their places or being darkened, the sea being no more, and the earth as being destroyed, or purified, or burned up by fire.

"We believe, according to the repeated declarations made by the Lord in the volume of His Word, that He hath created the earth and established it that it may abide for ever; that He hath given it fixed foundations that it cannot be moved; that He made it to be inhabited, and that He hath given it as a permanent possession to the children of men. 'One generation passeth away and another cometh, but the earth abideth for ever.'

"We are told by Swedenborg that the object which our heavenly Father has in view is the formation of a heaven out of the human race, which may go on increasing in purity, in happiness, and in numbers to eternity. The earth, therefore, is required as a seminary for heaven—as a place for the birth and education of the human race—as a place from which the population of heaven may be continually increased by the emigration of good people from this world to the other through the process of natural death.

" Hence we believe that the earth will endure; that men will not cease to be born and grow up on this planet. No outward change will come to break up the onward flow of human history. The nations will go on and develop as heretofore. The stars will move on in their courses, and all the visible heavens remain as they are. The solid framework of the globe will abide. Its surface will remain undisturbed, save as it may be gradually altered by the operation of certain geological forces which are constantly at work. The population of the globe will increase, and one who should revisit this earth a thousand years from now—a hundred thousand years from now—will find it much as it is at present in its essential features; only more populous, civilization more advanced, and more widely extended, the Gospel more diffused, more unity of sentiment on the great themes of religion, and men on the whole, at the end of each great cycle, possessed of more wisdom and endowed with greater degrees of goodness, morality, and social order.

"It will naturally be asked, then, How do we dispose of the two classes of passages in Scripture commonly understood to predict the destruction of the world? And to this question we will endeavor briefly to reply.

" 1. When we lay aside our common translation of the Bible and turn to the Greek Testament, we do not find the ' end of the *world* ' foretold at all. There is no such expression there. Nor is there any phrase or expression that answers to it.

" There is in the Greek a common and familiar word to express our idea of the visible world. And that word is *Kosmos*. It is peculiarly and distinctively fitted to translate it, standing in the Greek mind for just the idea that our common word *world* does in the English mind; meaning sometimes visible nature, and sometimes also the men inhabiting visible nature. Now this word was familiar to the writers of the New Testament in just this sense, and they constantly employed it in this sense. Whenever they desired to speak of the world of nature, or of the world of men inhabiting nature, they used the term *Kosmos*. It occurs no less than a hundred and ninety-one times in this sense in the New Testament, and is always so translated in our common version. We see, therefore, what they said when they wanted to say *world;* they said *Kosmos*.

"Now this phrase which we are here considering, 'end of the world,' occurs seven times in our copies of the New Testament; five times in Matthew, and twice in the Epistles of Paul. But in these seven cases the word *Kosmos* is not used. It is never said that the *Kosmos* is going to come to an end, but another term is employed. The word *Aiön* is introduced to denote that which closes up or comes to an end. It is always the end of the *Aiön* that is foretold, and of the *Aiön* only. Now this is a term which relates to time, expressing the idea of duration or length. It answers very nearly to our word *age;* and means the period or cycle through which anything lasts. This will be found by consulting the common lexicons of New Testament Greek. Different things have their aiön or age, the period through which they endure. Thus the age of man is said to be seventy years; a tree has its age; an empire has its aiön or period of endurance. And so there are great aiöns or ages, or periods in the Church, under successive Divine dispensations, and the aiön or age is the time during which a dispensation lasts. Thus the period from Adam to Noah constituted one of these ages or Divine dispensations, which was brought to an end by the flood. The Jewish aiön, age, or dispensation, commencing from the call of Abraham, or from Moses, was finished or came to an end when our Lord appeared in the world.

"In two of these seven instances where this phrase is used in the New Testament it is applied to the Jewish dispensation, viz.: 1 Cor. x. 11, and Heb. ix. 26. The Apostle refers to the termination of the Jewish age, the Jewish order of things in the Church, saying in one place, 'Now all these things happened unto them for examples: and they are written for our admonition, upon whom *the ends of the world* are come.' Here we see that the Apostle declares himself and brethren to be living at the time of the *end of the world,* if we accept the common translation. But he did not mean to say that. He says that they are living at the end of an *aiōn* or a series of *aiōns,* meaning thereby the end of the Jewish age or dispensation, and of those which had preceded; and hence Conybeare and Howson (clergymen of the Church of England, who have given us the best translation of the Epistles) render this passage, 'Now all these things befell them as shadows of things to come; and they are written for our warning, on whom *the ends of the ages* are come.' This is the proper translation.

"So, in the other passage, Heb. ix. 26, speaking of our Lord, the Apostle says: 'But now once in the *end of the world* hath He appeared to put away sin by the sacrifice of Himself.'

"Now, if we accept the common translation, the end of the world was to be then, at the first coming of our Lord. But it did not happen then. Nor did the Apostle mean to say that it would. Conybeare and Howson render this passage, 'But now once *in the end of the ages* hath He appeared, to do away sin by the sacrifice of Himself.' This is the correct translation, for the word here occurs in the plural, as in the other passage just cited. Dr. Robinson, in his lexicon of the New Testament, says that the Apostle in these two instances undoubtedly refers to the end of the Jewish dispensation; and such is the common consent of scholars.

In Matthew, in the five instances named, the word occurs each time in the singular, *the end of the age,* and is used by our Lord to designate the time when the last judgment should occur in the world of the departed, the first Christian age or apostolical dispensation cease, and the age and dispensation of the latter-day church, *i. e.* the New Jerusalem, should commence. In the writings of the New Jerusalem this phrase is translated *the consummation of the age*, which is equivalent to the closing or winding up of the dispensation; a rendering which is now everywhere concurred in by the best scholarship of the time.

"Thus, it will be perceived, that, in accordance with our Lord's words, we are not looking for the destruction of the world, nor for violent commotions in visible, material nature, but for important changes, and the commencement of a new order of things with respect to the church, both in the spiritual world and in the natural world; or in the world of spirits and in the world of men; a new age already commenced, and now progressing."

The material universe and all things in it having been created by the Lord, every natural thing and object corresponds, as we have seen, to spiritual things. We read in the holy Word that "the Lord God is a Sun," and Swedenborg assures us that He is the sun of the spiritual world, to which the natural sun corresponds. Thus, according to the science of correspondences, the material sun corresponds to the spiritual sun, or the Lord; the light from the sun corresponds to the divine truth, for truth is spiritual light; the heat of the sun corresponds to the divine love, for love is spiritual heat. The light and heat of the material sun illuminate and warm the body and material earth, as truth and love from the Lord do the spirit of man and the mental earth.

"Now, in the church, the first thing is charity, or more properly perhaps, love, heavenly love—love to God and love to man. This is the central principle. And when this love is vigorous and active and alive in the church, then the sun shines, for the Lord, who is the real sun of the spiritual universe, sheds down the light of His countenance upon us. We see Him as He is; while we are warmed and vivified by the rays of His Spirit."

The eyes correspond to the understanding, for they receive natural light as the latter does spiritual light, or truth. The heart corresponds to the will, or affections; for it is easy to perceive that it serves the same purpose in the material body that the will does in the spiritual body. Paul assures us that "there is a spiritual body, and there is a natural body." The material, being but the clothing of the spiritual, must correspond to the latter in every particular, for the material has been fashioned and moulded into form by the spiritual.

The natural clouds and atmosphere modify and adapt the light and heat of the natural sun to man's natural eyes; they therefore correspond to the clouds of heaven, or the literal sense of the sacred Scriptures, which modifies and adapts the divine truth and love, or spiritual light and heat, to man's spiritual vision. The clouds in which the Lord was to come, then, were the clouds of the letter of His Holy Word.

"Now the Lord makes His appearance in these clouds, the types and symbols of the letter of His Word, as soon as the heavenly meaning of the symbols are made clear, and they all are seen to relate to Him. In the revelation of the spiritual sense of the Word, which is everywhere veiled in its letter, every type, every figure, and every circumstance, in history or psalm or prophecy, is seen to relate to the Lord, and to represent His work for and within human souls. And it is in the accomplishment of this purely divine work of opening the Holy Scriptures, and revealing for the church the existence, nature, and particular truths of their spiritual sense that the Lord comes in the clouds of heaven. *He* comes, for the whole Word reveals Him, and His work; He comes in the *clouds* because they are the images of the letter of the Word, which, being interpreted, reveal Him. This is known because it is an accomplished fact; and the event has explained and proved the Apocalypse."—*Rev. L. P. Mercer.*

The sun which was to be darkened at His coming was

not the material sun, but the heavenly sun, or the Lord.
When darkness prevails in the world, it is not because the
sun does not shine, but because either the earth turns
from the sun, or some opaque object intervenes between
the sun and the earth. It is precisely so in regard to the
spiritual sun; for the Lord's truth and love, or spiritual
light and heat, ever flow down through the Holy Scriptures to man; but spiritual darkness is caused by man's
turning from the Lord and His Word to the traditions of
men, and his own self-derived intelligence, and coming to
love himself, power, money, and sensual gratifications
more than he loves the Lord and his neighbor.

"Thus, when charity wanes or dies out, or, as our Lord
expresses it, when true Christian 'love waxes cold,' then
it is said in the prophets that the sun goes down or becomes darkened; because, as we at such times withdraw
from the Lord, hiding, as it were, our faces from Him, the
light of His countenance fails to reach us, ceasing thus to
shine upon and influence us."

The moon, giving but a reflected light with comparatively little heat, corresponds to faith; and its becoming
as blood, denotes that true faith in the Lord would be
destroyed.

"That is, when there is an eclipse of faith in the church,
when there is doubt and obscurity, and only a half-way belief in the higher spiritual truths taught in the Scriptures,
men knowing hardly what to believe, then the moon is
said to withdraw her shining, or to be turned to blood, the
appearance presented in a literal eclipse."

The stars of heaven, which were to fall to the earth,
were not the material stars, but the knowledges of goodness and truth, or spiritual stars, seen and revealed in the
sacred Scriptures to guide our footsteps in states of mental
darkness and doubt, and to which our Saviour appealed in
hours of temptation. These glorious truths, or stars, do
indeed fall to the earth when man drags them down to the
justification of a perverted, sensual, earthly and evil life,

expecting to escape the legitimate consequences of his acts, and to reach heaven in the end by an easier way than by striving daily and earnestly to live a life according to the commandments and the Lord's sayings.

"When the knowledges of Divine and heavenly things, the teaching of Holy Scripture, fade from the memories of men, and they forget them, no longer recurring to them in thought, but grope on without them, immersed in the thought and feeling of selfish and worldly things, then the stars are said to fall from their places, or to cease from shining, and so disappear. For at such times the whole heaven becomes dark; men no longer look up. There is no longer any illumination as to spiritual things. And He who came to be the light of the world is no longer able to shine at such times, or in such a class of minds, by any of the lamps of His truth.

"Such being the meaning of this symbolism, therefore, at one place in the Prophet Isaiah, where the New Jerusalem is spoken of, after it shall have arrived at its full, and so, a happy and prosperous state of the church is depicted as coming in the latter times, there a contrary form of speaking is employed; and to the church there addressed it is said, 'Thy sun shall no more go down, neither shall thy moon withdraw itself; for the Lord shall be thine everlasting light, and the days of thy mourning shall be ended;' whereby is signified and meant the last or full state of the true Christian Church in the latter times; described also in the last chapter of Revelation, in which charity or love shall no more decay, nor genuine, rational, and living faith become extinct."

It will be seen, as has already been intimated, that the coming of the Son of Man in the clouds of heaven was not to be in the material clouds of earth, but in the Word in its literal sense—which constitutes the clouds of heaven—revealing its spirit and life; for it is through the letter of the Word that man receives spiritual light and heat, or truth and love, as he receives natural light and heat through the natural clouds and atmosphere.

The Holy City, New Jerusalem, which was to descend from the Lord out of heaven, at the time of His second coming, was not to be a literal city of twelve thousand furlongs, of equal length, breadth and height, but a new church or dispensation to be established by the Lord at the end of the first Christian Church or dispensation. A city corresponds to a church as to doctrine, for men dwell in a city naturally as they do in a church spiritually. The gates of a city correspond to the introductory truths which lead to the church; the streets of a city correspond to all things of truth which lead to good, or all things of faith which lead to love and charity, in which men should abide, and whereas truths become of good, and thus trans, parent from good, the street of the New Jerusalem is said to be pure gold as transparent glass. The foundations of a wall signify the knowledges of truth, whereupon doc trinals are founded, and the walls of a city correspond to the truths and doctrines in the letter of the sacred Scrip tures by which the church is defended and preserved. That Jerusalem signifies the church in the language of the sacred Scriptures has been recognized among Christians, and it is manifest that the New Jerusalem must signify a new church.

There are not wanting commentators, who, within the last few years, simply by studying the Scriptures, without a knowledge of the revelations contained in the writings of Swedenborg, have come to the conclusion that the lan guage predicting the end of the world, and the Second Coming, is figurative or symbolical. "Thus," says Rev. Wm. B. Hayden, "writers increase who give up all belief in a physical catastrophe. An opening of the Divine prophecies according to the laws of correspondence ren ders clear all the subjects to which they relate; it removes the obscurities and brings us face to face with those great realities of which the Bible treats. It enlightens our minds by disclosing the actual meaning of the Scriptures and placing before our thought the enduring truths of heaven and the church.

"We have already seen they are the interpretations which the Scriptures themselves, when rightly examined, induce us to put upon them. They are the Lord's own commentary on His own book. They express exactly what the Bible says and means when it is allowed to bring out its whole thought.

"It is the mode of interpretation that our Lord and His apostles applied to the Old Testament Scriptures when they came and told the Jews that they were no longer to look for the establishment of a great earthly kingdom, but only for a new spiritual kingdom ; that the Messiah, instead of being a great earthly Monarch, of vast power and influence, sitting upon the literal throne of David, was a spiritual Monarch, ruling by the convincing power of His truth, and through the influences of His Spirit upon the hearts of men. It seems to us that Christianity is a broader, more interesting, more real, more important fact than a universal Jewish empire would have been though it had covered the whole earth ; while the spiritual fact is far more useful to mankind than the literal fact would have been.

"And so now, we get clear, definite, rational, consistent views of the higher, nobler, and more enduring realities by opening our eyes to the spiritual sense and meaning of Divine prophecy and Holy Scripture, than by confining our thoughts to the mere letter or outward symbol of the Bible; the shell or husk in which the pure wheat of heavenly truth lies enclosed, and to some concealed.

"An event which affects the mental and spiritual states of mankind, operating to mould their character and their destiny through a succession of ages, is far greater, and holds a better place in the memories of men, than one which affects merely physical bodies, like convulsions of the earth. How little do we remember or care to recall the great eruption of Vesuvius which overwhelmed the cities of Pompeii and Herculaneum ! The simple preaching of Paul in the city of Rome was a more significant fact, and one which lives more vividly in the hearts of men."

If the reader would understand fully the prophecies in regard to the end of the world and the Second Coming of the Lord, and especially if he would understand the signs of the present times, and the wonderful age in which we live, he must read the writings of Emanuel Swedenborg, especially the "Apocalypse Revealed;" and a new world of affection, thought and beauty, will be opened to his astonished vision.

XXIX.

The Resurrection.

"There is a natural body and there is a spiritual body." In order that we may understand clearly the great doctrine of the Resurrection, it is all-important that we bear in mind this enunciation of the Apostle. He does not say there is now a natural body, and there shall hereafter be a spiritual body; but he says, there is a natural body, and there is a spiritual body. If we remember this great truth, the scriptural doctrine of the Resurrection will be found to be very clear and beautiful.

We should also bear in mind, that the Scriptures treat of two kinds of life, two kinds of death, two kinds of resurrection, and two kinds of graves. First, Of natural life, and of spiritual life or the life of regeneration—life of love to the Lord and the neighbor, the result of the new birth, or of being born again. Second, Death of the material body, and being dead in trespasses and sins—the state of man previous to regeneration; and finally, if man does not allow himself to be regenerated, the death of all heavenly affections or of love to the Lord and his neighbor in his soul, when he comes to be completely ruled by selfishness—the second death. Third, The resurrection of the spiritual body from the natural body when the latter dies, and the resurrection from the unregenerate state to the heavenly state, which results from the new birth. Fourth, The grave of the natural body, from which the spirit is raised when the body dies, and the grave denoted by the lifeless and dead state of those who are dead in trespasses and sins.

Man, while he lives here, is a spirit clothed with matter. The material body is constantly changing; particles are being worn out and cast off; and new ones are received, which take their place. The body increases during childhood and youth, remains comparatively stationary during adult life, and gradually withers as old age approaches. Why all these changes? Do the particles of matter, or the articles of food we eat, possess the power and capacity of changing themselves into living structures? and do they possess the intelligence to see when their services are no longer needed?

Every one can but see, that the power and intelligence to organize themselves into living structures are not contained in the materials from which our bodies are formed; but that there is a living force within the body, which moulds and organizes these natural substances into muscles, bones, nerves, and various other tissues. If this is so, it follows that this living principle must occupy every part of the body, or the part could never have been organized, and would not now be alive. The matter, then, of which our bodies are composed, is made alive by the indwelling spirit, and our material bodies are but the clothing of our spirits. It follows as a necessary consequence that the spirit is in the form of the body—that it is, in the language of St. Paul, "a spiritual body." We see daily manifestations of the quality or character of man's spirit in his external words and acts; for the body only speaks and acts as it is acted upon by the spirit; and the affections and thoughts which are manifested in acts and speech are spiritual and not material. Who does not see that a man is a man from the spirit and not from the material body?

With this view of man, it is not difficult to understand

what is meant by the resurrection from the dead, a..d when it occurs.   It is not difficult to understand the apostolic doctrine upon this subject, and the Apostle's beautiful illustrations. "It is sown a natural body, it is raised a spiritual body;" or perhaps, more correctly translated, "A natural body is sown; a spiritual body is raised; for there is a natural body, and there is a spiritual body," says the Apostle.

But previous to this positive assertion, the Apostle had been giving some familiar illustrations in regard to the resurrection, and the resurrection body. He says, "But some will say, How are the dead raised up? and with what body do they come? Thou fool, that which thou sowest is not quickened except it die. And that which thou sowest, thou sowest not that body that shall be, but bare grain, it may chance of wheat, or of some other grain." How clearly and unequivocally does the Apostle affirm, in the above passage, that the body which is cast off at death is not the body that is to be raised up; "but," says the Apostle, "God giveth it a body as it hath pleased him, and to every seed his own body." And, as if afraid some might mistake his meaning, and suppose that the natural body is to be raised, he continues: "All flesh is not the same flesh; but there is one kind of flesh of men, another flesh of beasts, another of fishes, and another of birds. There are also celestial bodies, and bodies terrestrial; but the glory of the celestial is one, and the glory of the terrestrial is another. There is one glory of the sun, and another glory of the moon, and another glory of the stars; for one star differeth from another star in glory. So also is the resurrection of the dead. It is sown in corruption, it is raised in incorruption; it is sown in dishonor, it is raised in glory; it is sown in weakness, it is raised in power" (1 Corinthians, 15th chapter).

All this is evidently intended to show that our material, natural bodies are not to be raised, but that they return to dust, nevermore to be required or desired by us. If this were not true, there would be no sense in his illustrations. The Apostle compares the death of the natural body, and the resurrection, to the sowing of grain; and a very beautiful illustration it is. We cast the kernel of wheat into the earth, and there is within it a living force, or spirit if you please; and there springs forth from the seed a new plant, capable of bearing seed in its turn. So long as the seed is not cast into the earth, its living force remains inactive; but when duly moistened and warmed, as the little seed is decomposed and disappears, there springs forth the new blade and leaf. Thus the Apostle would have us understand it is with man, when this natural body dies and returns to its mother dust; there then comes forth from it a spiritual body, as the new plant comes forth from the dying seed. The resurrection, then, takes place at death. Then the spiritual body or soul is raised from the dead body, and the latter is decomposed.

But let the kernel of grain be decomposed, and return to dust without a new plant arising as it dies, and we all know that there can be no resurrection; no new plant can ever come forth from the dust of which the seed or old plant was composed. Now, if the Apostle's illustration is correct, or a good one, so it must be with man; if his body dies and returns to dust, without there springing forth, or being raised from it, at the very time it dies, the spiritual body, there can be no resurrection.

It will be seen that the Apostle speaks of the resurrection in the present tense, as occurring at the time when the body is sown, and he does not speak of it as a future event.

We are nowhere in the Bible taught that the material body, when it is once put off at death, is ever to be raised again.

In the revelations made by the Lord, through Emanuel Swedenborg, to all who are willing to receive Him at His Second Coming, we are told that "man rises immediately after death, and then appears to himself in the body altogether as in the world, with such a face, with such members, arms, hands, feet, belly, loins; yea, also, when he sees himself and touches himself, he saith that he is a man as in the world." (*A. C.* 5078.)

Again we are told: "The spirit of man, after the death of the body, appears in the spiritual world in the human form, altogether as in the natural world; he enjoys also the faculty of seeing, of hearing, of speaking, of feeling, as in the world; and he is endowed with every faculty of thinking, of willing, and of acting, as in the world. In a word, he is a man as to all things and every particular, except that he is not encompassed with that gross body which he had in the world; he leaves that when he dies, nor does he ever resume it. This continuation of life is what is understood by the resurrection. The reason why men believe that they are not to rise again before the last judgment, when also every visible object of the world is (expected) to perish, is because they have not understood the Word; and because sensual men place their life in the body, and believe that unless this were to live again, it would be all over with the man. The life of man after death is the life of his love and the life of his faith; hence, such as his love and such as his faith had been, when he lived in the world, such his life remains to eternity. It is the life of hell with those who have loved themselves and the world above all things; and the life of heaven with those who have loved God above all things, and their neighbor as themselves. The latter are they that have faith, but the former are they that have not faith. The life of heaven is what is called eternal life; the life of hell is what is called spiritual death."—*N. J. D.* 223–7.

The Lord while on earth declared, "I am the resurrection and the Life; he that believeth in me, though he were dead, yet shall he live; and he that liveth and believeth in me, shall never die" (John xi. 26).

When a man is dead in trespasses and in sins, the Lord alone can raise him, when he sincerely believes on Him;

and when he does thus raise him, he shall never die: by
this we cannot understand that he is not to suffer natural
death, for we know that all men die naturally; but we are
to understand that he is not to suffer spiritual death, or to
become again dead in trespasses and sins. He will therefore live right on, for it is not in regard to natural death
that the Lord is speaking. Again, the Lord says: "Every
one that seeth the Son and believeth on him, shall have
everlasting life, and I will raise him up at the last day."
That is, he will transplant him into eternal life, when the
last day of natural life comes, and he shall live to eternity.

If we would understand the plain teachings of the
sacred Scriptures upon the subject we are considering, we
must ever remember, as we read, that when they speak of
death and the resurrection, they do not always refer to
natural death, and the resurrection of the material body
is not even noticed once, nor do they always refer to the
resurrection of the spirit of man from his worn-out body
at death ; but they often refer to the regeneration of man,
or to his being raised out of the low, ignorant, sensual, and
selfish state into which our race has sunken at this day,
up into a state of heavenly light and life by the Lord,
when man looks to Him, and hears and tries to keep His
sayings.

Therefore the Apostle says: "Awake, thou that sleepest,
and arise from the dead, and Christ shall give thee light"
(Eph. v. 14). No one will for a moment suppose that the
Apostle was addressing dead bodies, or the souls of dead
men.

In reading the writings of St. Paul, it is all-important
that we notice that the Apostle does not always clearly
separate, so that we readily perceive it, in his manner of
speaking, the idea of resurrection from that of regeneration; and it is often impossible to apply what he says
of the resurrection to any but the regenerate.

The Apostle distinctly teaches us, in this chapter, that

even if the material body should be raised, it could not enter heaven, for he says: "Now this I say, brethren, that flesh and blood cannot inherit the kingdom of God; neither doth corruption inherit incorruption" (1 Cor. xv. 50).

If we turn to the fifth chapter of 2 Corinthians, after having declared that our light affliction, which is but for a moment, worketh for us a far more exceeding and eternal weight of glory, the Apostle goes on to show that this is to be entered upon as soon as our earthly body dies. He says: "For we know that if our earthly tabernacle were dissolved, we have a building of God, a house not made with hands, eternal in the heavens." Consequently, by this house in the heavens, as opposed to the tabernacle of the natural body, he means the spiritual body, which, in his first epistle, he declares man already possesses, and in which the soul of the faithful will dwell after death to eternity. "For this," he adds, "we groan, earnestly desiring to be clothed upon with our house which is from heaven: if so be that, being clothed, we shall not be found naked."

How plain is the Apostle's teaching, that the true Christian, while working out his salvation with fear and trembling, as the work of regeneration progresses, is daily being clothed upon by his house which is from heaven. The beautiful garments of truth which he is receiving into his understanding from God's Word, and which convey to his heart the Divine love, and thus nourish his spirit, in accordance with the Lord's words when he declares that man shall not live by bread alone, but by every word which proceeds out of the mouth of God shall he live, are building up the house not made with hands; so that, when he is stripped of the natural body, his spiritual body shall not appear destitute of heavenly truths and graces, and present the form and image of all our natural corruptions, of which nakedness and shame are constantly predicated in the language of inspiration.

The Apostle continues: "For we that are in this tabernacle do groan, being burdened: not for that we would be unclothed;" that is, not anxious to escape from the cares and troubles of this world by death, until clothed upon by being invested by a truly heavenly as well as a spiritual form. And the reason which he gives for preferring to be clothed upon, to dying, is "that mortality might be swallowed up of life;" or that he might bring his natural appetites and passions under subjection to the spiritual or new man, and thus be prepared for such glorious investments as the faithful have a right to expect immediately after death. Accordingly he presently adds: "Therefore we are always confident, knowing that while we are at home in the body, we are absent from the Lord; we are confident, I say, willing rather to be absent from the body, and to be present with the Lord."

How clear it is that the Apostle expected when death should dissolve his earthly tabernacle or body, that he would immediately stand forth in the presence of the Lord, not naked, but clothed with a beautiful angelic form; a house not made with hands, but formed from the eternal and heavenly principles of goodness and truth from the Lord.

What a sublime and practical doctrine is this, dear reader! That we are daily, by every thought we harbor, by every word we speak, and every act we do, perfecting and building up an angelic form within us, and obscuring our spiritual nakedness, by being clothed by beautiful garments, or sublime truths from God's holy Word: or we are, on the other hand, becoming more and more naked, by neglecting and rejecting the truths of revelation, and more and more deformed by harboring evil thoughts, speaking false and harmful words, and doing evil acts.

The Apostle then teaches a practical doctrine in regard to the resurrection—that death in this world is resurrection into the next, or spiritual world—and if we examine we shall find that all Scripture, as well as reason, are in harmony with this doctrine.

The Lord, from the cross, declared to the penitent thief: "Verily I say unto thee, to-day shalt thou be with me in paradise" (Luke xxiii. 43).

In the parable of the rich man and Lazarus we read: "The beggar died, and was carried by angels into Abraham's bosom: the rich man also died, and was buried, and in hell he lifted up his eyes, being in torments, and seeth Abraham afar off, and Lazarus in his bosom. And he cried and said, Father Abraham, have mercy on me, and send Lazarus that he may dip the tip of his finger in water and cool my tongue; for I am tormented in this flame."

In this passage the Lord not only teaches that men arise immediately after death, and begin to receive their reward, according to the deeds done in the body, but he also teaches that a man's spiritual body has a bosom, tongue, finger, and consequently all the other organs which the natural body has here.

At the Lord's transfiguration we read: "And behold there talked with him two men, which were Moses and Elias, who appeared in glory, and spoke of His decease which he should accomplish at Jerusalem." Moses and Elias, although their natural bodies were long dead, were here seen as men, of course possessing spiritual bodies, by Peter and those who were with him (Luke ix. 30, 31).

The Lord Jesus, in His reply to the Sadducees, teaches most explicitly that the time-honored Prophets are not dead, but are living; of course in the spiritual world, raised up from their dead earthly bodies. He says: "But as touching the resurrection of the dead, have ye not read that which was spoken unto you by God, saying, I am the God of Abraham, and the God of Isaac, and the God of Jacob? God is not the God of the dead, but of the living" (Matt. xxii. 31, 32).

Now if it is true that God is the God of Abraham, Isaac and Jacob, as He declares He is, and if He is not the God of the dead, it follows necessarily that they are living.

How exactly does this accord with the teachings of Solomon, when he says: "If the silver cord be loosed, or the golden bowl be broken, or the pitcher be broken at the fountain, or the wheel broken at the cistern, then shall the dust return to the earth as it was; and the spirit shall return unto God who gave it" (Eccl. xii. 6, 7). We have not the slightest intimation that they are ever to be reunited, but we are assured that the dead body is to be returned to the dust as it was, and we see that it does steadily crumble back to its native elements.

The Apostle John, when caught up to heaven, "Beheld a great multitude which no man could number, of all nations, and kindreds, and peoples, and tongues, standing before the throne and before the Lamb, clothed in white robes," uniting with the angels in their everlasting song of praise. The Apostle asked who these persons were? The angel informed him, that they were "those who came up out of great tribulation, and had washed their robes and made them white in the blood of the Lamb." "Therefore," the angel adds, "they are before the throne of God, and serve Him day and night in the temple" (Rev. iv. 1, 6).

No one questions but that those were men, and in the human form, having bodies which could be seen by spiritual eyes. Can any one suppose that this vast multitude, enjoying angelic bliss as exquisite as can be conceived, are again to resume their bodies of clay? how absurd and opposed to Scripture is such an idea!

It may be well to notice a few of the passages which are supposed to teach a resurrection of the material body. And first the celebrated one from the nineteenth chapter of Job, 25, 26, 27. "I know that my Redeemer liveth, and that he shall stand at the latter day upon the earth; and though after my skin, worms destroy this body, yet in my flesh shall I see God, whom I shall see for myself, and mine eyes shall behold, and not another; though my reins be consumed within me." Job had been sorely afflicted,

with boils from the sole of his foot unto his crown; he
was wasted away to mere skin and bone as it were. He
says of his condition: "My bone cleaveth to my skin as
to my flesh, and I am escaped with the skin of my teeth."
And yet, notwithstanding all this, in his confidence in the
Lord, he expresses his conviction, in the passage we have
read, that he shall not die, but shall see God interposing
in his behalf, while he is still living in the flesh.

By looking at the passage which has been read from
Job, which is supposed by some to teach the resurrection
of the body, we will find that the words, worms and body,
are in italics; which denote that they were not in the
original, but were added by the translator.

If we turn to the last chapter of Job we read: "Then
Job answered the Lord and said: I know that thou canst
do everything, and that no thought can be withholden
from thee. * * * I have heard of thee by the hearing
of the ear; but now mine eye seeth thee." And we read
still further that the "Lord turned the captivity of Job,
when he prayed for his friends; also, the Lord gave Job
twice as much as he had before." "After this lived Job a
hundred and forty years, and saw his sons, and his son's
sons, even four generations. So Job died, being old and
full of days." What a remarkable accomplishment of all
that he expected of the Lord, as expressed when he
exclaimed, "I shall see for myself, and mine eyes shall
behold, and not another."

In the fifth chapter of John the Lord says, "Verily,
verily, I say unto you, he that heareth my word and believeth on him that sent me, hath everlasting life, and
shall not come into condemnation, but is passed from
death unto life." In this verse the Lord is evidently
speaking to and of living men; therefore He cannot mean
that they have passed from natural death unto a resurrection of the body, or even of the spirit. He manifestly is
speaking of the spiritual regeneration of man, or of his
passing from a low and dead state, spiritually, to a living

state, by hearing and believing on the Lord and keeping his sayings.

If we would correctly understand what follows, in the next few verses, it will be well to bear in mind that we have in the verse just read positive evidence that the Lord is not speaking of natural death and life. In the next verse we read:

"Verily, verily, I say unto you, the hour is coming, and now is, when the dead shall hear the voice of the Son of God; and they that hear shall live."

Now if we understand that he refers to those who are dead in trespasses and sins, it is all very plain; for wickèd men, while they live in this world, may hear the voice of the Son of God and live, for they are yet enjoying a state of probation.

But if he referred to those who are dead physically, and to the resurrection of their dead bodies, we may certainly inquire what has become of their resurrected bodies; did they again die? and, if so, is there any hope of their again being raised? How manifest it is that the Lord is not speaking of those who died naturally, or of the resurrection of the natural body; but he is speaking of the dead who are yet living in this world, and the life to which he refers is not physical life. Let us read on:

"For as the Father hath life in Himself, so hath He given to the Son to have life in Himself." Surely he does not here refer to physical life. "And hath given Him authority to execute judgment also, because He is the Son of man. Marvel not at this; for the hour is coming in the which all that are in their graves shall hear His voice, and shall come forth; they that have done good, unto the resurrection of life; and they that have done evil, unto the resurrection of damnation."

We have found that the Lord in these verses is not speaking of natural death and life; and we shall find that it is equally clear that he does not refer to natural graves, and the resurrection of the natural body, in the passage just read. He evidently refers to a judgment about to be performed, for He declares that authority is given Him to execute judgment, and He does not say that the hour will come at the end of hundreds or thousands of years, but that the hour is coming—that is, it is near at hand— when this judgment is to be executed. If we turn over to the 12th chapter of John, 31st verse, he assures us that that judgment was then being performed, for he declares:

"Now is the judgment of this world; now shall the prince of this world be cast out." Here then, beyond the possibility of a doubt, the hour of which he spoke as coming, had arrived, when all that were in the graves should hear his voice and come forth; they that had done good, unto the resurrection of life, and they that had done evil, unto the resurrection of damnation.

For judgment came He into the world. All that were in the graves heard his voice; the good came forth to the resurrection of life, the evil unto the resurrection of damnation. Then was the prince of this world cast out.

Were the natural bodies of those who were dead raised at that judgment? or were their natural graves disturbed at all? We know that they were not; for most of us have doubtless seen, as Egyptian mummies, the dead bodies of those who died long before that judgment, still invested in their winding sheets. And another circumstance worthy of our most serious attention attended that judgment and resurrection. The time of that judgment was unknown to and unnoticed by the great mass of mankind; in fact, by all except the few to whom the Lord was speaking. Men, we read, are to be judged according to the deeds done here in the body. It follows, of course, that this can only be done after the completion of man's natural life, and therefore the judgment must take place in the spiritual world; so that it was not strange that mankind generally knew nothing about that judgment.

The case of Elijah is supposed to form some proof of the possibility of the resurrection of the material body, and also that it will be raised. In reply we cannot do better than to make a quotation from that excellent work, "An Appeal to the Reflecting of all Denominations," by Rev. Samuel Noble. He says: "Quite evident, then, it is, that whatever became of Elijah's material body, it was not carried up into heaven; for quite evident it is, though the circumstance is generally overlooked, that the translation of Elijah was not seen by Elisha with the eyes of his body, but with those of his spirit. * * * Elisha had asked that a double portion of his master's spirit might be upon him; to which Elijah answered: 'Thou hast asked a hard thing; nevertheless if *thou see me* when I am taken from thee, it shall be so unto thee; but *if not*, it shall not be so' (2 Kings ii. 10). Elijah knew that the miraculous event about to take place would be imperceptible to any man in his natural state, and could not be beheld by Elisha, unless by special divine favor the sight of his spirit were opened to behold it; the granting then to Elisha of the favor of the opening of his spiritual sight was to be to him the earnest of the granting to him likewise of the other favor which he had requested. This therefore was done and distinctly recorded. 'And it came to pass, as they still went on, and talked, that behold there appeared a chariot of fire and horses of fire, and parted them both asunder; and Elijah went up by a whirlwind into heaven.' Certain it is that this chariot and horses of fire did not belong to the natural world, but that they were a spiritual appearance, and consequently not visible to the sight of man, unless he were put into a spiritual state proper for beholding it. That Elisha, then, was put into such a state is intimated by its being immediately added: 'And Elisha saw it,'—that is, saw the whole transaction, both the fiery chariot and horses and the transit of Elijah; 'and he cried, my father, my father, the chariot of Israel, and the horseman thereof.'"

Now if Elijah's natural body was to have been translated, there would have been no difficulty in Elisha's seeing it with his natural eyes. While in spiritual vision Elisha would know little of the things of the natural world, and Elijah's dead body might have been carried off by a natural whirlwind, or Elisha may have wandered from it, and therefore have seen it no more; or again, seeing its real occupant depart, he may have regarded it as worthy of no further consideration or remark.

If the reader would like to see every passage in the sacred Scriptures which is supposed to teach the doctrine of the resurrection of the natural body carefully examined, both as to translation and its true meaning, he will do well to obtain and read "Noble's Appeal."

The resurrection of our Lord and Saviour Jesus Christ occurred on the third day. "The crucifixion occurred on Friday afternoon, and early on the following Sunday morning a company of angels was seen around the tomb, and they gave the information that He had already risen, and was with *them* in their world. He soon appeared, too, to the women and to the other disciples. He became visible to them in His glorified body by an *opening of their spiritual eyes,* as we plainly read in Luke xxiv. 31, where it is said that, as He brake bread in their company, '*their eyes were opened,* and they knew Him.'

"Now, if our Lord's resurrection is a type of ours (and from the Scripture we know that it is), then our resurrection occurs on or about the third day after the decease of the mortal part, as soon as the spirit has had time to be entirely withdrawn from its former body, and the mind has recovered its wonted action.

"So the Prophet Hosea, in the sixth chapter, speaking of this subject in a passage that has been generally overlooked, says distinctly—first referring to the dissolution which the Lord works upon our mortal frames through disease, causing death—

'He hath torn, [but] He will heal us;
He hath smitten, [but] He will bind us up;

After *two days* will He revive us;
In the third day He will raise us up;
And we shall live in His sight.'

"What can be plainer than this? Though our mortal frames *are* dissolved, and we are *dead* in the sight of *men,* yet 'after *two days* He will revive us; on the third day He will raise us up, and we shall live in His sight,' and in the sight of angels, agreeably to our Lord's words already quoted, that '*to* HIM *all are living.'"—Light on Last Things.*

Death, we see, is not an instantaneous process, according to the Divine Word. So Swedenborg informs us that the separation between the soul and body is generally completed, and the resurrection occurs, about the third day after apparent death; but with more or less variety as to time in different cases, owing to the character of the disease, or the cause of death.

The Lord provides that the highest, or celestial angels, shall be present with every one, be he good or bad, when he dies, so that his first reception in the next life is most kind. And, says Swedenborg, "The celestial angels who thus minister to the resuscitated person, do not leave him, because they love every one; but if the spirit is such in quality that he cannot longer continue in the company of celestial angels, he feels a desire to depart from them. When he does, angels from the Lord's spiritual kingdom come to him."

So that the Lord and His angels never forsake the spirit; but if he is not satisfied with any angelic society, where love to the Lord and neighbor, and of obedience to the Divine commandments prevails, he voluntarily seeks his like in hell, or among those where selfishness, in its various forms, is predominant. But the Lord does not forsake him even there; for he permits suffering and punishments, restrained by angelic influences within reasonable bounds, to follow his thinking and doing evil, in his

10

new abode, to prevent him from sinking to lower depths
of evil, and consequent suffering.

The reader will find Swedenborg's "Heaven and Hell"
an exceedingly interesting and profitable book to read, if
he has any care for his eternal welfare; and to that work
we must refer him.

> " There is no death ! what seems so is transition,
>   This life of mortal breath,
> Is but a suburb of the life elysian,
>   Whose portal we call death."—*Longfellow.*

XXX.

State of Infants in the Other Life.

WHAT parent is there who has lost a little child by
death that has felt no interest in the fate of their
darling after it had left the tender care of its earthly
parents? The writer well remembers, although about
thirty years have passed since the sad event, watching
carefully with his wife the sick and, as the event proved,
dying couch of our then only child, a little boy about one
year old—a beautiful and promising child as we thought.
With what feelings of sadness and sorrow we closed his
eyes in death! and then, O then! the uncertainty, the
veil that was between us and the object of our affection!
Into whose keeping had he gone? how was he cared for?
why should the Lord place us in such darkness? were but
questions which had arisen with thousands thus circum-
stanced before us. With many tears we laid the mortal
remains of our dear one in an earthly grave—dust to dust.

One night my wife awoke from sleep in the greatest
excitement, sprang up in bed, and declared that she saw
our little boy; that he was sitting upon her lap, when a
beautiful lady appeared, one whom she recognized and
called by name, a playmate and companion of her younger
days, but who had died several years before this event.
She, with the most pleasant and kind expression, beckoned

our darling boy to come to her; he raised his little arms
and with expressions of joy passed to her, and was clasped
in her loving arms. At this instant the excitement was
too great, the curtain dropped, and my wife awoke as
above. It was all so real, so life-like, that we felt that it
was more than a dream and were comforted. How much
this event-had to do in preparing us for the full reception
of the disclosures in regard to the spiritual world, and the
doctrines of the New Jerusalem revealed by the Lord in
the writings of Emanuel Swedenborg, the reader will
perhaps be able to judge after reading the few extracts
which we propose to make from the above writings.

"As soon as infants are raised from the dead," says
Swedenborg, "which takes place immediately after their
decease, they are carried up into heaven, and delivered to
the care of angels of the female sex, who in the life of the
body loved infants tenderly, and at the same time loved
God. Since those angels when in the world loved all
infants from a sort of maternal tenderness, they receive
them as their own; and the infants also, from an affection
implanted in them, love them as their own mothers."—
Heaven and Hell.

Up into heaven, means not up in material space, but in
spiritual state. The angels attendant on little children,
we read, do always behold the face of our Father in the
heavens.

"Some believe," says Swedenborg, "that only the infants
who are born within the church are admitted into heaven,
but not those who are born out of the church; and they
assign as a reason that children born in the church are
baptized, and are initiated by baptism into the faith of the
church. But such persons are not aware that heaven is
not imparted to any one by baptism, nor by faith either;
for baptism is only instituted as a sign and memorial that
man is to be regenerated, and that it is possible for those
to be regenerated who are born in the church, since the
church possesses the Word, in which are contained the

divine truths by means of which regeneration is effected, and in the church the Lord is known, by whom it is accomplished. Be it known, therefore, that every infant or little child, let him be born where he may, whether in the church or out of it, whether of pious or wicked parents, is received when he dies by the Lord, and is educated in heaven, where he is instructed according to Divine Order, and is imbued with affections of good, and, through them, with knowledges of truth; and that afterwards, as he is perfected in intelligence and wisdom, he is introduced into heaven and becomes an angel. Every person who thinks from reason may be aware, that no one is born for hell, but all for heaven, and that if man goes to hell the blame is his own, but no blame can attach to infants or little children.

"When infants die, they are still infants in the other life. They possess the same infantile mind, the same innocence in ignorance, and the same tenderness in all things. They are only in rudimental states introductory to the angelic; for infants are not angels, but become angels. Every one, on his decease, is in a similar state of life to that in which he was in the world; an infant, in the state of infancy, a boy, in the state of boyhood, and a youth, a man, or an old man, in the state of youth, manhood, or old age. But the state of every one is afterwards changed."—*Heaven and Hell.*

"Many persons may imagine that infants are for ever infants among the angels in heaven. They who do not know what constitutes an angel, may be confirmed in this opinion from the images which are sometimes seen in churches, where angels are exhibited as infants. But the case is altogether otherwise. Intelligence and wisdom constitute an angel; and so long as infants are without intelligence and wisdom, although they are associated with angels, they are not yet angels. When they become intelligent and wise, then they first become angels. I have, indeed, been surprised to see that they then no longer appear as infants, but as adults, for they are then no longer of an infantile disposition, but of a more mature angelic character. Intelligence and wisdom produce this maturity. Infants appear more adult in proportion as they are perfected in intelligence and wisdom, and thus as youths and young men, because intelligence and wisdom constitute essential spiritual nourishment. That which nourishes their minds nourishes also their bodies, from correspondence, because the form of the body is nothing but an external form of the interiors. It is to be observed, that infants who grow up in heaven do not advance beyond early youth, but remain in that state to eternity. That I might be assured of this, it has been granted me to converse with some who were educated as infants in heaven, and who had grown up there. I have also spoken with some when they were infants, and afterwards with the same when they had become young men, and heard from them the progression of their life from the one age to the other." (*Ibid.*) .

As the child, we are told, grows up to, but does not advance beyond early youth, so, Swedenborg informs us, that those who die in old age, return gradually in appearance to the state of early youth, and remain thus forever.

XXXI.

On the State and Condition of the Heathen and Gentiles in another Life.

WE cannot do better than to make a few short extracts from a communication recently published from a Hindoo convert to Christianity, Dadoba Pandurung, of Bombay, entitled "A Hindoo Gentleman's Reflections respecting the works of Swedenborg, and the Doctrines of the New Jerusalem." He says:

"What parents, whether Christians or Heathen, I ask, would not feel a most heartfelt consolation in the fate after death, as it is described by Swedenborg, of the little

children, and of the millions of heathens who are daily
and hourly ushering into the next world, but who, from
their helpless and unavoidable condition, are precluded
from the benefits accessible to grown-up Christians of
mature age and consideration?

"Christianity, as is now taught and preached to the
world, appears to me to be almost silent on the important
question touching the fate and future destiny of that vast
and incalculable number of human beings who have died,
and who at this day are daily dying in total ignorance of
its voice ; not to speak of that inconceivable number of
human beings who had occupied and left this our earth
during a period of thousands of years previous to the
advent of the Lord Jesus Christ.

"But I am here thinking, and thinking quite naturally,
of those millions of millions of heathens who have died
and are daily dying for want of the requisite good in their
case, viz.: the blessings of Christianity. I am not referring to those who have led wicked and sinful lives—to
the avaricious and worldly men who have never turned to
their God with a penitent heart, for the fate of such persons is the same, whether they be in Christendom or in
heathendom; but I refer particularly to such Gentiles as
have led a virtuous life, of which it may be predicated that
it cannot be otherwise than pleasing in the sight of the
Lord, nor can it ever be affirmed that heathendom is altogether devoid of pious, good, and virtuous men and women,
for such an assertion, in my opinion, amounts to a gross
blasphemy. In reference to such queries as these, in order
to remove our over anxiety on the subject, we are no doubt
sometimes shown such small passages in the Old and New
Testament as Deut. x. 17; 2 Chron. xix. 1; Prov. xxiv.
12; Matt. xvi. 27; Rom. x. 6 to 14; Gal. vi. 7, 8; 1 Peter
i. 17, in the assurance that they will satisfy our curiosity.
But these are shown with such trembling hands and flat-
tering words, as to leave the general impression on the
minds of the heathens, that eternal damnation is their in-

evitable lot. In this state of universal diffidence and despondency, which affect the mind if not the heart of many a Christian minister in a greater or less degree, according to his natural temperament, when expressing his opinion on this point, the Church of the New Jerusalem comes forward with a degree of boldness and assurance which the Gentiles will surely hail with welcome, to promulgate its true doctrine on this most momentous question. This church explicitly teaches us that the heathens and Gentiles who have led a virtuous life will receive the truth in the world of spirits, have as much right to enter into the gates of heaven as the Christians themselves. In the case of the heathens there is a course of Christian knowledge and instructions which they have to go through, and which they had not had an opportunity to obtain while on the earth: but which the universal benevolence of the Heavenly Father of all mankind has provided for them in the intermediate state, under the loving care of ministering angels. These appear to me to be not only noble but correct sentiments, which must surely be confessed by those Christians who have not allowed their minds to be contracted by the preaching of bigoted and narrow-minded ministers.

"Then Swedenborg goes on reasoning very cogently, showing in the relation of his vision of heaven that good and pious heathens have as easy an entrance into heaven as the good and pious Christians themselves; of course, after their being perfected in the knowledge of the Lord, and of His unalterable mercy in having so far condescended as to have assumed the form of a man on our earth, to show to the whole human race the way of salvation—a fact on which most of the Christians have but a vague and imperfect notion. In one place in the same chapter, Swedenborg says, and says not without sufficient reason, that the Gentiles of the present day enter heaven more easily than Christians themselves in accordance with these words of the Lord in Luke: 'Then shall they come from

the east and from the west, and from the north and from
the south, and shall sit down in the kingdom of God.
And, behold, there are last—who shall be first, and there
are first who shall be last' (chapter xiii. 29–30). In these
words, and in fact in the whole description of his 'Heaven
and Hell,' Swedenborg appears to me to have actually taken
away the very sting out of the dread of eternal punishment, which the preaching and writing of a great body of
the Christian clergy appears to inflict on the whole of
heathendom, and on by far the greatest portion of Christendom; for according to their teaching no one shall be saved
except those few who conform themselves to the dogmas
of their respective churches.   Strictly speaking, according
to the spirit of Protestantism, the whole of the Roman
Catholic world, and, according to the Church of Rome,
the whole of the Protestant world, as heretics, and to both,
the whole of the still wider world abroad, as infidels and
heathens, are indiscriminately destined to everlasting per-
dition; with this exception, that the Romish Church offers
a kind of respite in the shape of their purgatory, in which
their opponents might take breath, and repent of their
folly, while Protestantism peremptorily demands of you an
unconditional surrender.   In this dilemma the Church of
the New Jerusalem appears to me as coming forward for
our rescue, showing us the true state of things; by offering
for our consideration both sides of the question, very fairly
and reasonably, that we may with alacrity enter on the
long but narrow path upwards, which ultimately leads us
to heaven, there to enjoy all the degrees of a blessed and
happy life, and also to shun the short but broad path
downwards, which leads us—if our nature be so incorrigi-
bly perverse as not to be reclaimable even in the spiritual
world—to hell."

"In his 'Arcana Cœlestia' the illustrious author has
devoted full seventeen numbers (from No. 2589 to No.
2605) to this important question—'Concerning the state
and condition in another life of the nations and people

who are born out of the pale of the church.' I cannot here make full extracts of these; but the following short ones, in addition to what I have already given, will amply show the true position which the heathens occupy under the teaching of the New Jerusalem. Swedenborg says:

"'I have had abundant information that the Gentiles who have led a moral life, and have been obedient, and have lived in mutual charity, and have received somewhat like conscience agreeable to their religion, are accepted in another life, and are there instructed by the angels with the utmost care in the goodness and truth of faith.— *Arcana Cœlestia*, No. 2590.   *   *   *   *   *
For with respect to Christians and Gentiles in another life, the case is this: Christians, who have acknowledged the truths of faith, and at the same time have led a life of good, are accepted in preference to the Gentiles" (*quite true*), " but such Christians at this day are few in number" (*very true indeed*); "whereas the Gentiles who have lived in obedience and mutual charity are accepted in preference to the Christians who have not led a good life'—(*undoubtedly*).

"Thus Swedenborg goes on to say many things concerning the heathens and Gentiles whom he conversed with in the spiritual world, as is amply shown in his grand work, 'The Arcana Cœlestia,' in his 'True Christian Religion,' and in his 'Heaven and Hell.' They claim the perusal and consideration of the Christians and heathens alike. It is not to be understood from my above and other observations in this address, which, I comprehend, may be considered as expressive of my excessive and undue sympathy for the fate of the heathens, that I entertain any lurking wish to exonerate my brethren, the heathens, from the great and awful responsibility which attaches to their position as sinners and answerable beings before the tribunal of God, or rather liability to suffer the consequences of their sins and delinquency, and to make light of the burden under which they labor in common with Christians.

It is far from my avowed purpose to endeavor to screen
them, under the cloak of their ignorance of Christianity,
from the punishment which they duly deserve in the other
world ; or, on the other hand, in any way to encourage
them to seek for refuge under the comfortable asylum of
that ignorance, in defiance of the loud calls which Christianity makes to them from outside for a thorough investigation of its claim, as it is said to be the only religion
revealed by God to man for his salvation, and if satisfied
with the validity of its claim, to seek eagerly for that salvation which it holds out to sinners.   But my chief object
in thus evincing sympathy, if it be so called, in the cause
of the heathens in the present address, is to seek to excul-
pate such of them, and them only, whose ears its call has
not reached, nor eyes its light seen, from the hard and
awful denunciation with which they are menaced by a
large and inconsiderate portion of the Christian preachers.
But it is to be clearly understood that to those who have
no such excuse to urge in their defence it is not in my
contemplation to extend any sympathy at all.   They shall
have their own cause to answer and plead before the tribunal of God, if they stand convicted of this most culpable
negligence in a case which concerns the vital interest of
their own souls in the world to come."

We will close this section with a few extracts from
Swedenborg's own writings:

"The church of the Lord exists with all in the universe
who live in good according to their religious principles,
and acknowledge the Divine Being ; and they are accepted
of the Lord and go to heaven."

"It is a common opinion, that those persons who are
born out of the limits of the church, and are called Gentiles or heathens, cannot be saved, because they do not
possess the Word, and thus are ignorant of the Lord ; and
it is certain that, without the Lord, there can be no salvation.   Nevertheless, that salvation is open to these also, is
a truth which might be inferred from these considerations

alone: That the Lord's mercy is universal, or extends to every individual; that they are born men, as really as those who are born within the church, who are but few in comparison; and that their being ignorant of the Lord is no fault of their own. Every person who thinks from a rational faculty, in any degree enlightened, may see clearly that no man can be born designedly for hell; since the Lord is Love itself, and His Love consists in desiring the salvation of all. On this account He provides that all should be attached to some religion, and should possess, by means of it, the acknowledgment of a Divine Being and interior life, since to live according to a religious belief is to live interiorly; for a man then has respect to a Divine Being, and so far as he does this he does not look to the world, but removes himself from the world, consequently from the life of the world, which is exterior life."

"That Gentiles are saved as well as Christians, may be known to those who are aware what it is that constitutes heaven with man; for heaven is in man, and those who have heaven in themselves go to heaven after death. It is heaven in man to acknowledge a Divine Being, and to be led by him. The first and chief essential of all religion consists in acknowledging a Divine Being; and a religion which does not include this acknowledgment, is no religion at all. * * * It is known that the Gentiles live a moral life as well as Christians, and many of them better. Men live a moral life, either from regard to the Divine Being, or from a regard to the opinion of the people in the world; and when a moral life is practiced out of regard to the Divine Being, it is a spiritual life. Both appear alike in their outward form, but in their inward they are completely different; the one saves a man, but the other does not; for he that lives a moral life out of regard to the Divine Being, is led by Him; but he who does so from regard to the opinion of people in the world is led by himself."

"The Gentiles cannot profane the holy things of the

church like Christians, because they are not acquainted with them." "They are afraid of Christians on account of their lives." "Those who have lived well, according to their religious principles, are instructed by the angels, and easily receive the truths of faith, and acknowledge the Lord," "for they have not formed for themselves any principles of falsity opposed to the truths of faith, which would need to be first removed."

"Although Gentiles are not in genuine truths during their life in the world, they receive them in the other life from a principle of love. The Africans are most beloved in heaven of all the Gentiles, for they receive the goods and truths of heaven more easily than others. They particularly desire to be called obedient, but not faithful; Christians, they say, may be called faithful, because they possess the doctrine of faith ; but they themselves not so, unless they receive that doctrine, or, as they express themselves, are able to receive it."—*Heaven and Hell.*

"Many in the other world, who come from parts of the globe outside of Christendom, and who have been worshippers of idols, have the utmost horror of hatred and adultery, and are afraid of Christians who indulge in these vices, and make no scruple of torturing their fellow creatures. * * * Gentiles who have lived morally, being in mutual charity and innocence, are regenerated in the other life. During their abode in the world, the Lord had been present with them in charity and innocence, both of which proceed wholly from Him. He had also endowed them with conscience of what is right and good according to their religious principles, and into that had insinuated innocence and charity; and when these are present in the conscience, persons easily become principled in the truth and faith grounded in good."—*Arcana Cœlestia.*

XXXII.

The New Jerusalem.—The Church of the Future. —The Crown of all Churches.

THERE is but one Saviour—our Lord Jesus Christ— and there is but one road to heaven, and that is a spiritual road which every man must perseveringly and faithfully travel for himself, or he will never reach the Heavenly City. We enter that road when we, in acknowl- edgment of a Divine Being, sincerely repent of our evil deeds, and we walk in it when we earnestly strive to live a life according to the commandments, shunning evils as sins against God, and act honestly and justly towards our fellow-men, and endeavor to do good to all as opportunity offers. The Lord Jesus Christ, or God manifest in the flesh, the one God in one Divine Person, is the corner- stone of the New Jerusalem. This is a central doctrine around which all true doctrines revolve like the planets around the sun. Let us cease following men and look to the Lord Jesus Christ for salvation and to the sacred Scriptures for light to guide us, and especially to the latter as unfolded by the Lord in the writings of Emanuel Swedenborg for this incoming new age, and the truth will make us free from the shackles of sectarianism, and from sect and man worship. The exaltation of faith and the doctrines which a man believes, and the sect to which he belongs, above the life which he lives, together with the claiming and usurpation of spiritual dominion in matters of faith by man over his fellow-man, and denying to men religious freedom, has brought the first Christian Church to its end and split it into its innumerable fragments. In the beautiful allegory of creation in the first chapters of Genesis, where, in the spiritual sense, the regeneration and fall of man are described, Cain denotes faith and Abel charity; and when Cain destroyed Abel he became a fugitive and a vagabond, and thus faith ever becomes when it destroys charity; it separates, puffs up, alienates and arrays man against his fellow-man, and sect against sect. The seer for the New Jerusalem informs us that if charity had retained its proper place in the Christian Church differences of belief would not have separated and divided the church, but men would have been allowed in freedom to hold their own views so long as they lived good lives. Every man should look to the Lord, and read and judge for himself; for it is only that which he in freedom intelligently perceives to be true, and carries out in his daily life, which tends to build up a heavenly life within him. A blind assent to doctrines and creeds, or a blind following of teachers, amounts to little. In this new dispensation men are to receive truth because they perceive it to be true, and not on the authority of a man, or men, or of a church even. Teachers must prove their doctrines true and good, or prepare to see them rejected.

The Christian should recognize but one leader—the Lord; but he should not fail to recognize a brother in every man who believes in a Supreme Being and is striving to lead a good life; for the Lord is no respecter of persons, and the Christian's charity should manifestly extend to all of his Father's children.

The prevalence of a spirit of genuine charity—a charity which thinketh no evil, but strives to excuse rather than accuse, and can tolerate in a fellow-man an honest difference of opinion, without offence, is to be one of the characteristics of the church of the future, or of the New Jerusalem, and another is Freedom; for spiritual liberty, Swedenborg has shown us, has been restored to man. " How has such liberty been restored to man ? " the reader may inquire.

If we read carefully the fifth and twelfth chapters of John, we shall find that the Lord, when on earth, executed a general judgment, for He declared : " Verily, verily, I say unto you, the hour is coming, and now is, when the dead shall hear the voice of the Son of God, and they that hear shall live." "Now is the judgment of this world: now shall the prince of this world be cast out." This judgment of course took place in the spiritual world, where all last judgments are executed, for man is to be judged for the deeds done in the body. It is a recognized doctrine that the New Testament predicts another general judgment. This, like the judgment which occurred when the Lord was on earth, was to take place in the spiritual world; but something must be said in regard to that world, that one not versed in the new revelation may understand the subject.

Swedenborg found the inhabitants of the spiritual world divided into three grand divisions, which he denominates the world of spirits, heaven and hell. The ruling love of every individual here governs his destiny hereafter; and as most individuals when they leave this world are neither angels nor devils, but are in preparation for one or the other of these states of life (as all angels and devils are from the human race), it follows that they cannot at once enter either heaven or hell. Therefore they tarry in the world of spirits, which is an intermediate state, until the good are cleansed from all false doctrines, ideas, and thoughts, and purified from all evil inclinations, when they are received into heaven. The evil confirm themselves more and more fully in their false views and evils, until they have put away even the semblance of genuine truths and heavenly desires, when they go voluntarily or from choice among their like in hell, for they cannot be happy in heaven. All the inhabitants of heaven, he found, acknowledge and worship our Lord Jesus Christ as the one only God and Saviour, and are actuated by love to the Lord and neighbor in all their acts, words, and thoughts, each striving to do good to all; consequently no penal laws or punishments are required, for every one is striving to keep the Divine commandments, love to the Lord and neighbor constituting heaven. All in hell deny the Lord and His Word; deny that a

man can act from any higher motive than selfishness, and
are actuated in all they do, say, and think, by some selfish
love. The supreme love of self, or of ruling over others,
or of wealth, display, or of sensual gratification, in hell, as
in this world, arrays man against his fellow-man, and can
never be fully gratified ; but it must be restrained there,
as here, by laws and punishments, or life in hell would be
unendurable, in fact, worse than no existence. Self-love
and supreme selfishness constitute hell, as love of the
Lord and neighbor do heaven. Heaven is not a place
into which a man can be let as a matter of favor;
but heaven must be in us, and heavenly affections must
rule us, before we can enter heaven, and the way to heaven
is a life according to the Commandments. It will be seen
that the knowledge of the spiritual world and the life of
men there, contained in the revelations made through
Swedenborg, has a practical relation to the life of men
here, and shows us as in a glass that our every-day acts,
words, and thoughts are developing our very souls into
the image of heaven or hell, and we are now journeying
towards the one or the other state of life slowly but surely.
The evil-doer shall not go unpunished, nor the honest
and good man fail of his reward, but every one will receive
a just reward and recompense for all the deeds done here.
God was in Christ, reconciling the world unto Himself,
and His tender mercies are around all His creatures, as
well in hell as in this world and heaven ; but He compels
no one here to love Him and his neighbor supremely;
and He cannot do it hereafter, without destroying the
manhood of man, and this He never does.

Previous to the Lord's first coming, and between that
and His second coming, Swedenborg informs us, those
who left this world unprepared for either heaven or hell,
remained in the world of spirits, or the intermediate state,
and formed vast societies there, or imaginary heavens;
and, as the world of spirits is immediately associated with
man, in the course of time influx from them into the

minds of men began seriously to endanger man's spiritual freedom.

It was in this intermediate world that Babylon the Great was gradually developed. Those whose externals appeared holy, whilst their internals were profane, who transferred the merit and righteousness of the Lord, and attributed Divine things to themselves, dwelt there. There, in that great city, self-love, and love of rule and dominion from self-love, were predominant, and held dominion over and imprisoned the simple good, in that world, as well as their votaries have done in this world; destroying their freedom and rationality, until their cry went up: "How long, O Lord, holy and true, dost thou not judge and avenge our blood on them that dwell on the earth?"

Then, in the fullness of time, the Lord came for judgment, and now Babylon the Great has fallen—fallen to rise no more forever. The freedom of man in spiritual things was endangered in this world by the selfish love of rule in his fellow-man, and the Lord has interposed for his rescue.

"Emanuel Swedenborg, servant of the Lord Jesus Christ, happened to be the man endowed and commissioned to observe and report it; not by his own seeking, but by Providential allotment; not on account of any superior innate merit existing in him, but simply for the sake of the truth, and the consequent well-being of all Christian men. To a single seer was given the wonderful vision which, 'by signs' sent from Jesus Christ, prefigured and described all these extraordinary things 1600 years in advance; and so to another single seer was it given to behold their fulfilment; looking through the 'veil' while they were going on, that he might note them, record them, and publish them, as an epistle 'to the churches.' He was in a state of the spirit, and, like John, enjoyed an open or sensible communion with the beings of the other world."—*Light on Last Things.*

Swedenborg assures us that he witnessed this judgment in the spiritual world. That it was commenced and fully ended during the year 1757; and that hereafter, all men are judged as they leave this world. He wrote a small work entitled, "The Last Judgment," in which he carefully described that judgment as it was executed on the various Christian societies and heathen nations in the world of spirits. Those who were interiorly good, were separated from those who were interiorly evil; the former class were removed to heaven, the latter to hell. And thus was the world of spirits renovated, and the dense clouds of evil spirits, which threatened the freedom and very existence of mankind by interrupting the inflowing of truth and love from the Lord and the angels, were removed.

The reader may inquire, how were these two classes of spirits separated, and why were they not permitted to dwell together as good and evil men do in this world, and as they had been previously doing in the world of spirits? The truth judges. When the Lord came for judgment and there was a new inflowing of truth into the minds of the inhabitants of the world of spirits, unveiling the hypocrisies, the pretenses, and the shams, so that the real intentions and motives were apparent to every one, we can very readily see how and why they separated. The hidden things, the lust for dominion over his fellow, for selfish gratification, the envying, jealousies, and real hatreds were proclaimed upon the housetop. In such an unveiling of man's interior life, it is evident that like will turn to the society of like, for they can find no other congenial associates. We know that even in this world similarity of tastes, habits, pursuits, and character draw people together.

The Rev. Chauncey Giles, in his very interesting work, entitled "The Nature of Spirit and Man as a Spiritual Being," says:

"The doctrines of the New Jerusalem simply carry out this universal principle to its legitimate conclusions. They have the logic of the Divine order, as it is embodied in the creation and in the hearts and minds of men. It is a conclusion also which every good and every wicked man must desire, if he understands his own nature. A wicked man cannot be happy in the presence of the good. "Heaven would be a perfect hell to him. What delight could a supremely worldly and selfish man find in loving the Lord and the neighbor? in doing good to others? What pleasure could the impure find in purity? the proud in humility? the ambitious and tyrannical in serving others? Their whole nature must be reversed before they could find any delight in these heavenly virtues. What we inmostly and really love is what we call good. It is and ever must be the measure of our good, and must determine its quality. We can no more escape from it than we can escape from the laws of gravitation. Men desire to escape hell because it is a place of torment; and to go to heaven because they think it is a place of happiness. But they forget that what is happiness to one is torment to another. They forget that freedom from punishment is not happiness. If every law was abolished in the land, and every penitentiary leveled with the ground, it would have no effect in making wicked men delight in what is good. They would rejoice, no doubt, that they could freely indulge in their wicked desires. But these would soon react upon them in some form of punishment, and in the end they would gain no happiness by it. No. If those heavenly principles, which constitute the kingdom of God, are not formed within us—if we have not made them our own, by actual life—we can never taste a heavenly joy. We pronounce judgment upon ourselves, in the spiritual world, in the same way we do in this world. The wicked man seeks hell there as he does here, because he is drawn to it by his infernal delights—the only delights he is capable of enjoying; and he is drawn to it by the current of his desires, as a vessel is drawn to the ocean by the current of a stream."

But the reader, unacquainted with the revelations made

by Swedenborg, may reasonably inquire: "If such a wonderful event as the long-expected Last Judgment took place in the world of departed spirits more than a century ago, what signs have we of it, for it would certainly seem time that some results or effects of such a great change should be seen in this world?"

In reply to the above we will first call the attention of the reader to the changes in the state of mankind on earth, which Swedenborg and the angels anticipated at the time, or soon after the Judgment, would and must follow; then the reader will be able to judge whether those anticipations are being realized or not. Swedenborg says:

"The great change which has been effected in the spiritual world, does not induce any change in the natural world as regards the outward form; so that the affairs of states—peace, treaties and wars, with all other things belonging to civil communities, in general and in particular—will exist in the future as they have existed in the past. * * * But with respect to the state of the church, this will be dissimilar hereafter. It will be similar, indeed, in the *outward form,* but dissimilar in the *inward.* To outward appearance divided churches will exist, and their doctrines will be taught, as heretofore; and the same religions will exist among the Gentiles as at present. But henceforth the man of the church (that is, the men of Christendom generally) will be in a more free state of thinking on matters of faith, that is, on spiritual things which relate to heaven, because spiritual liberty has been restored to him. * * *

" I have often conversed with the angels respecting the state of the church hereafter. They said they did not know the things that were to come, since such knowledge belongs to the Lord alone; but that they did know that the slavery and captivity in which the man of the church was formerly, is removed; and that now, from restored liberty, he can better perceive interior truths if he wishes to perceive them, and thus be made more internal if he desires it." (*L. J.* n. 73, 74.)

"The state of the world and the church before the last judgment was as *evening and night;* but after it, as morning and day."—"For since communication with heaven has been restored by the last judgment, man is able to be enlightened and reformed; that is, to understand the divine truth of the Word, to receive it when understood, and to retain it when received; for the interposing obstacles are removed." (*Contin. L. J.* n. 12.)

Again he says:

"After the last judgment was accomplished there was light in the world of spirits, because the infernal societies which *were removed* [by that judgment], had been interposed like clouds which darken the earth. A similar light also then arose in men in the world, giving them new enlightenment." (*Ibid.*, n. 30.)

How wonderfully the above expectations have been and are being realized in the recent history of the world! Physical slavery has been largely abolished, and ere long, it is manifest, it will only be known in history. Ecclesiastical despotism is rapidly passing from the face of the earth. We have seen the most formidable manifestation of this power which the world has ever witnessed, stripped of its civil power in our day, and its ability to persecute and oppress in a great measure destroyed. Take courage, ye lovers of freedom, for God wills the overthrow of both civil and religious despotism and slavery. He has overthrown their central power in the spiritual world, and they cannot long retain an existence in this world. What can the puny arm of man do to prevent this great and wonderful change, which is so rapidly progressing in our day. Fear not; God is mightier than either civil or ecclesiastical despots, and physical and mental slavery are never to be re-established, but men are to be free, in the church of the future—the New Jerusalem—and are to claim their freedom, especially in matters of religion ; for without religious freedom there can be no progress. Every man should insist on the right of private judgment in religious matters, as a right too sacred to be surrendered. Swedenborg says:

"The dogma that the understanding is to be held in subjection to faith, is rejected in the New Church; and in its place this is to be received as a maxim, that the truth of the church should be *seen* in order that it may be understood; and truth cannot be seen otherwise than rationally. How can any man be led by the Lord and conjoined to heaven, who shuts his understanding against such things as relate to salvation and eternal life? Is it not the understanding that is to be illumed and instructed? And what is the understanding closed by religion but thick darkness, and such darkness, too, as rejects the light that would illumine?" (*A. R.* 564.)

"The understanding truly human, when it is separate from what is material, sees truths as clearly as the eye sees objects. It sees truths as it loves them; for as it loves them it is enlightened. The angels have wisdom in consequence of *seeing* truths; therefore when it is said to any angel that this or that is to be believed although it is not understood, the angel replies, Do you think that I am insane, or that you yourself are a god whom I am bound to believe?" (*Ap. Ex.* 1100.)

"Since the Lord desires that everything which comes from Himself to man should be appropriated as man's own (for otherwise there would be no conjunction of man with the Lord), therefore it is a law of the Divine Providence that a man's understanding and will should not be at all compelled by another." (*Ap. Ex.* 1150.)

Thus the New Jerusalem is as free, as we shall presently see, as it is catholic. It encourages the largest liberty of thought, the utmost freedom of religious inquiry. It would have us acknowledge no master but the Lord Jesus Christ as He reveals Himself to our individual consciousness, as we search the Scriptures in the light of this new day. Its language is, " Every one should be led in freedom according to reason."

In his work on the " Divine Providence," " Swedenborg declares more emphatically than any other writer has ever done, that freedom and rationality are the distinguishing feature between man and beast, and that in these two faculties, the very human principle consists."—*Rev. R. L. Tafel.*

It is not simply in the restoration of human freedom that the consequences of the Last Judgment, and of the Lord's Second Coming, are alone to be seen; for as a recent writer truly says : " Results such as no human fore-sight could have ventured to predict are around us on every side in a profusion which baffles every effort of array or description. Science, art, thought, in every direction, has been stimulated by the new impulses thence communicated. Society wears a new aspect; we live in a new world. Never has there been so full and so ample a confirmation of any man's saying as that which has followed Swedenborg's declaration that in his time a new age and new dispensation were commencing, which would prove to be the culminating, crowning day and dispensation of the world's history. Were we to maintain that the one hundred and twenty years since has done more for the cause of human improvement than the whole five thousand years that went before, it would be a difficult matter to gainsay the assertion. That this short period has done more in this direction than any previous one thousand years that have gone before, no one will be inclined to doubt. In other words, the very *first century* of the Lord's *second* advent has done more to elevate and redeem mankind than any *ten* centuries of His first advent were able to accomplish."—*Light on Last Things.*

Swedenborg says : " In the spiritual world to which every man goes after death, it is not the character of your faith into which inquiry is made, nor of your *doctrine,* but of your *life,* whether it has been of this character or that;

for it is known that such as a man's *life* is, such is his faith—nay, more, such is his doctrine; for life forms its doctrine and faith for itself." (*D. P.* 101.) "For the good of life according to one's religion contains within it the affection of knowing truths, which such persons also learn and receive when they come into the other life."— (*A. C.* 455.)

"Evils which belong to the will, are what condemn a man and sink him down to hell; and falsities only so far as they become conjoined with evils; then one follows the other. This is proved by numerous instances of persons who are in falsities, and yet are saved." (*Ibid.* 845.)

"There are two things to be remembered. First, that a person may love God and his neighbor, and yet believe some things that are false. Under such circumstances, untruth does not hurt him. False doctrine is, indeed, a deadly thing; but all deadly things do not hurt; for our Saviour says of his true disciples, *If they drink any deadly thing, it shall not hurt them.* Secondly, a person may have no love of God, and yet maintain true doctrine. In this case he is, nevertheless, not a true disciple of Christ. The first has within him the essence of a true church, but not the perfect doctrinal form; the second has the doctrinal form, but not the real essence. A church composed of individuals such as the latter, would nevertheless not be a church; there might be an outward appearance of life and health, but inwardly there would be nothing but death and corruption."

"When love to the Lord and charity toward the neighbor, that is, the good of life, are regarded as the *essentials,* then, however many churches there be, they make one. This also is the case in heaven, where there are innumerable societies, all distinct from each other, but still constituting one heaven because all are principled in love to the Lord and charity toward the neighbor. But the case is otherwise with churches that make faith (or belief) the essential thing—imagining that if people know or think

such and such things they will be saved, be their life what
it may. Then several churches do not make one, nor
indeed *are* they churches."

Again Swedenborg says: "There are two things which
conjoin the men of the church, viz: Life and doctrine.
When life conjoins, doctrine does not separate them; but
if only doctrine conjoins them, as at this day is the case
within the church, then they mutually separate, and make
as many churches as there are doctrines: when yet doctrine is for the sake of life, and life is from doctrine. If
only doctrine conjoins, they separate themselves, as is
evident from this, that he who is of one doctrine, condemns another person, sometimes to hell; but if life conjoins, doctrine does not separate, as is evident from this,
that he who is in goodness of life, does not condemn
another who is of another opinion, but leaves it to his
faith and conscience, and extends this rule even to those
who are out of the church; for he says in his heart, that
ignorance cannot condemn any if they live in innocence
and mutual love, as infants who also are in ignorance
when they die." (*A. C.* 4468.)

Yet Swedenborg does not leave us to infer that the
belief in false doctrines is harmless, especially if we
strongly confirm ourselves in such views; for it is exceedingly difficult and painful for a man, even a good man, to
get rid of such falses either in this world or in the next.
It is of great importance that truth should be united to
good in this world. Swedenborg says: "Those who are in
falses, and especially those who are in evils, are said to be
bound and in prison; not that they are in any bonds, but
because they are not in freedom; those who are not in
freedom being interiorly bound; for those who have confirmed themselves in what is false, are no longer in any
freedom of choosing and accepting the truth, and those
who have much confirmed themselves therein, are not
even in freedom to see it, still less to acknowledge and
believe it, for they are in the persuasion that what is false

11

is true and what is true is false; so powerful is this persuasion, that it takes away all freedom of thinking anything else, consequently it holds the thought itself in bonds, and as it were in prison. This I have had much opportunity of being convinced of experimentally from those in the other life who have been in a persuasion of the false by confirmations in themselves; they do not at all admit truths, but reflect or strike them back again, and this with an obstinacy proportioned to the degree of persuasion; especially when the false is grounded in evil, or when evil has persuaded them." (*A. C.* 5096.)

We have endeavored to give the reader a hasty glimpse of some of the prominent doctrines and teachings of the New Jerusalem; enough, we hope, to seriously call his attention to the writings of the Illuminated Scribe of the Church of the Future, Emanuel Swedenborg.

Rev. B. F. Barrett, one of the oldest and most diligent of the readers of Swedenborg's writings, says:

"Now, if I were called upon to indicate any single idea which was to distinguish pre-eminently that dispensation or church of which Swedenborg was the divinely appointed herald—any single idea that towers conspicuously above all others in his writings, I should say it is the idea of religion as a *personal* and *practical* thing; of religion embodying itself in good and useful deeds; of religion carried into all our human acts and relations, purifying them all, sanctifying them all, ennobling them all. And this idea of religion in our common every-day life, so eminently characteristic of the New Theology, is the very idea which has been steadily growing into favor for the last hundred years in nearly all the churches.

However similar, then, in their creeds and in outward appearance the churches of to-day may be to those of a hundred years ago, it is clear that they are very different internally. They have different ideas and purposes, and are animated by a different spirit. And every year this difference is increasing, and becoming more and more apparent.

"And thus it is that the New Jerusalem may be seen 'descending out of heaven from God, having the glory of God.' Thus may the Lord Himself be seen coming anew to the churches in the spirit and power of His now unsealed Word. Thus do we behold Him breaking through and dispersing the mists of naturalism, and gladdening the hearts of his sincere followers with a new manifestation of Himself;—'coming,' agreeably to his own prediction, 'in the clouds of heaven with power and great glory.' Thus may a New Church be seen slowly forming, not as a new visible institution—not as a separate and distinct organization, but rather as a new spirit and life entering into the great heart of humanity and moulding it anew; comparatively as the earth, on the return of each new spring-time, receives a fresh influx of the solar rays, and so becomes a new earth clad afresh with verdure and beauty. A church not antagonistic to existing organizations, but cordially sympathizing with and reanimating them all."—*The Golden City.*

The late Rev. John Clowes, Rector of St. John's Church, Manchester, England, who for many years, without ever being required to sever his connection with the Church of England, openly and boldly taught the doctrines revealed through Swedenborg, and translated many of his works into English, says:

"Nothing, therefore, can be plainer, than that the New Jerusalem Dispensation is to be universal, and to extend unto all people, nations, and languages on the face of the earth, to be a blessing unto such as are meet to receive a blessing. Sects and sectarians, as such, can find no place in this General Assembly of the ransomed of the Lord. All the little distinctions of modes, forms, and particular expressions of devotion and worship, will be swallowed up and lost in the unlimited effusions of heavenly love, charity and benevolence with which the hearts of every member of

SKEPTICISM AND DIVINE REVELATION.

this glorious New Church and Body of Jesus Christ will overflow one toward another. Men will no longer judge one another as to the mere externals of church communion, be they perfect or be they imperfect; for they will be taught that, whosoever acknowledges the incarnate Jehovah in heart and life, departing from all evil, and doing what is right and good according to the commandments, he is a member of the New Jerusalem, a living stone in the Lord's new Temple, and a part of that great family in heaven and earth, whose common Father and Head is Jesus Christ. Every one, therefore, will call his neighbor *Brother*, in whom he observes this spirit of pure charity; and he will ask no questions concerning the form of words which compose his creed, but will be satisfied with observing in him the purity and power of a heavenly life."

What a glorious prospect does this New Dispensation open to our race !

"The last great campaign of the kingdom of heaven upon earth is opening before us, and the inmost heart of Christianized humanity is beating in unison with the movement; while the utterances of the ancient prophets become the sacred watchwords of the hour, the inspired directions for the march, and the songs of holy joy that are set to the music of the camps." * * *

"All nations whom Thou hast made shall come and worship before Thee, O Jehovah, and shall glorify Thy Name." * * *

"The wilderness and the solitary place shall be glad, and the desert shall rejoice and blossom as the rose. * * *

"In the days of these kings shall the God of heaven set up a kingdom that shall never be destroyed : it shall break in pieces and consume all these kingdoms, and it shall stand forever."

"And there shall be given him dominion and glory, and a kingdom, that all people, nations, and languages, should serve Him; His dominion is the dominion of an age which shall not pass away, and His kingdom that which shall not be destroyed." * * *

"The earth shall be full of the knowledge of the Lord, as the waters cover the sea." * * *

"After those days, saith the Lord, I will put My law in their inward parts and write it in their hearts; and I will be their God, and they shall be My people; they shall all know Me from the least unto the greatest, saith Jehovah, for I will forgive their iniquity, and I will remember their sin no more."

"Thine eyes shall see Jerusalem a quiet habitation, a tabernacle that shall not be taken down; not one of the stakes thereof shall ever be removed, neither shall any of the cords thereof be broken." "Behold, the tabernacle of God is with men."

"I, John, saw the holy city, New Jerusalem, coming down from God out of heaven."

"'Let us be glad, and rejoice, and give the glory unto Him,' that our lot is cast in these latter times; that we are permitted to live at the day in which all these things are beginning the march of their fulfillment, and that, in His merciful provision for human want, the Lord has caused to break forth from the bosom of His Word a system of theology and philosophy, not man-made but heaven-descended, which leads—by a thousand years—the highest aspirations of human thought, fitted to the age—to serve as a lamp to the movement; 'the glory of God to lighten' us, and to instruct us aright in these great themes."

"And let us, one and all, lend our hearts and our hands to this movement; working where we stand in aid of its fulfillment, and helping, as far as in us lies, to bring about in our time some of its blessed results."—*Light on Last Things.*

The senders of this pamphlet desire again affectionately and earnestly to call your attention to the writings containing these new revelations, from our ever-blessed Lord and Saviour Jesus Christ.   Three large volumes, from among the most important of Emanuel Swedenborg's writings, you will perceive by the attached circular on the second page of the cover, are furnished to Protestant clergymen and theological students studying for the ministry without money and without price, they having only to call and get them, or pay the postage or express charges on them, and request them to be sent, to receive them.   That every clergyman and theological student studying for the ministry who has not already done so, will immediately order the above works, is the desire of those who are giving them, and that the Lord may open their understandings and hearts for the reception of the heavenly doctrines of the Holy City, New Jerusalem, now descending from God out of Heaven, prepared as a bride adorned for her husband, is the earnest prayer of every disciple of the New Dispensation.

It was apparently the opinion of Swedenborg that his writings would be read by the clergy, who would teach the doctrines therein contained to their congregations, and thus the glorious truths for this new era or crowning church, would be spread among the people; for, in speaking of the descent of the New Church or New Jerusalem, from God out of Heaven, he says it can only take place "in proportion as the falses of the former church are removed, for what is new cannot gain admission where falses have before been implanted, unless those falses are first rooted out; and this must first take place among the clergy, and by their means among the laity."

We thank the Lord for the abundance of evidence that this process is rapidly going on around us in all the churches, and to do what we can to hasten on this great and noble work, or to be humble instruments in the Lord's hands for aiding in its accomplishment, is our sole aim in sending these few words—a brotherly message—to you. Not as sectarians do we send them, for the New Jerusalem, as we have abundantly shown in the preceding pages, is not a sect, but a New Dispensation of divine truth for the benefit of all sects and all men.

XXXIII.

The Divine Promise to those who Receive the New Jerusalem at the Second Coming of the Lord.

(BY REV. WM. B. HAYDEN.)

"Remember therefore, how thou hast received and heard, and hold fast, and repent." * * *

"I know thy works: behold I have set before thee an open door, and no man can shut it: for thou hast a little strength, and hast kept my word, and hast not denied my name." * * *

"Him that overcometh will I make a pillar in the temple of my God, and he shall go no more out: and I will write upon him the name of my God, and the name of the city of my God, which is New Jerusalem, which cometh down out of heaven from my God: and I will write upon him my new name" (Rev. iii. 3, 8, 12).

The Lord Jesus Christ is at this day doing a remarkable work; in some respects one of the most remarkable He has ever performed. He is effecting His Second Advent, and is beginning to establish in the world His new and final church, which in His Word He calls the New Jerusalem.

He has caused the volume of His Word to be opened more fully to human apprehension, the prophetic portions of the Bible being explained as to their spiritual and heavenly meaning; while that pure and perfect system of True Christian Doctrine, which the angels of heaven derive from the Divine Word, has been revealed for our use and instruction, and written out in the language of men by Emanuel Swedenborg, a man specially illuminated by the Lord for this purpose.

This wonderful system of heavenly truths He has caused to be printed and circulated in books, not only in Latin, but in nearly all the Christian tongues, so that they may be freely promulgated in every part of Christendom, that whoever will may partake of this pure river of water of life freely.   And these heavenly truths are slowly gathering together the New Church, for they are freely offered to all, and all who will may receive them in obedience with affection, and confess them openly before and among men.

Included in this opening and explanation, is this Book of Revelation, given through John, the last great Book of the sacred canon; the enigma of Christian scholars; now, with its seals taken off, and all its dark sayings made plain, in clear, rational, heavenly light; the meaning of every chapter, verse, and single symbol plainly given, so that he who runs may read; a feast of fat things, full of marrow, to the spiritually-minded seeking for heavenly instruction and longing to know more of the Master's will.

The Apocalypse or Book of Revelation is the especial book of this New Church, for it is the book devoted to the Second Coming of the Lord, predicting the particularity of this Advent, with all the attending circumstances, and in it the New Jerusalem is foretold and described. In its pages, therefore, now illuminated by the glory of their own heavenly meaning, we have a divine commentary on the events by which we are surrounded, on the wonderful fulfillments of prophecy now taking place, and the New Age or Dispensation of Christian light now progressing in our midst.

In these epistles which John was commanded to write to the seven churches then located in Asia Minor, in their spiritual or prophetic import, we behold all the different classes of believers in Christendom in our day addressed. Addressed, too, in earnest tones and decided terms, by our Lord Himself, speaking to us out of heaven. All capable of exercising religious affection and religious thought are here appealed to, being enjoined to lift up their eyes and to come.

One thing particularly is noticeable in these missives to the churches; in each there is a call to repentance.

Many other things likewise are spoken of. Each church has a special and pointed teaching addressed to its peculiar wants, but this one feature is common to them all—they all command repentance. This reveals a leading characteristic of the New Dispensation; which is that now there is to be required a closer conformity to the divine commandments than ever before. All men are called upon to put on more fully the spirit of true religion. Not only emotional piety, but also practical obedience in daily life is required. Entrance into the New Jerusalem therefore implies a step forward for every one who comes, a new degree of religion, and advance in real holiness of life and character.

No matter where these new heavenly truths find us, whether in much good or little good, whether we are professed Christians already, or indifferent, or unbelievers, the call is to all alike, to leave our present state whatever it is, and put on something more of pure and true religion, leaving the fallacies of the senses and the cupidity of the natural man still further behind us. New and greater spiritual attainment is forcibly insisted upon, and the way given to attain it.

Then, after having risen up and entered this New Jerusalem through interior amendment of life, each class of religious men finds in these seven epistles some instruction fitted to its own state. Their own peculiar shortcomings are pointed out, and they are clearly told how they may grow in grace and spiritually progress towards the angelic state of life.

"*Remember therefore how thou hast received and heard, and hold fast.*" These words are addressed to those who are already in the external worship of the church, to nominal or professed believers in the truth. They are remarkable words, and of very impressive import. They are meant particularly for us, receivers of these heavenly doctrines, professed believers in this New Age and Dispensation; and they are calculated to arouse the conscience and stimulate a holy zeal in the heart of every true and earnest believer. We who have heard and listened to the Truth, who have heard the words of the New Jerusalem, who know that the Lord has come a Second time, gathering His flock and setting up His final kingdom, are enjoined to remember *how we have received and heard, and hold fast.* The Lord would impress upon us the importance of holding fast to these new truths, proclaiming and obeying them.

As we go away from the Sanctuary, or the Word and the Writings, back into our worldly employments, and often into our natural selfish and worldly states of thought and feeling, our minds become cloudy. We are apt to think remotely of our religious privileges. We think lightly of holy truth ; comparatively lightly of the heavenly truths now revealed, to regard slightingly our obligations to them, our obligation to heed them, to value them, to uphold them, to promulgate them, to obey them, and to openly confess them before men.

But from all we read in His Word, and all we know, the Lord Himself does not so lightly regard them. We hear no such indifferent or easy-going language on His part. Not any Laodicean—neither cold nor hot—state finds favor in His eyes. On the contrary, all His words on the subject come forth with emphasis. Search the Bible through, and nowhere else will you find such strong and impressive language, or appealing more forcibly to the heart and the conscience, than this employed in the Book of Revelation with respect to the truths of the New Jerusalem. The whole heaven is powerfully moved and affected by the utterances. The Lord Himself is deeply in earnest when He proclaims them to the angels, deeply in earnest when he sends them into the world to reclaim men and overturn the kingdom of darkness, and deeply in earnest, too, when He calls upon us to receive and obey them.

And again, closely following these deeply freighted calls of admonition and injunction, what blessed words of encouragement and promise fall from the same lips, to the steadfast and obedient! Such as have been held out to no church before, such as are found nowhere else in the Bible. Hear them: *"Behold, I have set before thee an open door, and no man can shut it."* An "open door!" Do we realize what this means? In view of *all* it implies, how comprehensive the sense! An opening such as has never been vouchsafed to mankind before, such as the previous ages have never seen, and yet an opening promised in the Word, and the hope of good men in the Christian centuries of the past.

1. "A door into heaven opened."

The heavenly world laid open to view, and described for our use and instruction. Not to satisfy vain curiosity, or make an empty show; but to make immortality real, and encourage purity of life by showing that only the really pure and good can enter there. Life among the angels considered and described, in its most general forms, as comprehensible by men, as involved in the teachings of the Holy Word, and rendered clear by a more exhaustive study of its pages. The blessedness of heaven brought near; the mutual love reigning among its inhabitants, their conjunction of heart and mind with the Lord our Redeemer, the glorious light in which they dwell, their practical wisdom, their ineffable innocence and peace of mind, their elevating employments, doing the Lord's will in innumerable offices of love and good use to members of the heavenly kingdom, as well as to mankind on earth— all unfolded in clear rational light, for our quickening and encouragement.

Then, the constitution of the human soul, its connection with the body, its close association with the unseen world, the grounds and principles of future judgment, with the miserable results which persistent sin inflicts, all made known for our admonition and warning, to separate us more and more from disobedience, and attach us more firmly to the kingdom of the Lord; the whole involving such an opening of the unseen world and the future state of existence, as could scarcely be conceived of before it had come, though desired and waited for by spiritual men in all ages of the church.

And this door never again to be shut: this elevating knowledge of the heavenly world and its order, recorded in printed books, never again to disappear from the thought and memory of man.

2. The Great Book opened. The seven seals taken off from the Bible, its heavenly interpretation written out; wherein all its divine prophecies find their true and final exposition; its obscure passages cleared up, its dark sayings brought forth in light, the clouds of its letter everywhere illuminated with the heavenly glory of their spiritual meaning, and all its pages shown to testify concerning the Lord Jesus Christ. The real nature of the Divine Word explained, showing that as to its deeper, inner ground, it is the very Divine Truth itself. The difference between *Letter* and *Spirit* made clear, and how the spiritual sense, like a soul, dwells everywhere within the Letter, which is the body; and thus the real nature of Divine inspiration exposed, from its inmost ground. As the Lord, with His constant presence, dwells in the Word, in its interior meaning and essence, and the angels are also present in its spiritual sense, bringing with them a heavenly sphere of mental light and heat, the Divine Word becomes the medium among men of the Presence of the Lord and His Holy Spirit, and a medium of communication with heaven through which animating floods of illustration and warmth may flow into the heart and mind of the believer and reverent, faithful student. And this Holy Word, thus opened, never again to be closed up, but to remain forever as an open door to heavenly and eternal things.

3. Then, again, our Lord and Saviour declares Himself to be the Door; a door in the Supreme sense; the living door; the great avenue or medium of access to Supreme, unapproachable Divinity. And how *this* Door is opened to us in these new heavenly or angelic Doctrines! In

which the one eternal Saviour and Redeemer, our Lord Jesus Christ, reveals Himself to us at length in all the fullness of His ineffable glory, as the One supreme and only object of our love and worship. Declaring to us from the very letter of His Word that He is indeed Jehovah Himself, not three persons, not the second among three, but the Only One; dwelling by Himself from all eternity, and then in the fullness of time condescending and coming down to seek and to save that which was lost, assuming humanity for our sakes and appearing in the world as Immanuel, God with us. Thus walking our earth, not as a consecrated and holy man merely, but the Lord Himself, clad in the outward garments of a man. Glorifying, by His indwelling Divinity, all the originally frail elements derived from the virgin mother, putting them off, perfecting their nature by filling all their forms with pure divine substances, thus making even His human part perfectly divine in essence, organizing all its substance anew, so that at length the fullness of the whole Godhead dwelt bodily in that Human Form, without confining or contracting its infinity. In this Glorified Form He arose, and ascended into heaven, where He forever abides, seated on the Throne of the Universe, including in His own single Person all that is meant by Father, all that is meant by Son, and all that is meant by Holy Spirit: the three in One Person. His own supreme, eternal, unapproachable Divinity being called Father; the Humanity which He assumed in order to appear in the world, and which while in the world He glorified and made Divine, being called the Son; and that new powerful and personal presence and influence which since the Incarnation He vouchsafes to faithful, obedient believers, being called the Comforter, Paraclete, Advocate, or Holy Spirit. Summing for us in this last book of the Sacred Canon the final doctrine concerning Himself in these memorable words: "I am the Alpha and the Omega; the Beginning and the End; the First and the Last; the one who is and who was and who

is to come, the Almighty." And again in these, at the
very close of the volume: "I, Jesus, have sent Mine angel
unto you to testify these things in the churches." Declaring
also that He is both the Root and the Offspring of David.

Thus showing that the great object of the Biblical
Revelation, in its progressive development from end to
end, is to bring out by degrees as they have been able to
bear it, and at length make clear to the spiritual apprehension of the church, the great vital Supreme Truth that
God is One Person, one single Person, and that our Lord
and Saviour Jesus Christ is this One God.

Thus fulfilling at last, and in our day, that glorious
prediction and promise of the Apostle that the time would
come when the Saviour would vacate that subordinate,
mediatorial position, which to the partially-instructed
intelligence of that day He seemed to hold, and that God
would be seen to be One, the "all in all."

And this Door; this heavenly, angelic Doctrine concerning our Saviour as the One Only Lord and God—
never to be closed up or lost sight of. Now that it is
revealed, and clearly made known to the thought and
rational intelligence of men, it is henceforth the property
of the church universal forevermore. No human power
can prevail against it. It solves the great problem of the
Godhead; and no human power can ever drive it back or
push it out of the world. It is the corner-stone, the stone
of power, which the prophet Daniel in holy vision saw cut
out of the Rock without hands, which became a great
mountain and filled the whole earth.

4. The Way of Life opened. In these heavenly Doctrines the way and means of salvation are most distinctly
set forth. The true ideas of justification and imputation
are unfolded. And *a life according to the Divine Commandments of the Holy Word*, clearly shown to be the
only true ground of hope and the only means of salvation.
Faith is commanded, Charity or Love is commanded,
Good Works are commanded. All are required; and

neither one is to be emphasized to the disparagement of the others. Without the acknowledgment of the Lord and Saviour there is no salvation, for no man of himself can attain the holy life, and regeneration and the gift of the Holy Spirit are from the Lord alone.

Those who, from the acknowledgment of a Divine Being, are in the good of life, who through ignorance do not acknowledge the Lord in His Divine Humanity in this world, will in the next, before they can enter the kingdom of heaven. The ground of forgiveness is the Divine Goodness, Clemency, or Mercy, while the simple condition on man's part is Repentance and actual departure from evil. Salvation is a thing of degrees; the further we are lifted out of Sin the more are we saved, while the merit or righteousness of Christ is imputed to the believer just as fast, and to the degree, that he actually *appropriates* that righteousness—in his own character, putting on the image and exemplifying the spirit of Christ in his own life.

The way of salvation therefore is growth in holiness, which is measured exactly by our ceasing from sinful acts and affections, and our practical conformity to gospel precept. "He that hath my commandments and *doeth* them, he it is that loveth me." And hence the great blessing pronounced in the New Jerusalem is, " Blessed are they that DO His commandments, that they may have right to the Tree of Life, and may enter in through the gates into the city."

And in these doctrines all questions are answered which Christians desire to ask, most lucid and extended expositions being given of all the vital doctrines of grace and life; Repentance, Regeneration, Charity, Faith, Good Works and the Holy Spirit; so that no one is any longer left in the dark, or in obscurity, or doubt with respect to any vital or practical point of religious experience.

And this door, opening thus into the onward and upward way to heaven, never again to be obscured by day, nor shadowed by the night. These heavenly disclosures concerning the secrets of the regenerate or holy life never again to be taken away from the knowledge of men, but through the divinely provided instrumentalities of the printing-press and the pulpit, to be widely circulated and diffused for the free use of all.

5. And then, the Two Holy Sacraments which the Lord has given for the safety and nurture of His Church, opened and explained. Their ineffable, heavenly uses made clear: their inner meaning brought out: the divine symbolism of their forms and elements declared, and in what manner they connect with the unseen world, and, when worthily celebrated, bring down invisible blessings thence to the hearts and minds of the recipients and partakers. What way they are helps, and why they are calculated to ward off evil and feed and strengthen man's spiritual part, clearly and rationally shown. Wherein it is seen by the Christian reason that they are indeed truly Divine ordinances, channels of grace and blessing, having a permanent and living connection with the Lord and the heavenly world.

And lastly, what a reward to obedience is held out! Enough to beget and inspire effort and diligence to learn and know these heavenly truths, and then with God's help to insure our steadfast faithfulness and perseverance unto the end. No church before has had such promises, no church before has had such helps placed within its reach, no church before has had given it such lofty assurance of hope. These words alone are worthy of more space than can be spared for this whole section, and yet their own divine simplicity far outweigh anything that could be added by human language.

"Him that overcometh will I make a pillar in the temple of my God, and he shall go no more out: and I will write upon him the name of my God, and the name of the city of my God, which is New Jerusalem, which cometh down out of heaven from my God: and I will write *him my* new name." "He that hath an ear, let him hear what the Spirit saith unto the churches."

XXXIV.

Emanuel Swedenborg, the Seer.

"THIS eminent servant of the Lord Jesus Christ was born at Stockholm, on the 29th of January, 1688, and departed this life on the 29th of March, 1772, in the 85th year of his age.

"He was the son of Jasper Swedborg, Bishop of Skarra, in Sweden, and was educated in the most pious and affectionate manner. He says of himself, that he was delighted, when a child, to hear his father and friends speak of God, faith, and salvation; and his father says of him, that such were the pious and remarkable sayings of his son Emanuel, that they often thought angels spoke by his mouth. He was educated, and highly distinguished himself, at the University of Upsal, and was so much remarked for his extraordinary mathematical attainments that, in 1716, at the age of 28, he was offered the choice of a professorship, or the office of assessor, or superintendent extraordinary, of the Board of Mines, by the King of Sweden, Charles the Twelfth. He chose the latter, and, during the thirty-one years which he spent in that office, combined with his travels in every country of Europe, he acquired such a fund of learning as astonished and delighted all who admired and promoted philosophic study; and he was made a member of almost all the learned societies in Europe. During this period he produced seven works on various scientific subjects, and, at length, his great work in three volumes, folio, entitled 'Opera Philosophica,' all written in Latin. He subsequently composed four other works, 'The Prodromus,' 'The Economy of the Animal Kingdom,' 'The Animal Kingdom,' and 'On the Worship and Love of God.' In these works he forestalled many of the sublimest and grandest discoveries which have since immortalized the names of several of our greatest men. He anticipated Dalton in the atomic theory, Wollaston in crystallography, Monro in the anatomy of the brain, Wilson in the character and vitality of the globules of the blood, and Gauss, Hansteen, Sabine, Humboldt, and others in the magnetic theory of the universe. He was the discoverer of the following sublime facts and doctrines:

"1. The precise situation of our sun, with its planetary system, in the starry universe to which it belongs. 2. The progressive advancement along the Milky Way, from west to east, of our sun with his spheres, and all the starry host of the visible heavens.

"After having exhibited this wonderful excellence in natural knowledge, and holding a very high position in the very first ranks of philosophy, in 1743, when he was in his fifty-fifth year, his mind became gradually opened to perceive the objects of the spiritual world; and during two years this state of development was going on, until it was completed in 1745, when the Lord himself appeared to him, and commissioned him to make known the science of correspondences, which explains the spiritual sense of His Word, and which he could fully perceive verified in heaven. He learned, also, the laws of the eternal world, and the true doctrines of the Word for the New Jerusalem. That such a state is possible, all the cases of those whose visions are recorded in the Bible prove. This state, which was that of a Seer, was continued during the rest of his life, that is, nearly thirty years. He had the constant privilege of seeing the inner, or spiritual world, as well as the outer, or natural world. He wrote, during this period, works in explanation of the spiritual sense of the Word of God, equal to twenty volumes; unfolding, sentence by sentence, the whole of Genesis, Exodus, and the book of Revelation, and introducing and explaining so many passages from the rest of the Bible, as to open to the devout and spiritually-minded reader the interior sense of the whole Divine Word.

"He wrote also his 'Treatise on Heaven, Hell, and the World of Spirits;' and in several of his other works he describes his experience derived from his acquaintance with the spirit life, giving a rational and harmonious account of it, and of the constitution and life of the human soul. Besides these, he composed works on Christian Doctrine, from the Four leading Doctrines—of the Lord, the Sacred Scripture, Faith, and Life—for the New Jerusalem, to his last work, 'The True Christian Religion.' These relieve the doctrines of Christianity from those oppositions to reason, which, hatched in the dark ages, have rendered religion, which should be the light and the hope of the soul, perplexing to all, and impossible to be embraced by millions of well-disposed thinking men.

"Few, who know anything of his pure, truthful, pious life—of his system, which is entirely an embodiment of truth and love—and of his calm declaration on his deathbed, will imagine he was an impostor. His life, through his long career, is declared by a host of witnesses—by all, in fact, who have testified to their knowledge of him—to have been what Sandel, the nobleman who made the oration in his praise after his death in the Swedish House of Nobles, Oct. 7, 1772, said: 'Never did he allow himself to have recourse to dissimulation. He was the sincere friend of mankind; and in his examination of the character of others, he was desirous to discover in them this virtue, which he regarded as an infallible proof of the presence of many more. He was cheerful and agreeable in society. He enjoyed the most excellent health, having scarcely ever experienced the slightest indisposition. Content within himself and with his situation, his life was, in all respects, one of the happiest that ever fell to the lot of man, till the very moment of its close.'

"The clergyman who attended Swedenborg during his last illness, the Rev. Mr. Ferelius, after having asked whether he thought he should die, and been answered by Swedenborg that he should, made a very solemn appeal to him to say if his writings were entirely true. Swedenborg raised himself in his bed, and placing his hand on his breast, said, with great zeal and emphasis, 'As true as you see me before you, so true is everything I have written; and I could have said more had I been permitted. When you come into eternity, you will see all things as I have stated and described them, and we shall have much to discourse about them with each other.' He then took the Holy Supper, and presented the clergyman with a copy of his 'Arcana Cœlestia.' This is not the life and death of a deceiver. His works, though so numerous, are consistent and harmonious throughout. His system is a grand whole—every principle having its place, and the whole being complete, magnificent, and beautiful, beyond anything the world can elsewhere show. It is, at the same time, fully scriptural, and always in harmony with science; and, above all, the universe is seen to have been created, and to be sustained, by the infinite love, wisdom, and power of the Divine Man, the Lord Jesus Christ, who from eternity was the Father, in time for man's redemption became the Son, and whose spirit is the Holy Spirit. This system gives a complete and rational account of the laws, life, and scenery of heaven—the land of the blessed; answering all our inquiries respecting our children, our departed friends, and the merciful arrangements of Divine Providence for their resurrection. It affords a plain and rational account also of hell, and shows it to be the result of unjust and unholy principles wrought out to their extremes of sin, folly, and misery. It informs us also of the intermediate state—not purgatory, but the world of spirits, the land of judgment; the world, too, where the mistakes of ignorance and of false doctrines in religion are corrected; so that our blessed Lord may, out of the good of all religions, form one fold, with one Shepherd— a grand spiritual house with many mansions."

www.ingramcontent.com/pod-product-compliance
Lightning Source LLC
Chambersburg PA
CBHW020849270326
41928CB00006B/613